# 5000

## AMAZING FACTS
Incredible but true facts about
## EVERYTHING!

This edition published by Parragon Books Ltd in 2015

Parragon Books Ltd
Chartist House
15–17 Trim Street
Bath BA1 1HA, UK
www.parragon.com

ISBN 978-1-4723-7933-7

Printed in China

# 5000

## AMAZING FACTS
### Incredible but true facts about
## EVERYTHING!

PaRragon

Bath · New York · Cologne · Melbourne · Delhi
Hong Kong · Shenzhen · Singapore · Amsterdam

# 8 MONKEY FACTS

South American monkeys have tails that can grip. They use their tails like a fifth limb as they swing through the trees. #0001

Monkeys live in groups called **troops**. Each monkey has allies and enemies within the troop. #0002

**Capuchin monkeys make different sounds to warn their troop of different predators.** They have one sound for snakes, another for leopards and another for eagles. #0003

Female baboons will **adopt** youngsters whose mothers have been killed. #0004

Howler monkeys have booming voices that can carry up to **5 km** through the forest. #0005

Squirrel monkeys **rub their feet with their own urine**. As they walk around, they mark their territory with the smelly pee. #0006

Studying rhesus monkey blood helped scientists to work out the different blood groups that humans belong to. #0007

**Monkeys went into space before people did, the first monkey was sent to space in 1949.** #0008

# 3 SPACE FACTS

Planet Earth is not **perfectly round,** but actually bulges in the middle. #0009

A satellite uses very little energy – about as much as **two ordinary light bulbs.** #0010

A rocket needs to travel at **40,000 km per hour** to escape Earth's gravity. #0011

# 10 GLOWING FACTS ABOUT THE MOON

Human footprints on the Moon will last for **millions of years,** because there is no wind to blow them away. #0012

The largest crater on the Moon is the South Pole-Aitken basin, which is almost **2,414 km across!** #0013

There are **no noises on the Moon,** because there is no air to carry sounds. #0014

As there was no wind, the American flag planted on the Moon by astronauts was **held straight with wire.** #0015

Only **12 people** have walked on the surface of the Moon. No one has been there since 1972. #0016

The Moon is moving away from Earth at the rate of **3 cm a year.** #0017

Moonlight takes **1.25 seconds** to reach Earth. #0018

We only ever see **one side of the Moon** from Earth. #0019

Temperatures on the dark side of the Moon fall to **-173°C!** #0020

Most scientists believe the Moon formed when a **collision** broke off a chunk of Earth. #0021

# If all the blood vessels in your body were laid out in a line, they would reach **TWICE** around the world. #0022

# 10 TOUGH BONE FACTS

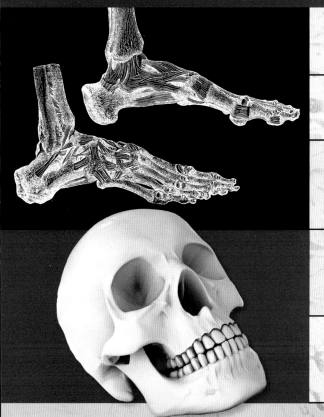

Human bone is stronger than **concrete** or **steel.** #0023

You have over **200 bones** in your body... #0024

... and **over half** of those are found in your **feet and hands.** #0025

People used to **drill holes in their skulls** to cure headaches. #0026

The ancient Aztecs used human thigh bones to make **musical instruments.** #0027

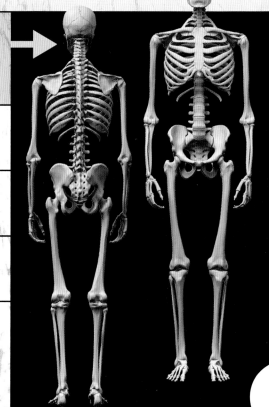

The rest of the body rots away after death, but bones can last for **thousands of years.** #0028

After the age of about 30, people's skeletons start to **shrink.** #0029

The **smallest bone** in your body is in your ears. It is just **0.3 cm long.** #0030

Your **bones** can repair themselves if they get broken, but your teeth can't. #0031

Your **funny bone** isn't actually a bone. It's a sensitive nerve running past your elbow joint. #0032

# 11 FACTS ABOUT
# FLIGHTLESS BIRDS

The giant moa of New Zealand stood nearly **3.6 m tall** – twice the height of an adult human. It died out about **500 years ago.** #0033

**3.6 m**

A **female kiwi** lays a single egg in a season. The egg is about **20 per cent** of the mother's body weight – the largest egg, proportionally, of any bird. #0034

The kiwi has **NOSTRILS** on the end of its long beak, which it uses to sniff out food in the undergrowth. #0035

On hot days, emus **ROLL AROUND** on their backs in streams to keep cool. #0036

An ostrich
can run at

# 72 KM/H. #0037

As it runs, an ostrich
## uses its wings
### to help it to steer. #0038

It travels up to **5 m** in one stride. #0039

An ostrich's
POWERFUL KICK
can kill a human.
#0040

An ostrich's eye is
larger than
its brain.
#0041

The ostrich has the **largest eye** of any land animal.

It is **5 cm across.** #0042

(5 cm)

Many **dinosaurs** had the same leg structure as ostriches.

Scientists study the way **ostriches run** to give them an

**understanding of how dinosaurs moved.** #0043

11

# 5 FACTS ABOUT INCREDIBLE JOURNEYS

**ARCTIC TERNS** migrate from the Arctic to the Antarctic and back every year, flying **70,000 KM.** #0044

**SALMON** are born in streams, then swim all the way to the ocean. Before they die, they swim back to the **EXACT SAME STREAM** they came from to lay their eggs. #0045

**MONARCH BUTTERFLIES** can find their way to the very same spot where their great-great-grandparents hatched out. #0046

**COCONUTS** have been known to float **10,000 KM** across an ocean before growing into a tree on another continent. #0047

Every spring, millions of **RED CRABS** on Christmas Island in the Indian Ocean migrate from **FORESTS** to the **SEA** to breed. A few weeks later, their babies migrate back again! #0048

# 3 WEIRD ANIMAL FACTS

**PLATYPUSES** and **ECHIDNAS,** furry and spiny burrowing creatures found in Australia and New Guinea, are the only **MAMMALS** that lay **EGGS.** #0049

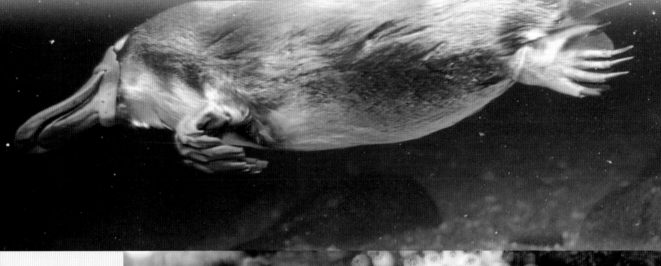

**Three-toed sloths** have **moths** living in their fur. #0050

Sea slugs are **hermaphrodites** – they have both male and female reproductive organs. This increases their chances of finding a mate! #0051

# 100 PIRATE facts

Piracy (attacking and robbing ships at sea) began thousands of years ago in Ancient Egypt and throughout the Mediterranean Sea. [#0052] **Julius Caesar** was captured by pirates. [#0053] He told them he would have his revenge and after he escaped he returned to kill them all. [#0054] Piracy became popular between **1620** and **1720**. [#0055] This time was known as the **Golden Age of Piracy**. [#0056] Pirates of the Mediterranean Sea were known as **corsairs**. [#0057] **Privateers** were legal pirates, given a licence to attack enemy ships by their government. [#0058] This meant they weren't punished for stealing, as long as they shared their profits with their government. [#0059] Pirates of the Caribbean Sea were known as **buccaneers**. [#0060] Spanish '**pieces of eight**' were silver coins used as currency. [#0061] Pieces of eight were made by Spain at mints in Peru and Mexico. [#0062] Fleets of ships carried the coins, and other treasure, back to Spain. [#0063] Pirates attacked Spain's treasure fleets as they crossed the Atlantic Ocean. [#0064] The Habsburgs ruled Spain and were the most powerful family in Europe at the time. [#0065] Pirate ships could be small, fast-moving **sloops** (sailing ships), or **galleys** (rowing ships). [#0066] **Galleons** (heavy, slow-moving merchant ships) were the main target of pirates. [#0067] Although some pirates used the **Jolly Roger** flag (skull and crossbones) on their ships, most flew a plain design. [#0068] A black flag showed that, as long as a ship surrendered, no one would be killed. [#0069] A red flag indicated that no mercy would be shown. [#0070]

According to myth, pirates were given earrings to celebrate successful voyages. [#0071] They believed earrings would improve their eyesight and cure seasickness. [#0072] Some pirates believed that having women on board their ship was bad luck. [#0073] If there was a chance that a pirate ship might be captured, the **captain** would change out of his expensive, flashy clothes. [#0074] That way he could pretend he was one of the crew and escape. [#0075] Every pirate got equal amounts of the loot captured, except for the captain and the quartermaster, who got the biggest share. [#0076] Pirates often got **scurvy**, an illness caused by a lack of vitamin C. [#0077] Symptoms of scurvy are teeth falling out, fatigue and aching legs. [#0078] If a pirate was caught, tried and found guilty, he was usually hanged in front of a large crowd of people. [#0079] Sometimes a pirate might even have his head cut off. [#0080] To put others off becoming a pirate, governments often put a pirate's head on a stick and placed it somewhere lots of people could see it. [#0081] The pirate saying '**shiver me timbers**' was invented for the book Treasure Island. [#0082] Piracy took place all over the world. [#0083] Port Royal in Jamaica was once known as the wickedest city on Earth. [#0084] In the 17th century it was home to an international band of pirates. [#0085] The town also served as the headquarters of the Royal Navy in the Caribbean. [#0086] The glory days of Port Royal ended in **1692** when an earthquake and tsunami caused much of the city to sink into the sea. [#0087] Madagascar in the Indian Ocean was another popular pirate haven and a great place to raid European and Asian ships. [#0088] It was safer than the Caribbean Sea because it was less heavily patrolled. [#0089] **Bartholomew Roberts**, also known as **Black Bart**, was one of the most successful pirates ever. [#0090] He turned to piracy after being captured by a gang of pirates led by Captain **Howell Davis.** [#0091] Not long after, Davis was killed and Black Bart was voted in as captain. [#0092] His first raid was to avenge the death of his former captain. [#0093] He captured about 400 ships before he was killed in battle. [#0094] When England and Spain were at war, **Elizabeth I** encouraged privateers **Sir Francis Drake** and **Sir John Hawkins** to attack and capture Spanish ships. [#0095] **John Hawkins** also captured Africans and traded them as slaves. [#0096] In **1571** he became a Member of Parliament (MP) for Plymouth. [#0097] In **1578** he went on to become Treasurer of the Royal Navy. [#0098] He helped the English defeat the Spanish Armada and was rewarded with a knighthood. [#0099] His cousin **Sir Francis Drake** accompanied him on many of his voyages and both men died on their last voyage to the West Indies. [#0100] One of the most successful privateers in history was **Henry Morgan**. [#0101] Born in Wales around **1635**, Morgan started life as a soldier. [#0102] He later turned to piracy and led raids on Panama, Maracaibo and Portobello in South America and the Caribbean. [#0103] He was rewarded by the British government with the role of Lieutenant Governor of Jamaica. [#0104] He died in **1688**, at the age of 53, of alcohol poisoning. [#0105] The pirate **William Dampier** was born in **1651**. [#0106] He introduced many new words into the English language including avocado, cashew, chopsticks, posse, snug and barbecue. [#0107] He was also an explorer, naturalist and writer. [#0108] Captain **William Kidd** was born in **1645**. [#0109] He started out as a pirate hunter but couldn't find many pirate ships to attack. [#0110] He switched sides and became a pirate himself. [#0111] He buried some of his treasure on Gardiners Island off the coast of the United States. [#0112] He tried to use it as a bargaining tool after being caught. [#0113] It didn't work and he was hanged in London. [#0114] His body was displayed in a cage on the River Thames to deter other pirates. [#0115] During the War of the Spanish Succession, 1701–1714, **Olivier Levasseur** was a privateer for the French crown. [#0116] After the war ended he ignored orders to return with his ship to France. [#0117] Instead he joined the **Benjamin Hornigold** pirate company. [#0118] After a year of successful raids, he left to try raiding on his own. [#0119]

He was eventually captured and executed in **1730**. [#0120] During his execution, he threw a message written in code into the crowd, telling them to find his treasure. [#0121] People are still looking for the bounty today. [#0122] **Anne Bonny** was born about **1700** in Ireland. [#0123] After moving to the United States, she ran off with Captain **Calico Jack** to join his pirate crew. [#0124] When attacking other pirate ships she dressed as a man. [#0125] Calico Jack was named after the calico trousers he wore. [#0126] He became a captain following a mutiny. [#0127] His crew turned on Captain **Charles Vane** after he fled an attack on a French ship, and made Jack their captain instead. [#0128] Vane was infamous for his cruelty to those he captured. [#0129] He also sometimes broke the pirate law, refusing to share loot with his crew. [#0130] He was hanged in **1721** at Gallows Point in Port Royal. [#0131]

# 20 EXPLOSIVE VOLCANO FACTS

A **volcano** is a cone-shaped land form with a crater at the top, through which molten lava, rock, ash and gas might erupt. #0152 The name 'volcano' comes from the name **Vulcan**, the god of fire in Roman mythology. #0153 **Magma** is molten rock inside a volcano. #0154 Pressure builds up under the surface causing the molten rock to erupt through narrow cracks in the Earth's crust. #0155 Once the magma erupts through the Earth's surface it is called **lava**. #0156 The temperature of lava ranges from 700°C to 1,200°C. #0157 There are around 1,510 active volcanoes in the world. #0158 Over half the world's volcanoes are in a line around the **Pacific Ocean** called the **Ring of Fire**. #0159 As well as the danger from hot lava, an erupting volcano can trigger tsunamis, flash floods, earthquakes, mud flows and rock falls. #0160 Around 1 in 20 people live within danger range of an active volcano. #0161 Scientists have estimated that at least 200,000 people have lost their lives as a result of volcanic eruptions during the past 500 years. #0162 The world's largest active volcano is **Mauna Loa.** #0163 Mauna Loa is 4,170 m above sea level on the island of **Hawaii**. #0164 It has erupted roughly every six years since **1,000 BC.** #0165 In **1815** the eruption of **Mount Tambora** in **Indonesia** spread an ash cloud around the world. #0166 In **1883** the eruption of a volcano in Indonesia produced the world's loudest-ever bang, which was heard in **Australia**, 4,800 km away. #0167 In **1943** a new volcano in **Mexico** grew five storeys high in a week. #0168 **Mount Paricutin** is now around 3,000 m tall. #0169 Over 60 per cent of volcanoes erupt underwater. #0170 The eruption of **Vesuvius** in **Italy** in **AD 79** perfectly preserved the Roman city of **Pompeii** under a layer of ash. It lay buried for 1,700 years. #0171

**Earthquakes** involve the powerful movement of rocks in Earth's crust. #0172 They are caused when pressure on the Earth's plates forces rocks to shift or break. #0173 The rapid release of energy creates seismic waves that travel through Earth. #0174 **Seismometers** are used to measure the magnitude of earthquakes. #0175 The Richter Scale, which runs from 'less than 2' to 'greater than 9' is used to describe the strength of an earthquake. #0176 You are unlikely to feel a magnitude 1 to 3 earthquake. #0177 The most powerful earthquake ever recorded on Earth was in **Valdivia** in **Chile**. #0178 It occurred in **1960** and had a magnitude of 9.5. #0179 More than a million earthquakes rattle the world each year. #0180 Earthquakes can be felt over large areas although they usually last less than one minute. #0181 A **tsunami** is a large ocean wave usually caused by an earthquake or volcanic explosion. #0182 More rarely, a tsunami can be generated by a giant meteor landing in the ocean. #0183 About 80 per cent of tsunamis happen around the edge of the Pacific Ocean. #0184 The first wave of a tsunami is usually not the strongest; later waves get bigger and stronger. #0185 Tsunamis can travel at speeds of up to 900 km/h, almost as fast as a jet plane. #0186 When tsunamis hit shallow water they slow down but become taller. #0187 Tsunamis can maintain their energy even while they travel across entire oceans. #0188 In **2004** the **Indian Ocean** tsunami was caused by an earthquake which was as powerful as 23,000 atomic bombs. #0189 After the earthquake, deadly waves radiating from the epicentre reached the coastlines of 11 countries. #0190 A **tornado** is a rapid spinning of air that

touches both the ground and the clouds above. #0191 Most tornadoes are formed by **thunderstorms**. #0192 Around 1,300 are reported around the world each year. #0193 Three out of every four tornadoes happen in the **United States**. #0194 More than 30 tornadoes are reported every year in the UK – but they rarely cause serious damage. #0195 The **Enhanced Fujita** scale measures the power of tornadoes. EF0 tornadoes cause minimal damage and EF5 ones are the deadliest. #0196 Tornado winds are the fastest winds on Earth. #0197 Extreme winds can reach almost 500 km/h. #0198 Most tornadoes travel just a few kilometres before exhausting themselves, but the largest can travel hundreds of kilometres. #0199 A tornado's colour usually matches the colour of the ground – if the ground is red the tornado would be too! #0200 A tornado that forms over water is called a waterspout. #0201

# 30 NATURAL DISASTER FACTS

# 8 MIGHTY WHALE FACTS

Bowhead whales can live for up to **200 years** – the longest lifespan of any mammal. #0202

Humpback whales **sing to each other**. A humpback whale's song can be heard by other humpback whales **thousands of kilometres away**. #0203

Sperm whales have **no sense of smell**. #0204

Sperm whales **dive** to depths of **up to 3 km** in search of food. #0205

## SPERM WHALE

Sperm whales **feed on giant squid**. The whales often have scars from battles with squid. #0206

# BOWHEAD WHALE

The bowhead whale has the **largest mouth of any animal**. When open, it measures **up to 4 m** from top to bottom. #0207

Unlike other whales, the beluga whale has a **flexible neck** that allows it to turn its head in all directions. #0208

## BELUGA WHALE

## HUMPBACK WHALE

The male narwhal has a **sword-like spiral tusk** that grows up to 2.7 m long. #0209

## NARWHAL

19

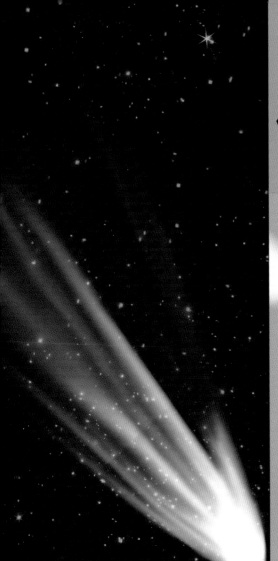

# 4 FACTS ABOUT CRAZY COMETS

**COMETS** speed up as they approach the Sun, to over **1.6 MILLION KM PER HOUR.** #0210

A **comet** is a ball of ice and dust. As it shoots through space a comet's tail always points away from the Sun. #0211

The longest comet tails are over **10 MILLION KM LONG,** resembling a streak of light across the sky. #0212

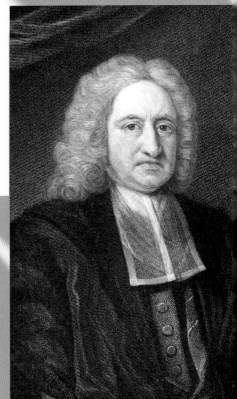

Halley's Comet appears every **76 years.** It will next be seen in 2061. #0213

# 5 FACTS TO ROCK THE GALAXY

Scientists believe there are over **100 BILLION GALAXIES** in the Universe. #0214

The galaxy nearest to our own is the **ANDROMEDA GALAXY.** Starlight from this galaxy takes 2 million years to reach us. #0215

The Milky Way and Andromeda Galaxy may collide in about **5 BILLION YEARS' TIME** to form one huge galaxy. #0216

All the stars in a galaxy are held together by **GRAVITY.** #0217

The Milky Way is estimated to be around **13.2 BILLION YEARS OLD.** #0218

# 10 SUPER-SMART FACTS ABOUT ANIMALS

An **African grey parrot** named Alex learned to count, sort out **shapes** and say 150 different words. #0219

Kanzi the **bonobo,** a type of chimpanzee, can understand around **3,000 English words.** #0220

A clever crow named Betty worked out how to make a **wire hook** to fish food out of a jar. #0221

**Chimps** poke sticks into termite nests, wait until termites crawl onto them and then lick them clean. #0222

Some **Japanese macaques** wash potatoes in seawater to clean them and add salty seasoning. #0223

**Ants** can use their antennae to tell other ants how to **solve a maze.** #0224

**Bonobos** use plants and minerals as **medicines** to treat worms, diarrhoea and stomach ache. #0225

**Killer whales** have been found to enjoy looking at **books!** #0226

An **octopus** can open a **screw-top jar** with its tentacles. #0227

An **elephant** can recognize itself in a **mirror.** #0228

# 4 AWESOME ANIMAL FACTS

Sociable **weaver birds** use grass to build huge nests with space for **200 or more birds.** #0229

How many times have you moved house? **ORANGUTANS** build themselves a new **NEST** of leaves and branches **EVERY NIGHT!** #0230

When **BEAVERS** build a **DAM,** they can completely change the **DIRECTION OF A RIVER.** #0231

A **giant squid's oesophagus** (the tube that food passes through to get to the stomach) runs right through its **brain.** #0232

# 5 GEESE FACTS

When they migrate, Canada geese fly in a
## 'V' FORMATION
as this is the most aerodynamic arrangement.

#0233

The birds take turns flying at the
**FRONT OF THE 'V',** dropping
back when they get tired.

#0234

With the right wind, geese
can cover 2,400 km in
## 24 HOURS. #0235

A flock of 50 geese produces **2.5 tonnes of poo** in a year, which is heavier than two large cars.

#0236

Canada geese look after their young in **communal crèches,** which may contain over 100 goslings.

#0237

# 7 FACTS ABOUT DUCKS & SWANS

A fear of swans is called **CYGNOPHOBIA.**

#0238

Swans' beaks have **JAGGED EDGES** to help them catch fish.

#0239

Swans are **highly intelligent,** and can remember **who has been kind to them and who hasn't.**

#0240

The female mallard lines her nest with downy feathers that she **plucks from her own undercoat.**

#0241

A duck covers its outer feathers with OIL made in a gland near its tail. The oil **MAKES THE FEATHERS WATERPROOF.**

#0242

**Twice a year,** mallards shed their flight feathers. They are unable to fly for several weeks while **NEW FEATHERS GROW.**

#0243

Just one day after hatching, **ducklings can run, swim and forage** for their own food.

#0244

# 103 DANGEROUS DINO

The first dinosaurs appeared around 228 million years ago. **#0245** For the next 165 million years they ruled our planet. **#0246** Dinosaurs roamed Earth for 820 times longer than modern humans have existed. **#0247** During the time of the first dinosaurs there was just one landmass – a supercontinent called Pangaea. **#0248** Over millions of years, Pangaea broke up into separate continents to form the world we know today. **#0249** Dinosaurs lived between 228 and 65 million years ago, during the Mesozoic era. **#0250** The period that they lived in is sometimes called the Age of Reptiles. **#0251** Dinosaurs are part of a large group of animals called Dinosauria. **#0252** More than 700 different types of dinosaur have been discovered so far. **#0253** Dinosaurs were land animals. **#0254** The prehistoric skies and seas were filled with reptiles, but they were not dinosaurs. **#0255** The word 'dinosaur' means 'terrible lizard' but dinosaurs were not actually lizards. **#0256** Dinosaurs were a type of land reptile. **#0257** Unlike modern-day lizards and crocodiles, a dinosaur's legs were set directly under its body rather than sticking out from the sides. **#0258** All dinosaurs had four limbs, though some walked on four legs and others on two. **#0259** Dinosaurs were land animals, but some would wade through water. **#0260** Dinosaurs laid eggs. **#0261** Some dinosaurs, such as **Compsognathus**, were as small as a chicken. **#0262** Others, such as **Amphicoelius**, were longer than four buses lined up end to end. **#0263** Large dinosaurs had powerful leg muscles to support their enormous weight. **#0264** Dinosaurs were either lizard-hipped (saurischians) or bird-hipped (ornithischians). **#0265** Many dinosaurs stood and walked on their toes. **#0266** Dinosaurs were slightly pigeon-toed and walked with their toes pointed inwards. **#0267** Dinosaurs that walked on two legs could move faster than those that walked on four. **#0268** Dinosaurs probably used their tails for balance. **#0269** Fossilized dinosaur tracks tell us that dinosaurs did not drag their tails behind them, but held them above the ground. **#0270** The first dinosaurs appeared during the Triassic Period, which lasted from 252 to 201 million years ago. **#0271** There was not a wide range of different dinosaurs in the Triassic. **#0272** The first dinosaurs were smaller than the dinosaurs that would develop later. **#0273** Dinosaurs, such as **Zupaysaurus**, **Eoraptor** and **Herrerasaurus** lived at this time. **#0274** **Eoraptor** was only about 1 m tall. **#0275**

**Melanorosaurus** was the largest Triassic dinosaur and was about 11 m long. **#0276** Its long neck allowed it to reach leaves high up in the trees. **#0277** Dinosaurs at this time lived alongside many other animals including reptiles and giant insects. **#0278** Prehistoric dragonflies could be as large as modern-day birds. **#0279** Many of the animals and dinosaurs that lived during the Triassic were wiped out in a mass extinction. **#0280** The dinosaurs that survived evolved into different kinds of dinosaurs during the Jurassic period that followed. **#0281** The Jurassic Period lasted 56 million years. **#0282** It began 201 million years ago and ended 145 million years ago. **#0283** Dinosaurs became much larger during the Jurassic Period. **#0284** Huge plant-eating dinosaurs known as sauropods appeared during this time. **#0285** Plants spread over large areas of the land, providing food for plant-eaters, which in turn provided food for new meat-eating dinosaurs. **#0286** During the Jurassic Period, many different types of dinosaurs existed, including **Diplodocus**, **Stegosaurus**, **Apatosaurus**, **Allosaurus** and **Ankylosaurus**. **#0287** Having huge bodies meant that dinosaurs had to spend a lot of time eating. **#0288** Allosaurus was a Jurassic predator that fed on stegosaurs and sauropods. **#0289** Meat-eating dinosaurs did not grow as large as plant-eating ones. **#0290** Allosaurus was the largest predator during the Jurassic. **#0291** Allosaurus was only about half the length of Apatosaurus. **#0292** To bring down larger plant-eating dinosaurs Allosaurus may have hunted in packs. **#0293** Stegosaurus used the spikes at the end of its tail to strike back at attackers. **#0294** Diplodocus could crack its long tail like a whip to scare off predators. **#0295** The tip of its tail could reach a speed of 1,300 km/h. **#0296** A Diplodocus egg was as large as a football. **#0297** When fully grown, a Diplodocus would have weighed about 1,000 times as much as when it hatched. **#0298** The Cretaceous Period followed the Jurassic and lasted from 145 to 66 million years ago. **#0299** The world became warmer with higher sea levels. **#0300** The Cretaceous Period is often known as the golden age of dinosaurs. **#0301** Dinosaurs that lived at this time included **Tyrannosaurus rex**, **Velociraptor, Iguanodon, Spinosaurus, Triceratops** and **Troodon**. **#0302** **Therizinosaurus** was a Cretaceous plant-eater with gigantic front claws that were almost 1 m long. **#0303** **Baryonyx** had large thumb claws up to 25 cm long

# facts

that it probably used to catch fish. #0304 **Deinonychus** was given a name that means 'terrible claw', because it had a retractable hunting claw on each foot. #0305 Few dinosaurs could have killed with claws alone, but claws could have helped to hold prey in a deadly grip. #0306 Tyrannosaurus rex was around 12 m long and around 6 m tall. #0307 Its name means 'tyrant-lizard king'. #0308 It had around 60 teeth in its huge jaws. #0309 Tyrannosaurus rex may have run at 30 km/h. #0310 Spinosaurus was the largest dinosaur predator. #0311 Its long narrow snout was suited to catching fish in the water. #0312 **Ankylosaurus** had a heavy club made of solid bone at the end of its tail that it could use as a weapon. #0313 **Parasaurolophus** may have blown through the hollow tubes in its skull to make trombone-like calls to others in its herd. #0314 Dinosaurs had thick, tough skin that was also sometimes protected by feathers or scales. #0315 Some dinosaurs were covered with feathers and looked similar to birds. #0316 Fossilized skin impressions tell us that **Carnotaurus**' skin had large pebble-like bumps. #0317 The first armoured dinosaurs had bony scales like crocodiles. #0318 From scales, dinosaurs evolved large plates of armour, spikes and clubs. #0319 The plates on Stegosaurus' back were covered in keratin, the same substance that human hair is made from. #0320 Ankylosaurs were heavily armoured with tough bony plates and scaly body protection. #0321 Some ankylosaurs were also covered with sharp spikes. #0322 **Euoplocephalus** had bony eyelids and two bone rings around its neck to protect it. #0323 **Pentaceratops** had five horns – a nose horn, two cheek horns and a horn above each eye. #0324 To understand the brains of dinosaurs, researchers study the brains of their living descendants – birds – as well as similar reptiles such as crocodiles. #0325 Many of the early giant plant-eaters had very small brains. #0326 Later plant-eaters like **Edmontosaurus** had slightly bigger brains, but their brains were still smaller than those of the predators that ate them. #0327 Predators that hunted prey at speed needed bigger brains. #0328 Tyrannosaurus rex had a bigger brain than any plant-eater. #0329 Velociraptor had a bigger brain for its size than Tyrannosaurus rex and had excellent eyesight and hearing. #0330 Troodon had a large brain for its small size and was probably one of the smartest predators. #0331 Duck-billed

dinosaurs, called hadrosaurs, had horny, toothless beaks with up to 1,000 cheek teeth in the sides of their jaws. #0332 Turkey-sized **Heterodontosaurus** had three kinds of teeth plus a beak. #0333 Its name means 'different-tooth lizard'. #0334 Heterodontosaurus had sharp incisors for cutting, chisel-like teeth for grinding and tusk-like teeth for defence! #0335 Carnivores like Tyrannosaurus rex used their huge sharp teeth to make a kill, usually biting the neck or belly. #0336 Tyrannosaurus rex's teeth were as big as bananas. #0337 They were strong enough to crush bone. #0338 All dinosaurs could grow new teeth to replace any that they lost. #0339 Troodon had large eyes, which were useful for hunting in low light levels at dusk and dawn. #0340 Plant-eaters often had eyes on the sides of their heads, which gave them a wide view and helped them to quickly spot danger. #0341 Meat-eaters, such as **Aucasaurus**, had larger, forward-facing eyes, which helped them to judge the distance to their prey. #0342 Some dinosaurs had bright feathers and crests so it is likely that they could see in colour, just as birds and most reptiles can today. #0343 All dinosaurs had ears with eardrums and inner ears, like humans. #0344 A dinosaur's inner ear, right inside its skull, was used as much for balance as it was for hearing. #0345 Meat-eaters didn't just track down living animals, their good sense of smell helped them find dead animals to eat, too. #0346 Plant-eaters may have used their sense of smell to find a mate. #0347

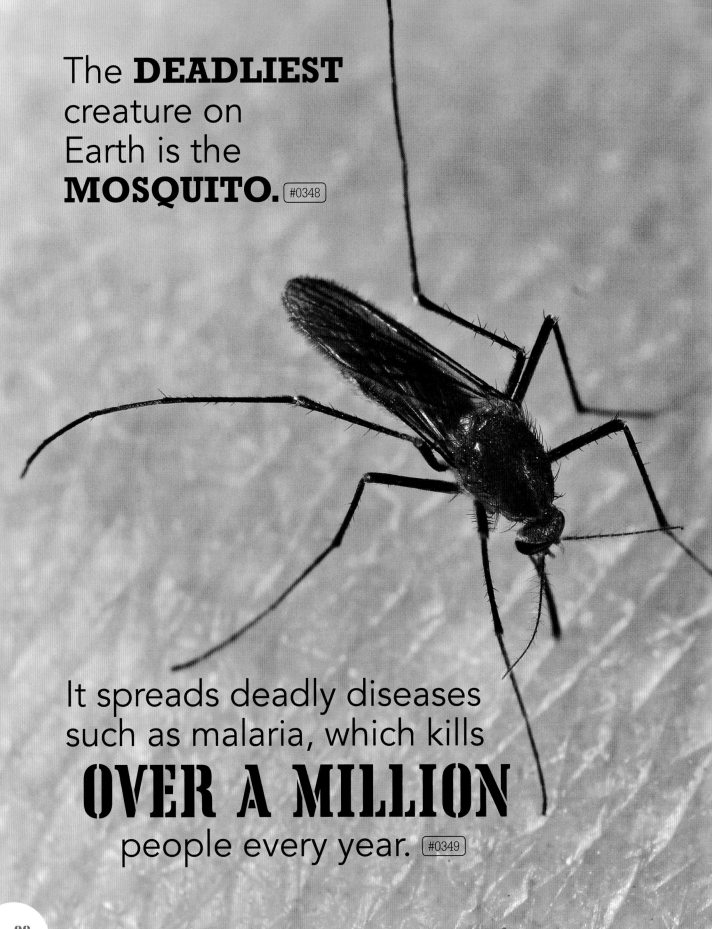

The **DEADLIEST** creature on Earth is the **MOSQUITO.** #0348

It spreads deadly diseases such as malaria, which kills **OVER A MILLION** people every year. #0349

# 10 BABY ANIMAL BRAINTEASERS

An **ostrich egg** is so **strong** that you could stand on it without breaking it. #0350

**Mice** breed so fast that in one year, two mice can multiply to become over **4,000 mice.** #0351

A newborn baby **kangaroo** is smaller than your **thumb.** #0352

The greatest number of **yolks** ever found in one chicken **egg** is nine. #0353

**Giraffes** give birth standing up, so their babies fall **2 m** onto the ground. Ouch! #0354

A **Surinam toad's** babies hatch out from under the skin on her back. #0355

**Sand tiger sharks** often start to **eat each other** inside their mum's body before being born. #0356

Baby **tortoise beetles** put predators off by covering themselves in their own poo. #0357

Baby **periodical cicadas** can live for **17 years** underground, yet once they become adults, they live only a **few weeks.** #0358

Baby **elephants** greet each other by **intertwining trunks**, and they like to play chase games! #0359

# 10 THOUGHT-PROVOKING BRAIN FACTS

The human brain can do about **100 trillion** (100,000,000,000,000) calculations per second. #0360

If you spread the wrinkly covering of your brain out flat, it would be as **big as a newspaper.** #0361

If someone cut into your brain with a **knife,** you wouldn't feel any **pain.** #0362

There is evidence that a person can remain conscious for a few seconds after having their **head chopped off.** #0363

A normal human brain can store more information than a **room full of books.** #0364

If **half** of your brain was removed... you could live quite normally! #0365

The brain can shrink up to **15 per cent** as it ages. #0366

**A newborn baby** already has all its brain cells. #0367

US scientist Chet Fleming has invented a device for keeping **a severed human head alive.** (It hasn't been built yet!) #0368

The brain works harder when you're **asleep** than when you're awake. #0369

Lee Redmond of Utah, USA, grew her **FINGERNAILS** to almost a

METRE LONG. #0370

(Unfortunately, they were then broken off in a car accident!) #0371

# 50 marvellous MUSIC facts

We hear because vibrations create sound waves that move through the air to reach our ears.
#0372

The scientific study of sound waves is known as acoustics.
#0373

Music can change the rhythm of your heartbeat.
#0374

Although music can be hard to explain, it is often defined as a pleasing or meaningful arrangement of sounds.
#0375

Hairs in our ears vibrate in a similar way to the source of a vibration, allowing us to hear many different sounds.
#0376

Mathematician **Pythagoras** first worked out the science of vibrating strings 2,500 years ago.
#0377

A song can shatter glass if the pitch of a note coincides with the natural frequency of vibration of the glass.
#0378

The pitch of a musical note depends on the frequency of the vibrations.
#0381

So-called 'gut strings', for acoustic Spanish guitars, were originally made from the small intestines of sheep.
#0379

Studies show that children who learn music are more likely to do well at school and work better in teams.
#0380

Composer **Ludwig van Beethoven** started to lose his hearing when he was just 25 years old.
#0382

Learning a musical instrument improves the way the brain breaks down and understands human language.
#0384

Guitar string material changed to nylon during World War II, when all available gut was used in the production of surgical thread for wounded soldiers.
#0385

Beethoven wrote many of his popular works when he was deaf.
#0383

To 'hear' sounds, Beethoven cut off the legs of his piano so the piano was on the floor – he could feel the vibrations it made when he played.
#0386

Warner Music owns the copyright to the song 'Happy Birthday' and makes more than £1 million a year from royalties, when it is sung in films and on TV shows.
#0387

**Wolfgang Mozart's** music is popular all around the world.
#0388

Composer **Pyotr Ilyich Tchaikovsky** wrote the ballet music for *The Sleeping Beauty* in 40 days.
#0389

**Tchaikovsky** also wrote the music for the popular ballets *Swan Lake* and *The Nutcracker*.
#0390

Famous composers **Johann Bach** and **George Handel** were both blinded by the same surgeon, **John Taylor**.
#0391

To win a gold disc, an album needs to sell 100,000 copies in Great Britain or 500,000 in the United States.
#0392

In May 1997, **Paul McCartney** broke his own world record by obtaining his 81st gold disc.
#0393

**The Beatles** are the biggest-selling band of all time.
#0394

All bird species have their own unique song.
#0395

The first pop music video was 'Bohemian Rhapsody' by **Queen**, released in **1975**.
#0396

When mosquitoes fall in love, they harmonize their buzzing sounds.
#0399

In 2009, **Taylor Swift** made history by selling more digital downloads than any other country music artist, ever.
#0400

The Beatles have sold more than 250 million records.
#0397

Canaries can sing two different songs at the exact same time.
#0398

Top-selling albums used to reach sales of 20 million copies before illegal Internet downloads became possible.
#0403

Singing exercises your heart and lungs, and releases endorphins that make you feel happy.
#0404

Greece has the longest national anthem. It has 158 verses.
#0405

**Taylor Swift** is the youngest singer to win a Grammy award for Album of the Year.
#0401

Spain is one of the few countries to have a wordless national anthem.
#0406

By 2009, album sales had dropped to about 5 million copies.
#0402

The world's oldest musical instruments are flutes made from bird bone and mammoth ivory.
#0407

The chills you get from listening to powerful music are called 'musical frisson'.
#0408

**Michael Jackson** was only five years old when he first performed with his siblings as The Jackson 5.
#0409

**Elvis Presley** didn't write any of his own songs.
#0410

A competition was held in **2007** to write words for the wordless Spanish anthem, but they proved so unpopular they were never sung.
#0411

**Coldplay's Chris Martin** plays guitar and draws with his right hand, but writes left-handed.
#0412

In 1968, **Louis Armstrong** reached number 1 in the UK Chart with his song What a Wonderful World' – he was 66 years old.
#0413

Louis Armstrong holds the record for being the **oldest chart-topper**.
#0414

Monaco's orchestra is bigger than its army.
#0415

The highest note ever whistled was by **Walker Harnden** from the United States.
#0416

Left-handed guitar player **Jimi Hendrix** actually wrote with his right hand.
#0417

The harmonica is the world's best-selling musical instrument.
#0418

Musician **John Lennon's** eyesight was so poor that he was legally blind without his glasses.
#0419

The earliest instruments are around 42,000 years old – they were found in a cave in Germany.
#0420

Walker Harnden whistled a B7, which is the second top note on a piano keyboard.
#0421

33

# **3** FACTS ABOUT
# CRABS AND LOBSTERS

## LOBSTERS
can live for at least **60 years,** and may live for up to **100 years.**

#0422

As they grow, crabs and lobsters **moult their old shells and grow new ones.** #0423

The red crab only lives on Christmas Island in the Indian Ocean, but there are

# 120 MILLION

of them there. #0424

# 4 FACTS ABOUT THE HERMIT CRAB

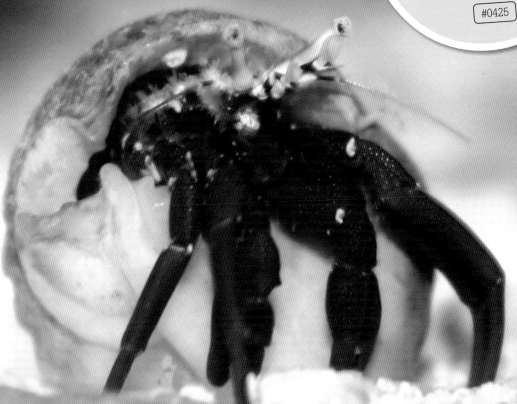

Hermit crabs have **soft bodies,** and climb into empty shells for **protection.**

#0425

The shape of their body changes to fit their shell. #0426

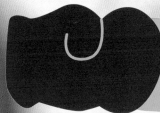

Hermit crabs will **fight each other** for the best shells. #0427

As it grows, a hermit crab must find itself a **larger shell.** #0428

35

# 3 BIZARRE BODY FACTS

In 1848, a railway worker named Phineas Gage survived having an **iron bar blown through his brain** by an explosion. He lived until 1860. #0429

People with **synaesthesia** get their senses mixed up – they may see sounds, feel colours or taste musical notes. #0430

A man grows about **5 m** of **beard** hair in a lifetime. #0431

# 10 HIGHLY SENSITIVE SENSES FACTS

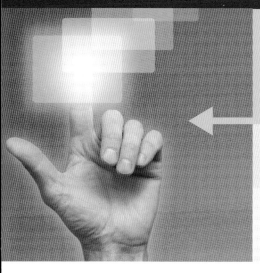

When you touch something, a message zooms from your fingers to your brain at **150 km per hour** – as fast as a **speeding train.** #0432

Some people can **pop their eyeballs** right out of their head. #0433

You can't **taste** things if your tongue is **dry.** #0434

People who've lost an arm or a leg sometimes feel pain as if it's still there. It's called a **'phantom limb'.** #0435

Children's **hearing** is better than adults'. #0436

Some blind people can sense where objects are by using **echolocation**, as bats do. #0437

Your nose can remember **50,000** different scents. #0438

Human eyes can detect over **a million** different **colours** and **shades.** #0439

All your life, your **nose** and **ears** very slowly keep getting **bigger...** #0440

... but your **eyeballs** stay almost the same size for your whole life. #0441

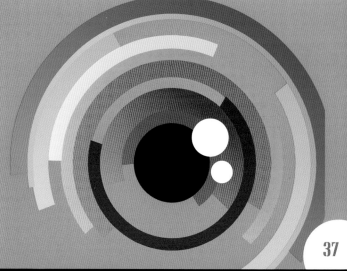

# 5 ELECTRIFYING THUNDER AND LIGHTNING FACTS

A bolt of lightning heats the air around it to **30,000°C**. #0442

Lightning travels downwards at **220,000 KM PER HOUR** and even faster upwards. #0443

Right now, there are about **2,000 THUNDERSTORMS** raging around the world. #0444

Lightning is very dangerous – it **KILLS AND INJURES** more people each year than hurricanes or tornadoes. #0445

People in the town of Tororo in East Africa hear thunder about **250 DAYS A YEAR.** #0446

# 2 UNDERGROUND FACTS

The temperature rises around **30°C** for every km you travel towards the centre of Earth. #0447

Vast **underground lakes** lie beneath some of the Earth's greatest deserts, including the Sahara. Some of the water is being tapped for farming and cities. #0448

# 101 FACTS
## that will make your SKIN CRAWL

**Cockroaches** can live for weeks without their heads. #0449 There are about 4,000 different species of cockroach but only about 30 are considered pests. #0450 Cockroaches can eat just about anything, including glue, paper and soap. They can survive for long periods of time without any food at all. #0451 Insects and bugs can be useful in creating honey, wax, silk and other products. #0452 But they can also be killers, destroying some crops and carrying disease. #0453 When they are finished with their webs, **spiders** eat the silk to recycle it. #0454 **Tarantulas** can live for up to 30 years. #0455 Female **nursery web spiders** often eat the males. #0456 They do this after mating with them. #0457 Spiders have huge brains for their size. Some spiders' brains spill over into their legs. #0458 The **crab spider** can change colour to match its surroundings to help catch its prey. #0459 The largest spider in the world is the **Goliath birdeater tarantula** with a leg span of 30 cm. #0460 The total weight of all the ants in the world is greater than the weight of all humans. #0461 There are more than 12,000 species of ant. #0462 An **ant** can carry more than 50 times its body weight – the equivalent of a human lifting a small truck. #0463 Queen ants may live as long as 30 years. #0464 Only three types of animals fight battles in formation. They are humans, crows and ants. #0465 The **Maricopa harvester ant** is the most venomous insect in the world, with a sting equivalent to that of 12 honey bees. #0466 Worker, soldier and queen ants are all female. #0467 Male ants have just one job – to mate. #0468 In Thailand, **weaver ants'** eggs are eaten with salad. #0469 **Termites** first appeared on Earth about 65 million years ago – that's 100 million years before the first dinosaur. #0470 Soldier termites have such huge jaws they cannot feed themselves. They are fed by worker termites. #0471 Worker **bees** are sterile females that usually do not lay eggs. #0472 Bees dance to communicate with each other, often to explain where to find food. #0473 The honey bee stores the pollen it collects from flowers in pouches behind its legs. #0474 Honey bees visit between 50 and 100 flowers during one trip. #0475 A honey bee's wings beat about 11,400 times per minute. This is what makes the buzzing sound. #0476 Africanized honey bees will chase you for 100 m if they feel threatened. #0477 Honey bees can only sting once as their stingers get stuck in the victim's body. #0478 A queen bee can lay up to 200,000 eggs per year. #0479 Only **female wasps** have stingers. #0480 Unlike bees, they can sting more than once. #0481 Some wasps sleep while hanging by their teeth. #0482 The most brightly coloured wasps are usually the ones with the most painful sting. #0483 There are more than 30,000 species of wasp. #0484 Most species of wasp live alone, and about 1,000 wasp species live in colonies. #0485 **Scorpions** can live in extreme conditions and some can even survive a night in a freezer. #0486 Some scorpions can slow their body down and survive on just one meal a year. #0487 A female scorpion carries her young on her back until their skeletons harden. #0488

## BRILLIANT beetles

About one third of all animal species are beetles – more than 350,000. #0489 Some female beetles may lay 1,000 eggs in their lifetime. #0490 Beetles have poor eyesight and communicate mostly using smells. #0491 **Stag beetles** take their name from their huge jaw, which looks like a stag's antlers. #0492 Beetles are found on every continent on Earth. #0493 The **fringed ant beetle** is the smallest known beetle. It grows to just 0.25 mm in length. #0494 The largest beetle is the **Titan beetle** at 17 cm long. #0495 The heaviest beetle is the **Goliath beetle**, which weighs 100 g. #0496 The **Hercules beetle** is really strong. It can carry 100 times its own body weight. #0497 **Dung beetles** feed on balls of poo. #0498

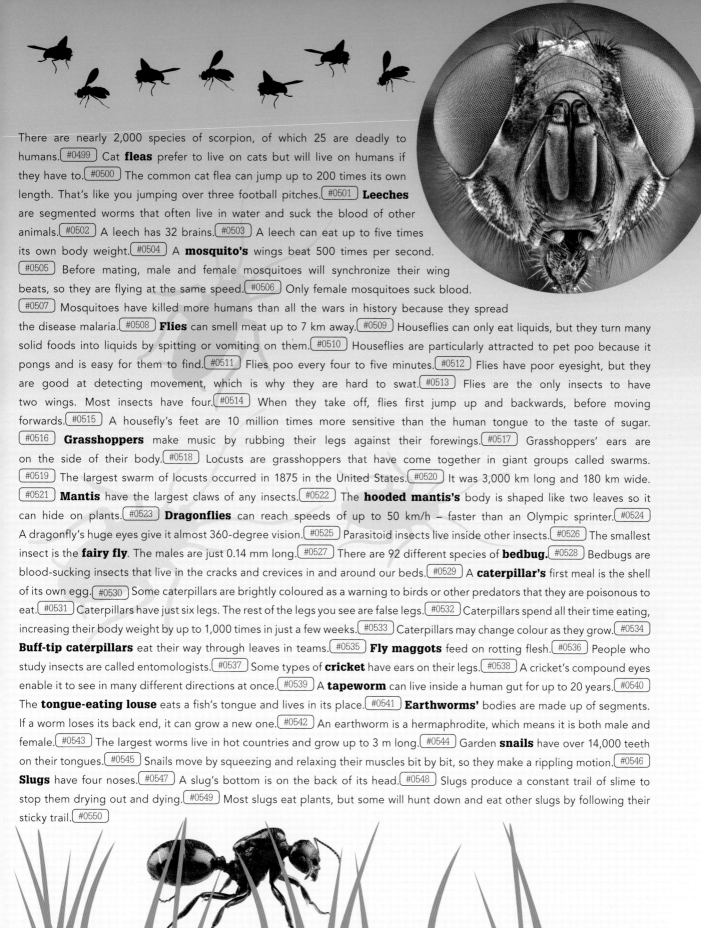

There are nearly 2,000 species of scorpion, of which 25 are deadly to humans. #0499 Cat **fleas** prefer to live on cats but will live on humans if they have to. #0500 The common cat flea can jump up to 200 times its own length. That's like you jumping over three football pitches. #0501 **Leeches** are segmented worms that often live in water and suck the blood of other animals. #0502 A leech has 32 brains. #0503 A leech can eat up to five times its own body weight. #0504 A **mosquito's** wings beat 500 times per second. #0505 Before mating, male and female mosquitoes will synchronize their wing beats, so they are flying at the same speed. #0506 Only female mosquitoes suck blood. #0507 Mosquitoes have killed more humans than all the wars in history because they spread the disease malaria. #0508 **Flies** can smell meat up to 7 km away. #0509 Houseflies can only eat liquids, but they turn many solid foods into liquids by spitting or vomiting on them. #0510 Houseflies are particularly attracted to pet poo because it pongs and is easy for them to find. #0511 Flies poo every four to five minutes. #0512 Flies have poor eyesight, but they are good at detecting movement, which is why they are hard to swat. #0513 Flies are the only insects to have two wings. Most insects have four. #0514 When they take off, flies first jump up and backwards, before moving forwards. #0515 A housefly's feet are 10 million times more sensitive than the human tongue to the taste of sugar. #0516 **Grasshoppers** make music by rubbing their legs against their forewings. #0517 Grasshoppers' ears are on the side of their body. #0518 Locusts are grasshoppers that have come together in giant groups called swarms. #0519 The largest swarm of locusts occurred in 1875 in the United States. #0520 It was 3,000 km long and 180 km wide. #0521 **Mantis** have the largest claws of any insects. #0522 The **hooded mantis's** body is shaped like two leaves so it can hide on plants. #0523 **Dragonflies** can reach speeds of up to 50 km/h – faster than an Olympic sprinter. #0524 A dragonfly's huge eyes give it almost 360-degree vision. #0525 Parasitoid insects live inside other insects. #0526 The smallest insect is the **fairy fly**. The males are just 0.14 mm long. #0527 There are 92 different species of **bedbug**. #0528 Bedbugs are blood-sucking insects that live in the cracks and crevices in and around our beds. #0529 A **caterpillar's** first meal is the shell of its own egg. #0530 Some caterpillars are brightly coloured as a warning to birds or other predators that they are poisonous to eat. #0531 Caterpillars have just six legs. The rest of the legs you see are false legs. #0532 Caterpillars spend all their time eating, increasing their body weight by up to 1,000 times in just a few weeks. #0533 Caterpillars may change colour as they grow. #0534 **Buff-tip caterpillars** eat their way through leaves in teams. #0535 **Fly maggots** feed on rotting flesh. #0536 People who study insects are called entomologists. #0537 Some types of **cricket** have ears on their legs. #0538 A cricket's compound eyes enable it to see in many different directions at once. #0539 A **tapeworm** can live inside a human gut for up to 20 years. #0540 The **tongue-eating louse** eats a fish's tongue and lives in its place. #0541 **Earthworms'** bodies are made up of segments. If a worm loses its back end, it can grow a new one. #0542 An earthworm is a hermaphrodite, which means it is both male and female. #0543 The largest worms live in hot countries and grow up to 3 m long. #0544 Garden **snails** have over 14,000 teeth on their tongues. #0545 Snails move by squeezing and relaxing their muscles bit by bit, so they make a rippling motion. #0546 **Slugs** have four noses. #0547 A slug's bottom is on the back of its head. #0548 Slugs produce a constant trail of slime to stop them drying out and dying. #0549 Most slugs eat plants, but some will hunt down and eat other slugs by following their sticky trail. #0550

# 9 MARSUPIAL FACTS

Marsupials are mammals that **give birth to tiny, helpless babies** that develop in their mother's **pouch.** Examples of marsupials include kangaroos, koalas and quolls. #0551

A baby marsupial that lives in its mother's pouch is called a **JOEY**. #0552

A newly born quoll joey is the size of a **grain of rice.** #0553

All the mammals that are native to Australia are **MARSUPIALS.** #0554

Opossums are immune to most **SNAKE VENOM.** #0555

Koalas feed on **eucalyptus leaves,** which are **low in nutrition,** meaning that koalas have little spare energy. #0556

To save energy, koalas sleep for up to 18 hours a day. #0557

Wombat poo is **cube-shaped.** #0558

The feisty **TASMANIAN DEVIL** has pink ears, but they go red if you make the marsupial angry. #0559

# 4 FACTS ON CHINA'S SECRET ARMY

Emperor **Qin Shi Huangdi** of China (259 BC to 210 BC) wanted to **live forever,** so he built a huge burial mound to protect his body in the afterlife. #0560

At least **8,000 CLAY SOLDIERS** guard the tomb, as well as **130 CHARIOTS** and **670 HORSES.** #0561

The burial mound is believed to contain **booby traps to protect his body,** which is also surrounded by rivers of poisonous **mercury!** #0562

Every soldier's face was designed separately, so **no two warriors look the same.** #0563

# 10 FACTS ABOUT THE WORLD'S BLOODIEST BATTLES

The world's **longest war** lasted for **116 years**. It was between England and France, and started in 1337. #0564

The world's **shortest war** lasted just **38 minutes,** when a British fleet attacked the island of Zanzibar in 1896. #0565

Between **62 and 78 million** people died during World War II (1939–1945). #0566

During the Mongol conquests (1207–1472) **17 per cent of the world's population died.** #0567

Nearly **2 million** German and Russian soldiers were **killed or wounded** during a battle at Stalingrad (1942–1943). #0568

During the Battle of the Somme, on 1 July 1916, around **19,240 of the British army were killed**. #0569

Around **51,000** soldiers died in a **three-day battle** during the American Civil War (1861–1865). #0570

Confederate General 'Stonewall' Jackson was mistakenly **killed by his own men**. #0571

The **largest naval battle** took place at Salamis in Greece about **2,500 years** ago. #0572

The **largest tank and aerial battles** happened at the same time, at Kursk in 1942, between Germans and Russians. #0573

# 43 terrific **TOY** facts

## 7 TEDDY BEAR FACTS

Around **1890, Margarete Steiff** began to make soft toys in Germany. `#0574` In **1902** Margarete's nephew designed and created a soft cuddly bear to add to the other animals Margarete was selling. `#0575` In **1902** the President of the United States **Theodore (Teddy) Roosevelt** refused to shoot a bear when he was out hunting. `#0576` The tale of his kindness spread quickly and from **1906** the Steiff bear sold in the United States under the name 'teddy bear'. `#0577` Other companies created and sold their own bears and the teddy bear became a firm favourite with children around the word. `#0578` The most expensive teddy bear ever is the Steiff **Louis Vuitton** teddy bear. `#0579` It sold for £125,000 at an auction in 2000. `#0580`

The first recorded **doll's house** was made for the **Duke of Bavaria** around **1557**. `#0585` It was a copy of his own home. `#0586` In the 16th century, dolls' houses were a popular way for a home owner to show their wealth. `#0587` One of the world's most expensive dolls' houses is the Fairy Castle. `#0588` On display in the Museum of Science and Industry in Chicago, it's valued at around 7 million US dollars. `#0589` It was created for the silent movie star **Colleen Moore** in **1928**. `#0590` Around 700 different craftsmen worked on it, including lighting specialists and jewellers. `#0591`

The longest wooden toy **train** track is 2,607 m long. `#0592` It was built by Brio AB and Siemens AG Rail System Division in **2012**. `#0593`

During the 19th century in the UK, many children were not allowed toys on Sundays, except Noah's Ark because it was in the Bible. `#0594`

The oldest-known **rocking horse** was owned by **King Charles I** and dates back to the **1600s**. `#0595` It was bought in **2006** by the V&A Museum in London, England. `#0596`

The first video arcade game was **Pong**, introduced by Atari in **1972**. `#0581`

**Dolls** are considered to be the oldest types of toys in history. `#0582`

The **yo yo** is believed to be the second oldest toy in the world. `#0583` The name 'yo yo' comes from a Filipino expression meaning 'come come'. `#0584`

Rubber ducks were introduced as toys in the **1800s**. #0597 Early versions were a kind of chewing toy. #0598 By the 1940s the rubber duck had evolved into a floating toy. #0599 **Charlotte Lee**, from the United States, is believed to have the largest private collection of rubber ducks in the world. #0600 She has 5,631 ducks, which she has been collecting since 1996. #0601

One of the first jigsaw puzzles was made around **1760** by English map-maker **John Spilsbury**. #0604 The puzzle was a map on a wooden board with the countries cut out to teach children their geography. #0605 Up until the **1820s** all jigsaw puzzles were educational. #0606

The world's largest toy collection was created by **Jerry Greene** from the United States. #0607 His collection has around 35,000 toys and is said to be worth tens of millions of dollars. #0608

The average child in the United States will wear down 730 crayons by their 10th birthday. #0609

The word 'toy' comes from an old English word meaning tool. #0610

75 per cent of the world's toys are made in China. #0611

The **hula hoop** originated in Australia where it was simply a bamboo exercise ring used in gym classes. #0602 The largest hula hoop ever spun had a diameter of 5.04 m and was spun 3.75 times by Ashrita Furman at a high school in the United States in 2010. #0603

The game of **marbles** is estimated to go back 5,000 years and was played by Ancient Egyptians and Romans. #0612 Mass production of marbles began in **1915** thanks to a machine invented by **M. F. Christensen**. #0613 The largest game of marbles ever played was a tournament in 2010 in California. #0614 It was organized by Duncan Toys and the Boy Scouts of America and 876 players took part. #0615

The greatest number of consecutive jumps achieved on a **pogo stick** is 70,271. #0616 The record was set by **James Roumeliotis** in the United States in 2013. #0617

**Snakes and Ladders** developed from the 16th century Indian board game **Vaikuntapaali**. #0618 In the original version the purpose of climbing a ladder was to show players the value of good deeds. #0619

The United States buys the most toys in the world, followed by the UK and Canada. #0620

Toy soldiers have been played with and collected since Ancient Egyptian times. #0621 **Sergey Valentinovich Spasov** has the world's largest toy soldier collection. #0622 He has been collecting them since **1990** and has around 661 different soldier figures. #0623

# 5 FACTS ABOUT VOTES FOR WOMEN

In 1718, a small group of female Swedish craftworkers were the **first women in the world** allowed to vote in elections. #0624

In 1756, Lydia Chapin Taft became the **first woman voter in North America** when she voted in Massachusetts Colony, then ruled by Britain. #0625

The first country to give all women the vote was **New Zealand**, in 1893. #0626

**British** women aged 30 and over got the vote in **1918**, while women in **Switzerland** had to wait until **1971**. #0627

Women in **Saudi Arabia** were first given voting rights in 2015. #0628

# 3 ARTY FACTS

The world's **oldest painting** is over **40,000 years old** – a red sphere of paint and handprints on a cave wall in El Castillo in Spain. #0629

One of the most **expensive paintings** in the world is *The Card Players* by Paul Cezanne, which sold in 2011 for **£160 million.** #0630

The oldest pieces of **pottery** in the world were found in 2012 by Chinese archaeologists. At **20,000 years old**, they were made at a time when much of the world was covered with ice! #0631

# ELEPHANTS

**10 FACTS ABOUT**

There are **two kinds** of elephant: **African** and **Asian**. African elephants have much bigger ears. Their big ears keep them cool on hot days. #0632

Just as we are left- or right-handed, elephants are left- or right-tusked. The dominant tusk is usually more worn down than the other. #0633

Female African elephants have a gestation (pregnancy) that lasts **22 months** – longer than any other animal. #0634

Elephants use mud or sand as sun block. #0635

Elephants have **26 teeth**, which are usually replaced **6 or 7 times in their life**. They eat plants, and wear their teeth out through chewing. #0637

Elephants lift and spread their ears to signal to other elephants when they are alarmed. #0636

An elephant's heart beats only **25 times per minute** – about three times more slowly than the average human heart. #0638

An African elephant's trunk is about **2 m long**. #0640

Female elephants spend all their lives with their family group. **Each group is led by an old female called the matriarch.** #0639

Elephants can communicate by **stamping on the ground**. Other elephants sense the vibrations many kilometres away. #0641

# 3 FACTS ABOUT WONDROUS WALLS

**Hadrian's wall,** a **120-km wall,** was built for the Roman Emperor Hadrian to prevent attacks by raiders from the north of Britain. #0644

During the AD 770s, King **Offa of Mercia** in central England ordered a border to be dug to keep the Welsh out of his kingdom. The ditch is **20 m wide** and can still be seen today. #0643

The **ancient wall** that stretches round Rome is **19 km long, 16 m tall** and has **383 towers, 18 main gates – and 116 toilets!** #0642

# 10 FACTS ABOUT GODS AND EMPERORS

The Japanese believe that their emperor is a descendant of **Amaterasu,** the goddess of the Sun and the Universe. #0645

The current Japanese emperor, Akihito, is the **125th emperor of Japan.** #0646

The Chinese emperor was called the **'Son of Heaven'**. #0647

In 331 BC, **Alexander the Great** decided that the Egyptian sky-god, Amun, was his real father! #0648

**Napoleon Bonaparte** became Emperor of France in 1804. #0649

Napoleon made his **three brothers kings** and his **sister a grand duchess.** #0650

The Roman emperor, **Caligula,** went mad and appointed his horse, Incitatus, a priest. #0651

**Diocletian** was the first Roman emperor ever to resign. He retired to a palace in Croatia and grew cabbages instead. #0652

After he died in 44 BC, **Julius Caesar** was officially recognized as a **god** by the Roman State. #0653

When **Ogedei Khan** of the Mongol empire died in AD 1241, the Mongol armies fighting in Western Europe had to go home to Asia to elect a new emperor. #0654

The **LARGEST METEORITE EVER FOUND** fell in Namibia, south Africa, in 1920. It weighed over **60** tons – as much as **15 ELEPHANTS**. #0655

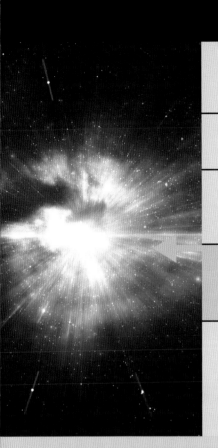

Distances between stars are measured in **light years** (the distance light travels in a year – about 10 trillion km). #0656

Stars called **supergiants** are 70 times larger than our Sun. #0657

**Our nearest star,** Proxima Centauri, is 4.3 light years away – about 40 trillion km. #0658

**The brightest stars** in the Milky Way shine 5 million times brighter than the Sun. #0659

In 1974, scientists searching for life on other planets beamed a message at a group of stars. It will take **25,000 years** for the message to arrive and **50,000 years for any reply.** #0660

A rocket travelling at the speed of the *Apollo* spacecraft would take **900,000 years** to reach Proxima Centauri. #0661

Stars appear to **twinkle** because of varying air currents in Earth's atmosphere. #0662

Our galaxy, the Milky Way, contains at least **100,000 million stars.** #0663

# 9 FACTS ABOUT HIPPOS

The name *hippopotamus* means **HORSE OF THE RIVER** in Greek. #0664

Hippo milk is **bright pink**. #0665

An **adult** hippo can weigh more than **3,000 KG** – as much as a medium-sized **elephant**. #0666

A hippo's eyes are covered with a special clear membrane. The membrane **acts like goggles** to help the hippo see underwater clearly. #0667

Nearly **3,000** people are **killed by hippos** every year. #0668

Hippo skin is **15 CM THICK.** #0669

The closest living relatives to hippos are actually **WHALES.** #0670

Its **HUGE** canine teeth are used for **fighting, not eating.** #0671

Hippos can **sleep underwater.** They bob up to the surface every few minutes to take a breath **without waking up**. #0672

# 5 RHINO
## FACTS

Rhinos welcome oxpecker birds because they **eat the itchy parasites** that live on the rhino's skin. #0673

Rhinoceroses can grow up to **3.5 m long** – as long as two adult humans lying toe to toe. #0674

There are only around **40** JAVAN RHINOS **left on the planet.** #0675

**Rhinos are very rare because humans hunt them. Nearly**

**700**

**were killed in South Africa in 2012.**

#0676

A rhino's **HORN** is made from keratin, the same stuff that our fingernails and hair are made from.

#0677

57

# 76 brilliant BIRD facts

There are about 10,000 species of bird. #0678 Birds have hollow bones that help them fly. #0679 Around 20 per cent of birds migrate long distances every year. #0680 **Green herons** will sometimes drop an insect in water, then catch the fish that eats the bug. #0681 **Crows** recognize human faces. #0682 They will attack people who have previously attacked them or a crow they know. #0683 Migrating crows will change their route to avoid a place where crows have previously been shot. #0684 In Japan, crows have learned to drop nuts at pedestrian crossings – passing cars crush the shells, and the crows wait for the green light to walk out and eat them in safety. #0685 **Scrub jays** pretend to hide their food if they know other scrub jays are watching,

In many species of bird, only the male has colourful feathers. #0686

The **peacock** fans his tail feathers to attract mates. #0687

His feathers can grow to more than 1 m long. #0688

They fall out and grow again each year. #0689

but they will really be taking it somewhere else. #0690 **Flamingos** can live in a variety of habitats, even salt lakes. #0691 Special glands near their beaks can filter out excess salt as they feed. #0692 **Malachite kingfishers** bash the heads of fish they have caught against tree trunks to kill them. #0693 The brightly coloured **macaw** birds mate for life. #0694 An **African grey parrot** has displayed an ability to think equivalent to that of a four-year-old child. #0695 The parrot was called Alex. #0696 When he was tired, Alex would give wrong answers on purpose to make tests (to measure his intellect) stop. #0697 The **toco toucan** is the largest of all toucans. #0698 Its bill makes up a third of its length. #0699 A **vulture's** head and neck are bald or covered in short feathers. #0700 This allows it to reach deep inside dead bodies as it feeds. #0701 On a hot day, vultures pee on their legs. #0702 This helps to cool them down. #0703 When a vulture feels threatened, it vomits. #0704 Up to six different species of vulture may feed on the same carcass. #0705 Each will feed on a different part of the body. #0706 Vultures have excellent eyesight. #0707 They can spot a dying animal on the ground several kilometres away. #0708 The wingspan of the **Andean condor** can be as long as 3.2 m. #0709 Each wing is as long as an average adult human. #0710 The condor uses its huge wings to soar high into the air on rising air currents. #0711 It can reach heights of over 4,000 m. #0712 Condors have one chick every other year. #0713 It takes them a whole year to rear the chick. #0714 A male **barn owl** will bring a female a gift of a dead mouse in an effort to win her affections. #0715 At night, male **nightingales** sing to impress the females. At dawn, they sing to defend their territories. #0716 The male **bowerbird** builds a display using twigs and brightly coloured objects to impress females. #0717 Male **frigatebirds** have giant red pouches under their bills that inflate to attract a mate. #0718 **Wandering albatrosses** incubate their eggs for 78 days. #0719 24 hens' eggs could fit into one **ostrich** egg. #0720 The European **blue tit** lays up to 16 eggs in one clutch. #0721 **Ospreys** lay three eggs, but the eggs do not hatch at the same time. The chick that hatches first is most likely to survive. #0722 Every autumn the **bar-tailed godwit** flies from Alaska to New Zealand, a distance of 11,000 km. #0723 The godwit does this journey in eight days and flies non-stop without a break. #0724 They build up fat reserves before the journey to use for energy as they fly. #0725 The **Arctic tern** starts its long journey from the Arctic to Antarctica after breeding each year. #0726 On the journey south, they stop for a while in the Azores to feed. #0727 The terns do not fly straight but follow an S-shaped route – this allows them to take advantage of prevailing winds. #0728 Iron-rich blood cells have been found in the tops of **homing pigeons'** beaks. #0729 Homing pigeons often follow roads on the ground as they fly home. #0730 They even turn off at junctions! #0731 During World War II, some aircraft carried pigeons on board. Airmen would send a message home attached to the pigeons if their planes were shot down. #0732 Homing pigeons use the position of the Sun to help them navigate. #0733 Eyesight is the most important sense for birds. Their vision is two to three times more detailed than humans'. #0734 Most birds have a poor sense of taste and smell. #0735 **Oilbirds** live in dark caves and use echolocation to find their way around. #0736 Weighing in at up to 18 kg, male **korl bustards** and **great bustards** share the record for the heaviest flying birds. #0737 **Rüppell's griffon vulture** is possibly the highest flyer, climbing to over 10,000 m. #0738 The **Australian pelican** has the longest beak, at up to 47 cm long. #0739 A flock of **starlings** is called a murmuration. #0740 Before they roost for the night, starlings form huge ball-shaped murmurations. #0741 Each bird tries to match its neighbours' speed and direction. #0742 The constant changing shape of the murmuration makes it difficult for birds of prey to attack any of the starlings. #0743 One murmuration in Goole, in England, included 1.5 million birds. #0744 Adult **sparrows** are vegetarian, but the young eat mostly insects. #0745 Sparrows have been known to nest in coalmines hundreds of metres underground. #0746 A pair of sparrows will raise two or three broods in one year. #0747 House sparrows live mainly in urban areas but may move to the countryside during harvest time. #0748 Sparrows have lived alongside humans since the Stone Age. #0749 A sparrow's place in the pecking order is determined by the size of its bib (the coloured part of its breast). #0750 Sparrows often steal other birds' nests rather than building their own. #0751 A **wren** will feed its young more than 500 spiders and caterpillars in a single day. #0752 The **Baltimore oriole** can eat up to 17 caterpillars in a minute. #0753

# 25 FUN FLYING ANIMAL FACTS

The **flying fox** isn't actually a fox, it's a bat. It is also called a fruit bat. #0754 Its wingspan is 1.5 m. #0755 A bat's knees bend the opposite way from human knees. This makes it easier to run on all fours. #0756 A bat's wing is so thin you can see the blood vessels running through it. #0757 Bats are the only mammals that can fly rather than glide. #0758 A **brown bat** can catch over 600 insects in 1 hour. #0759 **Vampire bats** feed on the blood of mammals. #0760 The bats bite their victims while they are asleep and lick the wound. #0761 Bats make high-pitched sounds and listen for the echoes to enable them to hunt in the dark. This is called echolocation. #0762 **Fruit bats** do not use echolocation but have big eyes to help them see in the dark. #0763 The **tube-lipped nectar bat's** tongue is 1.5 times longer than its body. It uses it to reach into plants and collect nectar. #0764 The **bumblebee bat** is actually smaller than some bees. #0765 Bracken Cave in the United States has a colony of 20 million bats living in it. #0766 The **flying gecko** can't actually fly but glides using skin flaps connected to its feet. #0767 **Flying snakes** glide from tree to tree for up to 100 m. #0768 They flatten their bodies to catch as much air as possible. #0769 They look graceful while in the sky, but usually crash-land. #0770 There are about 50 different types of **flying squirrel**. #0771 Flying squirrels can live for around 10 years in captivity and up to 6 years in the wild. #0772 They can make 180-degree turns during gliding. #0773 Thick paws help cushion their landing. #0774 Ballooning **spiders** use their silk to create floating parachutes to glide through the air. #0775 Parachuting is a dangerous mode of transport for spiders and is practised more by young, light spiders than older, heavier ones. #0776 **Colugos** are gliding mammals that inhabit forests in South-East Asia. #0777 Unlike other gliding mammals, even the spaces between their fingers and toes are webbed to increase the total surface area of their gliding skin. #0778

# RODENTS

About **40%** of all mammal species are rodents. #0780

**There are more than 2,000 species of rodent.** #0779

A mouse can **SQUEEZE** through a gap just **0.6 cm WIDE** – about the width of a pencil. #0782

Rodents have **four big front teeth.** The teeth never stop growing, and must be kept worn down by gnawing. #0781

A mouse's tail is **as long as the rest of its body.** #0783

The capybara's EYES, NOSE and EARS are all right at the top of its head. This allows it to swim with just the **top of its head above the water.** #0784

The capybara is the largest rodent, **weighing up to 66 kg** – about the same as an average adult human. #0785

**Naked mole rats can live for up to 20 years.**
#0786

The naked mole rat spends its entire life in **underground tunnels.**
#0787

Naked mole rats never develop cancer. Scientists study them to find out why this is. **IT MAY HELP US TO FIND A CURE.**
#0788

Naked mole rats can **run backwards** just as quickly as they run forwards.
#0789

A naked mole rat digs tunnels with its front teeth. It can **seal off its mouth completely** as it digs to stop dirt from getting in.
#0790

**GUINEA PIGS** are active for up to 20 hours a day.
#0791

**FLYING SQUIRRELS glide from tree to tree**, using flaps between their legs like the **wings of a glider.**
#0792

# 50 RAINFOREST facts

## THE BIG ONE: THE AMAZON

The Amazon rainforest is the **largest tropical rainforest** in the world. #0793 It covers around **5.5 million km².** #0794 Over half of the Amazon rainforest is in **Brazil.** #0795 It is also located in other South American countries including **Peru, Venezuela, Ecuador, Colombia, Guyana, Bolivia, Suriname** and **French Guiana.** #0796 **10 per cent** of the world's known species live in the Amazon rainforest. #0797 **20 per cent** of the world's bird species live in the Amazon rainforest. #0798 There are many dangerous species living there, like the **jaguar** and **anaconda.** #0799 Many of these dangerous species are insects such as **mosquitos, butterflies, spiders** and **beetles.** #0800 The loudest animal in the Amazon rainforest is the **howler monkey.** #0801 In **2005** and **2010,** the Amazon rainforest suffered severe droughts that killed off large amounts of vegetation. #0802 The **Amazon River** is around 6,400 km long. #0803 There are no bridges that cross the Amazon, mostly because the majority of the Amazon River runs through rainforests rather than roads or cities. #0804 During the wet season, sections of the Amazon River can reach over 190 km in width. #0805 There are over 3,000 known species of fish that live in the Amazon River. #0806 The Amazon River is home to many deadly animals including the **piranha, caiman** and **poison dart frog.** #0807 Indigenous people have been living in the Amazon rainforest for thousands of years. #0808 One of the most famous tribes living there is the **Yanomami** tribe. #0809 The tribe has around 40,000 people who speak four different languages. #0810 Around 26,000 of them live in Brazil and around 14,000 live in **Venezuela.** #0811 The Yanomami people are often at war with each other over food and territory. #0812 The Brazilian government recognizes the tribes as rightful owners of the land and have introduced them to better health care. #0813 Women do most of the work – they look after the children, cook, fish and gather plants. #0814 The men hunt and fight, and children are also expected to work with their parents from a young age. #0815 They live without clothes except for a small loincloth, and men and women all have the same round haircut. #0816

# AROUND THE WORLD

Rainforests are found on every continent except Antarctica. #0817 There are two types of rainforest, temperate and tropical. #0818 **Temperate rainforests** lie between the tropics (lines of latitude on either side of the equator) and the polar circles. #0819 They are found in several regions such as North America, south-eastern Australia and New Zealand. #0820 **Tropical rainforests** lie within the tropics. #0821 They are found in many areas near the equator, in Asia, Africa, Central America and the Pacific Islands. #0822 The **largest temperate rainforests** are found on North America's Pacific Coast and stretch from northern California up into Canada. #0823 Rainforests act as the world's thermostat by regulating temperatures and weather patterns. #0824 Rainforests maintain Earth's limited supply of fresh water. #0825 One fifth of the world's fresh water is found in the **Amazon Basin.** #0826 The trees of a tropical rainforest are so densely packed that rain falling on the tops of the trees can take as long as 10 minutes to reach the ground. #0827 A rainforest floor is usually very dark, with only about 1 per cent of sunlight making it through the tops of the trees above. #0828 In the moist rainforests of South America, **sloths** move so slowly that algae are able to grow in their fur. #0829

Some rainforest **monkeys** are omnivores, eating both animals and plants. #0830 More than 2,000 different species of **butterfly** are found in the rainforests of South America. #0831 Flying animals found in Asian rainforests include **frogs**, **squirrels** and **snakes.** #0832 The rainforests of **Central Africa** are home to more than 8,000 species of plant. #0833 80 per cent of the flowers in **Australian rainforests** are not found anywhere else in the world. #0834 1 out of 4 ingredients in our medicines originated from rainforest plants. #0835 Scientists believe that there may be millions of plant and insect species in rainforests that have yet to be discovered. #0836 More than 2,000 tropical rainforest plants have been identified by scientists as having anti-cancer properties. #0837 Rainforests used to cover 14 per cent of Earth's surface, but due to deforestation now only cover around 6 per cent. #0838 Rainforests are home to around half of the world's plant and animal species. #0839 An area of a rainforest the size of a football pitch is destroyed every second. #0840 About 2,000 trees per minute are cut down in the rainforests. #0841 More than 100 rainforest species are destroyed every day. #0842

# 10 BARMY BLOOD AND BREATHING FACTS

Your **heart** will beat between **2 and 3 billion** times over the course of a lifetime. #0843

If you spread all the breathing surfaces inside your lungs out flat, they would be the size of a **tennis court**. #0844

With every breath, you take in **air molecules** breathed out by **dinosaurs**. #0845

On deep dives without breathing equipment, a diver's lungs shrink to the size of **grapefruits.** #0846

Some people who've had **heart transplants** say they start liking the same food, hobbies and colours as their heart donor. #0847

The **heart muscles** squeeze so hard they could squirt blood **10 m** through the air. #0848

Blood is as salty as **seawater.** #0849

It takes about **45 seconds** for a blood cell to zoom around the body. #0850

**Blood cells** are made inside your **bones**. #0851

Octopuses have **blue blood** and insects have **yellow blood**. #0852

# 3 FACTS ABOUT HUMANS

**Urine** is mostly water, so it can be drunk for survival in an emergency! #0853

You make enough **SALIVA** each day to fill five teacups. #0854

If the **body's temperature** drops below **21⁰C,** it's usually fatal. #0855

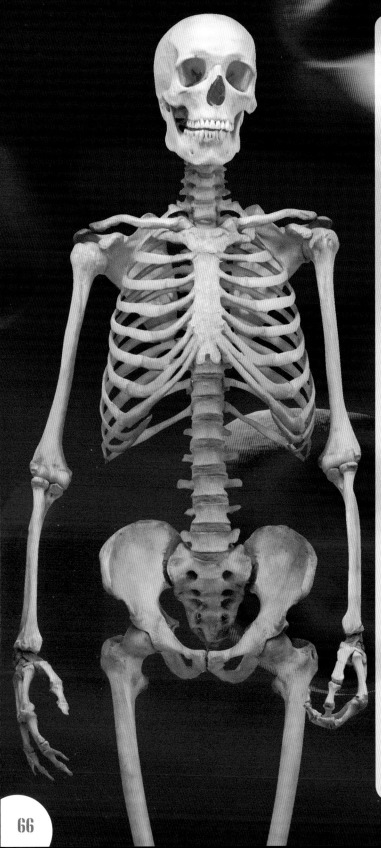

Over 60 per cent of your body is water. #0856 You can survive weeks without food, but only a few days without water. #0857 The average person produces about 1.5 litres of urine every day. #0858 You also lose about 0.4 litres of water in sweat, 0.4 litres as vapour in your breath and 0.1 litres in poo. #0859 You sweat when you are hot to cool the body. #0860 Skin has tiny holes, called pores, to let out the sweat. #0861 The sweat takes heat away from the body as it evaporates. #0862 The average person has about 2.6 million sweat glands. #0863 Around 250,000 of those glands are on the soles of the feet. #0864 If you suffer from excessive sweating, you have hyperhidrosis. #0865 You have about 5 million hairs on your body. #0866 Hair can grow everywhere apart from on the soles of your feet, the palms of your hands and your lips. #0867 Between 50 and 100 hairs fall out of your head every day. #0868 No hair lasts more than six years. #0869 Skin stops moisture from inside the body getting out. #0870 It also stops germs getting in. #0871 Tiny particles in your skin shield your skin from the Sun's harmful rays. #0872 A fingerprint is made by ridges of skin on each finger and thumb. #0873 The ridges form a line of loops, whirls and swirls. #0874 There are about 650 skeletal muscles in your body. #0875 Most actions like walking, running, sitting and smiling involve dozens of different muscles. #0876 The gluteus maximus in the buttock makes up 40 per cent of a man's body weight. #0877 Some muscles cannot push, they can only pull. #0878 This means they must work in pairs. #0879 Muscles are made of stretchy, fibre-like material. #0880 The more you exercise, the thicker and stronger your muscles become. #0881 Bones are made mostly of calcium and collagen. #0882 All your bones together are called a skeleton. #0883 All the bones of the skull, except the jaw, are fused together to make them stronger. #0884 A vertebra is a knobbly bone in your spine. #0885 The 33 vertebrae fit together to make a strong pillar, your spine, which carries your weight. #0886 The thigh bone (femur) is the longest bone in your body. #0887 It accounts for more than a quarter of an adult's height. #0888 Inside the larger bones is a criss-cross honeycomb. #0889 Blood vessels weave in and out of the bone, keeping the cells alive. #0890 Fingernails and toenails grow faster in hot weather. #0891 A fingernail grows about 1 mm every seven days. #0892

A nerve signal travels about 1 m per second in the slowest nerves. #0893 It travels about 100 m a second in the fastest. #0894 A chain of nerves carries a signal to and from the brain. #0895 Nerve endings send electrical impulses from one nerve cell to the next. #0896 Most people can hold their breath for about a minute. #0897 The enamel on your teeth is the body's hardest substance. #0898 Different teeth do different jobs. #0899 The broad, flat incisor teeth, at the front, slice food up when you take a bite. #0900 The pointed canine teeth grip and tear chewy food. #0901 The large premolars and molars, at the back, grind food. #0902 About 24 hours after swallowing food the waste, called faeces, is pushed out. #0903 The small intestine, which helps you digest your food, is almost 3 times as long as your whole body. #0904 The large intestine is a further 1.5 m. #0905 An adult eyeball is about the size of a golf ball. #0906 Most of it is hidden inside your head. #0907 Each of your two eyeballs gives you a slightly different picture, which combine to give you a 3D picture. #0908 The pupil becomes smaller in bright light to protect your retina (light-sensitive layer of tissue) from being damaged. #0909 It gets larger in dim light, to help you to see better. #0910 You blink to clean your eyes. #0911 The eyeball is covered with a film of salty liquid, so every time you blink the eyelid washes the eye. #0912 Two ears help you detect which direction sounds are coming from. #0913 The human nose can tell the difference between more than 10,000 different chemicals. #0914 The part of the brain that deals with smell is closely linked to the parts that deal with memories and emotions. #0915 That is why smells can make you remember things. #0916 By the age of 20 you will have lost 20 per cent of your sense of smell. #0917 By the time you are 60 you will have lost 60 per cent. #0918 Baby boys grow faster than baby girls in the first seven months. #0919 A baby's brain is the fastest-growing part of its body. #0920 Bones are so light they are only around 14 per cent of your body weight. #0921

## HEART FACTS

pump made mostly of muscle. #0943 Every day your heart beats about 100,000 times. #0944 A woman's heart beats faster than a man's. #0945 Electricity in your body makes your heart beat. #0946 The first heart cell starts to beat as early as 4 weeks. #0947 Regular exercise is the best way to keep your heart healthy. #0948 Every minute your heart pumps around 5 litres of blood. #0949 The arteries, veins and capillaries linked to your heart would stretch around the world – twice! #0950 The thumping sound of your heart is caused by the closing of the heart's valves. #0951 These valves make sure your blood flows in the correct direction in and out of your heart. #0952 The first successful heart transplant was performed in 1967 in South Africa. #0953 As long as it has a supply of oxygen, the heart will continue to beat even when separated from the body. #0954 Your heart does the most physical work of any muscle during your lifetime. #0955 Your heart is actually in the centre of your chest, not on the left. #0956

Bones get weaker as they get older. #0922 An empty stomach shrinks to a capacity of about 0.5 litres. #0923 A full stomach expands to hold up to 4 litres. #0924 Your lungs are like a pair of air-filled sponges in your chest. #0925 Your left and right lungs are different. #0926 The right lung is divided into three parts, the left lung is divided into two parts. #0927 The left lung is smaller to make room for your heart. #0928 There is usually at least 2.5 litres of air in your lungs. #0929 On average, you breathe in about 15 times a minute. #0930 When you exercise, this can increase to 80 times. #0931 Newborn babies breathe in about 40 times a minute. #0932 Your body has many barriers to stop germs entering. #0933 Itching, sneezing and vomiting are ways your body gets rid of unwelcome intruders. #0934 The largest artery (large tubes which carry blood) in the body is your aorta. #0935 It's about the size of a garden hose. #0936 Blood is made up of red cells, white cells and platelets, all carried in a liquid called plasma. #0937 Plasma is 90 per cent water. #0938 The smallest blood vessels in your body are smaller than a human hair. #0939 The amount of blood in your body depends on your size. #0940 If you donate blood, your body will replace the plasma within a few hours, but it can take weeks to replace the red blood cells. #0941

# ANTEATERS, ARMADILLOS AND SLOTHS

A giant anteater's **tongue** is longer than its head. It has **tiny hooks** on it to **catch insects**. #0957

The anteater uses its **huge claws** to dig into termite and ant nests. #0959

The giant anteater eats **35,000** insects every day. #0958

An anteater flicks its tongue out **three times a second,** scooping up insects. #0960

**NINE-BANDED ARMADILLOS** always give birth to **four identical quadruplets** – something no other **mammal** is known to do. #0961

Armadillos find their way around **at night** using **little hairs** on their sides and belly known as **CURB FEELERS.** #0962

Sloths hang from **branches** using their long, curved claws. They sometimes **don't fall off** even when they die. #0964

On the ground, sloths **cannot walk**. They drag themselves along with their **front arms**. #0965

Sloths come to the ground **once a week to poo**. #0966

Sloths can move more easily in **water** than on the ground, and may **swim from one tree to the next**. #0967

Some of the stones in the ancient circle of stones at **STONEHENGE** in southern England (constructed between 3100 and 1600 BC) weigh around **26** tons.  #0968

They are over **5** metres tall. #0969

# 10 FACTS ON FIERCE FEMALE RULERS

Despite her ruthless reputation, Russia's **Empress Catherine the Great**'s main interests were education and culture. #0970

The first woman to become a prime minister was **Sirimavo Bandaranaike,** who governed Sri Lanka from 1960–1965, 1970–1977 and 1994–2000. #0971

**Queen Victoria of England** was just 18 years old when she became queen. #0972

Many of Queen Victoria's **40 grandchildren** became kings and queens of other European countries. #0973

Margaret Thatcher was **Britain's first female prime minister** and was nicknamed **'The Iron Lady'** because of her strong-willed leadership style. #0974

**None** of the 43 American presidents and numerous vice-presidents have been women. #0975

The first woman to become a president was **Isabel Peron,** who governed Argentina in 1974. #0976

In 2012 **Queen Elizabeth II** celebrated 60 years on the British throne. #0977

Until 2013, women had ruled the Netherlands for **over 100 years**! #0978

**Mary Queen of Scots** was only six days old when she became Queen of Scotland in 1542. #0979

# 5 FACTS ABOUT JELLYFISH

**Jellyfish** don't have **BRAINS**.

#0980

Jellyfish do not have **gills**. They **absorb oxygen** through their **thin skin**.

#0981

In 2007, all the fish in a salmon farm off the coast of Northern Ireland were killed by a pack of **billions** of mauve stinger jellyfish.

#0982

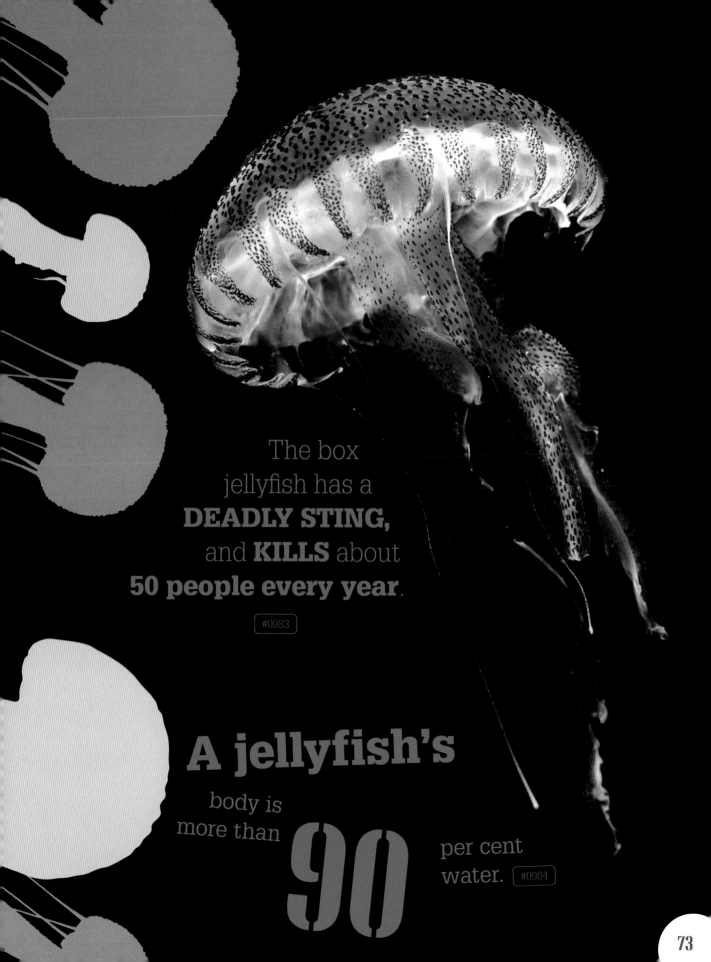

The box
jellyfish has a
**DEADLY STING,**
and **KILLS** about
**50 people every year**.

#0983

# A jellyfish's
body is
more than
**90** per cent
water. #0984

73

# 101 super SCIENCE

DNA, a material in our cells, carries information about how a living thing will look and function. #0985 Humans share about half of their DNA with a banana. #0986 Your DNA determines how you look, including your eye colour and the shape of your nose! #0987 99.9 per cent of your DNA sequence is the same as all other humans. #0988 Humans and chimpanzees share between 94–99 per cent of their DNA. #0989 *Apollo 11* was the first space mission to land men on the moon. #0991 The inventor **Al-Jazari** made automatic machines, like early robots, around **AD 1200.** #0992 The power of computers doubles every two years. #0993 There are around 17 billion devices connected to the Internet. #0994 That's more than two devices for every person on Earth. #0995 There is even Internet access on Mount Everest. #0996 A unit of length called the angstrom is equal to one ten-millionth of a millimetre. #0997 10 years is known as a decade, 100 years is known as a century and 1,000 years is known as a millennium. #0998 Milliseconds, microseconds and nanoseconds are very small units of time. #0999 One gigaparsec is about 3.26 billion light years. #1000 Match heads contain the poisonous chemical phosphorus. #1001 A match flame looks like a cone because gravity pulls the colder air down while hot air rises. #1002 There is less hot air, so the flame becomes thinner as it rises. #1003 Without gravity, hot air doesn't move upwards, so in space match flames look like balls of fire! #1004 Soap is made from animal fats or vegetable oil and

An electric eel uses its low-level charge like a radar to navigate and locate prey. #0990

If you crush a sugar cube in the dark, you can create flashes of light called triboluminescence, which means 'rubbing light'. #1006

The water we drink was once drunk by dinosaurs – it's recycled again and again. #1021

chemicals. #1005 Some types of rubber can be stretched 1,000 times beyond their original length before they reach their limit. #1007 The law of elasticity – the greater the stress, the greater the strain – is called Hooke's law. #1008 One measurement of time used by the Incas was based on how long it took to boil a potato. #1009 A laser is a beam of light energy. #1010 'Laser' stands for Light Amplification by Stimulated Emission of Radiation. #1011 Unlike the light we see from the Sun, light from a laser is made up of just one colour. #1012 Lasers are used in many places such as in hospitals, space exploration and communication. #1013 All solids are slightly elastic. #1014 Laser light is a 'coherent' source of light. #1015 This means the light waves are the same wavelength and in step with each other. #1016 The magnetic field of Earth reverses four or five times every 1 million years. #1017 This means that the North and South Poles swap over. #1018 At about 3,420°C, tungsten has the highest melting point of any metal. #1019 It gets its name from a Swedish term meaning 'heavy stone'. #1020 Most metals are shiny. #1022 They also conduct both heat and electricity well. #1023 Some metals are very tough but most can be easily shaped. #1024 There are billions of microbes (microscopic organisms) in just one teaspoon of soil. #1025 Japan has a network of roads that play music as you drive over them. #1026 The sound is created when cars drive over grooves cut out of the roads' surfaces. #1027 The average toilet seat is cleaner than the average toothbrush. #1028 This is because your teeth are home to millions of bacteria. #1029 The technology behind smartphones relies on around 250,000 separate patents. #1030 Mountains on Venus have been found to be capped with different types of minerals. #1032

Scientists can collect ice up to 800,000 years old in Antarctica. #1031

# facts

They include the minerals galena and bismuthinite. #1033 The pink thing in the corner of your eye is believed to be an evolutionary leftover from when we had an inner eyelid. #1035 Some birds and reptiles have inner eyelids today. #1036 A single bolt of lightning releases enough energy to cook 100,000 pieces of toast. #1037 Most people injured by lightning in their homes are talking on the telephone at the time the lightning strikes. #1038 Stars crush together hydrogen and helium under huge pressure. #1039 In 2006, scientists created a material that could one day be used to make invisibility cloaks. #1040 Common salt is made of sodium and chlorine. #1041 Both of these are dangerous to humans on their own. #1042 Astronauts lose 1 per cent of their bone mass for every month they spend in space. #1043 The force of gravity is not the same everywhere in the world because Earth is not a perfect sphere. #1044 Hudson Bay in Canada has lower gravity levels than other regions. #1045 Metal alloys are two metals mixed together. #1046 Berkelium is the rarest naturally-occurring element on Earth. #1047 Only 1 gram of the silvery white radioactive metal has ever been made. #1048 Around 1 per cent of the Sun's mass is oxygen. #1049 The Sun's enormous mass creates vast gravity, which puts its core under a lot of pressure. #1050 This pressure increases the Sun's temperature. #1051 If your body was the same size as the Sun, it would give out more heat. #1052 Uranus is the only planet in our Solar System that rolls on its side like a barrel – the other planets turn like spinning tops. #1053 Venus spins in the opposite direction to Earth. #1054 Water is a chemical compound, made up of two hydrogen atoms and one oxygen atom. #1055 Another name for water is hydrogen oxide. #1056 Unlike most substances, water expands when it freezes. #1057 An ice cube will take

Planet Earth would be the size of a marble if it had the same gravity as a black hole.
#1034

up to 9 per cent more volume than the water used to make it. #1058 If you drop a handful of salt into a full glass of water, the water level will go down, rather than overflow. #1059 There are about 250 g of salt in the human body. #1060 A pure element can take many forms. #1061 Diamond and graphite are both forms of pure carbon. #1062 Oxygen gas is colourless, but liquid oxygen is a pale blue colour. #1063 Around 95 per cent of the mass of the Universe is either 'dark matter' or 'dark energy'. #1064 It takes around eight minutes for light to travel from the Sun's surface to Earth. #1065 It takes about three minutes for light to reach Mercury. #1066 It takes light around five hours to reach Pluto. #1068 The Earth is around 4.6 billion years old. #1069 The dinosaurs disappeared before the Rockies and Alps formed. #1070 More germs are spread through shaking hands than kissing. #1071 The letter 'J' is the only letter that doesn't appear in the periodic table of elements. #1072 The metal gallium can melt in your hands. #1073 Every time lightning strikes, ozone gas is produced. #1074 This helps strengthen the ozone layer. #1075 Oxygen is the most abundant element on Earth. #1076 It's also about the third most common element in the Universe. #1077 The most common metal found on Earth is iron. #1079 This is because it makes up most of the Earth's core. #1080 If you yelled for around eight and a half years, you would produce enough sound energy to heat a cup of coffee. #1081 The faster an object moves, the smaller and heavier it becomes. #1082 The only rock that floats in water is pumice. #1083 Many physicists believe that there are wormholes (shortcuts through space and time) all around us. #1084 We can't see them, though, because they are smaller than atoms (the smallest particles). #1085

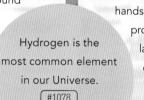

Bee stings are acidic.
#1067

Hydrogen is the most common element in our Universe.
#1078

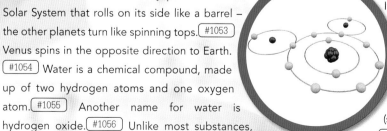

# 40 cool CULTURE and WORLD facts

## 10 UNUSUAL RULES AROUND THE WORLD

→ You can be fined for feeding the pigeons in St Mark's Square in Venice, Italy. #1086

→ It is illegal to run out of fuel on German motorways. #1087

→ Driving in flip-flops is a criminal offence in Spain. #1088

→ The Acropolis in Greece has banned visitors from wearing high heels. #1089

→ In Denmark you must always drive with your headlights on. #1090

→ It is illegal to step on bank notes in Thailand, because they feature an image of the king's head. #1091

→ If you pee in the sea in Portugal you would be breaking the law. #1092

→ In Canada, a set percentage of songs played on radio stations must be by Canadians. #1093

→ It is illegal to die in the Houses of Parliament (government buildings) in England. #1094

→ In Japan there is a law telling men and women how big their waistlines should be. #1095

The most commonly spoken language is Mandarin. #1096

English is the second most commonly spoken language. #1097

Spanish is the third most commonly spoken language. #1098

Papua New Guinea is the country with the highest number of spoken languages in the world – over 800 languages are spoken there. #1099 The official languages are Tok Pisin, English and Hiri Motu. #1100

More than 50 per cent of adults in Russia and Canada have a college degree. #1101

The United States has the most prisoners in the world. #1102 There are over 2 million people behind bars there. #1103

Niger, in Africa, has the youngest population in the world. #1104 Half of its population is under 15. #1105

Mongolia is the least densely populated country in the world. #1106

Norway has the lowest population density in Europe. #1107
It covers an area one-third bigger than the UK but has less than one-tenth the number of people living there. #1108
Japanese people live longest. #1109 On average, they live to be 84.6 years old. #1110
Singapore is the most religiously diverse country in the world. #1111
The United States spends the most on its military per head of population. #1112
It is a Spanish tradition to celebrate the new year by eating 12 grapes at midnight. #1113
It is custom that a Balinese baby must not touch the ground until it is six months old. #1114
Some Irish couples save a piece of their wedding cake to crumble and sprinkle on their first baby's head during its christening. #1115
Colombian school children learn that there are five continents, not seven. #1116 They put North and South America together as America, and Asia and Europe together as Eurasia. #1117
Many Finnish babies spend their first night in a cardboard box. #1118 The box is given to all Finnish mothers, along with a mattress, clothes, nappies and toys, to give each child an equal start in life. #1119
Norwegians usually eat their burgers with a knife and fork. #1120

Valentine's Day customs began hundreds of years ago in England. #1121 In Finland and Estonia, Valentine's Day is a celebration of friendship, rather than romantic love between two people. #1122
Halloween celebrations began in Ireland before spreading around the world. #1123 People would go from house to house in costume and be given food. #1124 This tradition was called 'guising'. #1125
A turnip was traditionally carved out to create a lantern. #1126 When the tradition arrived in America pumpkins were carved instead. #1127
When children lose their teeth in Greece, they throw them on the roof. #1128
The world's oldest international organization was set up in **1815**. #1129 Still running today, it's called the Central Commission for Navigation on the Rhine. #1130 Its headquarters are in France. #1131
The Red Cross was set up in **1863** after the Swiss businessman Henry Dunant witnessed the wounded lying on a battlefield and was appalled at the lack of care. #1132
Recognizing that the world could not afford a third world war, after World War II, the United Nations was formed in **1945** to promote world peace. #1133
UNICEF was set up in **1946** to help protect and promote the rights of children. #1134 It runs projects in around 190 countries and is the largest distributor of vaccines in the developing world. #1135

# 4 FACTS ABOUT ANIMAL ASTRONAUTS

In 1957, a Russian dog named Laika became **the first animal to orbit Earth**. Unfortunately, Laika did not survive her trip. #1136

Animals that have travelled in space include **mice, a rabbit, a frog and a tortoise.** #1137

French scientists planned to send a **CAT CALLED FELIX** into space in 1963, but he escaped. A replacement, Félicette, made the trip instead. #1138

The **first monkey in space** was called Albert II. Albert I sadly died before he got to take a trip. #1139

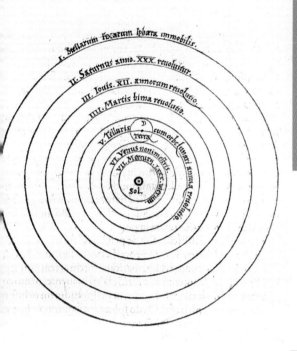

# 5 FACTS ABOUT EARLY IDEAS OF SPACE

In around 260 BC, Greek astronomer Aristarchus of Samos suggested the Sun was **THE CENTRE OF THE SOLAR SYSTEM**. It took 1,800 years to prove he was right. #1140

In the 1600s, you could be **THROWN IN PRISON** or even **TORTURED** for suggesting that the Earth was not the centre of the solar system. #1141

People believed the skies were unchanging until 16th century astronomer Tycho Brahe noticed a **NEW STAR IN THE SKY**. #1143

The word **COMET** comes from the Greek, for 'long-haired', as they were once thought to be '**LONG-HAIRED' STARS**. #1144

In 1543, astronomer Nicolaus Copernicus claimed the planets **MOVED AROUND THE SUN**. His book was banned until 1835. #1142

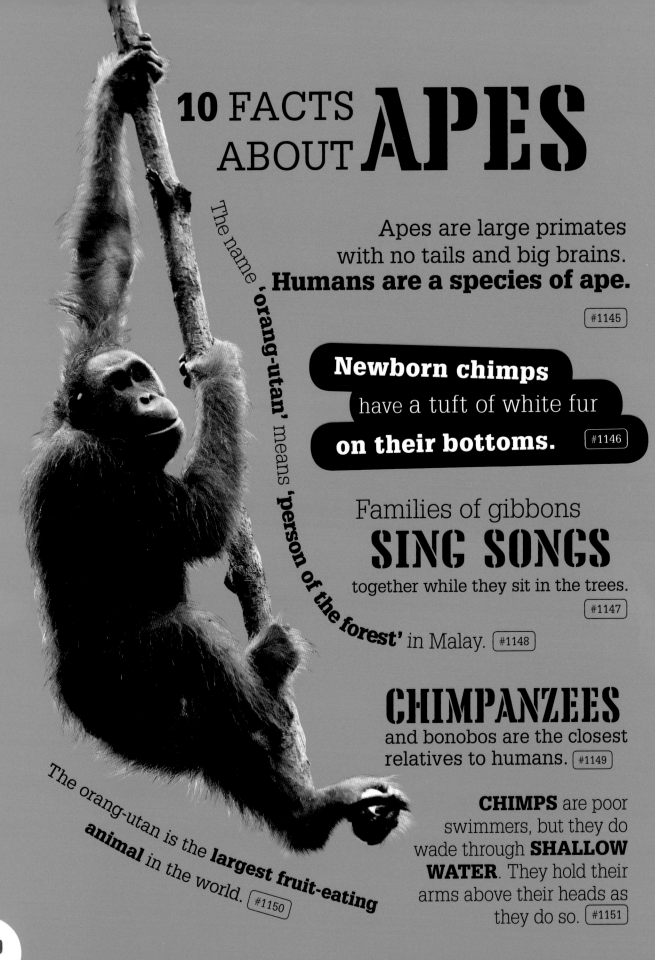

# 10 FACTS ABOUT APES

The name '**orang-utan**' means '**person of the forest**' in Malay. #1148

Apes are large primates with no tails and big brains. **Humans are a species of ape.**

#1145

**Newborn chimps** have a tuft of white fur **on their bottoms.** #1146

Families of gibbons **SING SONGS** together while they sit in the trees.

#1147

**CHIMPANZEES** and bonobos are the closest relatives to humans. #1149

The orang-utan is the **largest fruit-eating animal** in the world. #1150

**CHIMPS** are poor swimmers, but they do wade through **SHALLOW WATER**. They hold their arms above their heads as they do so. #1151

Mountain gorillas live in the high mountains of central Africa. They have **extra-thick fur** to keep them warm. #1152

**GORILLAS** are the largest **PRIMATES.** #1153

An adult male can weigh **200 KILOGRAMS** – that's heavier than two adult humans. #1154

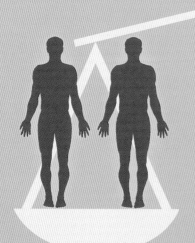

# 93 GROSS facts

You can tell when a camel is about to **spit** because its cheeks bulge. #1155 A single cow makes as much **saliva** as 200 humans. This helps it chew tough grass. #1156 Your nose runs when you cry because there is a lot more moisture going into it than normal, making the **mucus** more runny. #1157 **Earwax** keeps your ears moist and makes sure bugs and dirt can't get in. #1158 In the 19th century, magazines recommended using earwax as lip balm. #1159 Earwax is made from sweat, body oil and dead skin. #1160 The acid in your **stomach** is strong enough to eat through metal. #1161 Food needs three to five hours to dissolve in your stomach before it is ready to go into your small intestine. #1162 **Vomit** is very acidic and dissolves your teeth. #1163 Vomit contains half-digested food and bits of stomach lining. #1164 Fart gas is caused by swallowing air when you eat and the breakdown of certain foods in the large intestine by bacteria. #1165 One-third of **poo** is made of dead bacteria. #1166 Sweetcorn can pass straight through you and comes out looking exactly the same as when it went in. #1167 **Urine** is 95 per cent water. #1168 When it first comes out, urine is cleaner than spit. #1169 Male lobsters have bladders in their heads and shoot pee at each other. #1170 Swallowing air as you drink and eat can make you **burp**. #1171 Burping gets rid of a litre of gas from your stomach every day. #1172 Drinking through a straw can make you more likely to burp, as you swallow more air. #1173 The loudest burp ever recorded was as loud as a car alarm. #1174 Lots of **bacteria** live in your armpits and on your feet. They live off your sweat. #1175 **Sweat** is a mixture of water, salt and minerals that evaporates into the air. #1176 If sweat stays on your skin too long, bacteria start to eat it, creating the pongy chemicals that make you smell. #1177 **Dogs** hardly sweat at all and have to hang out their tongues to get rid of

body heat. #1178 **Hippo** sweat is red and acts as sunblock. #1179 Your feet shed dead skin cells all day. They mix with sweat to make a really smelly goo that is rolled into 'cheese' by your toes. #1180 The amount of **blood** that is pumped through an average human heart every day would fill about 85 baths. #1181 When you cut yourself, 16 different chemicals work together to turn blood into a jelly-like clot. After that, a **scab** can start to form. #1182 **Pus** is a gooey yellow gloop made from the dead white blood cells left over when your body attacks infection. #1183 The **skin** covering your body is your heaviest organ. #1184 Its three layers weigh 3.6 kg in total. #1185 If the average person stretched out all their skin, it would be about the size of a large bed. #1186 A **wart** is a knobbly clump of skin cells that grows when a virus gets into the skin. #1187 Four out of five teenagers get **acne**. #1188 This is a condition that causes bumps to appear on your skin. #1189 **Dandruff** occurs when your dead skin cells fall off faster than usual and become trapped by the hairs on your head. #1190 If your skin is rubbed for too long, it makes a little fluid-filled cushion called a **blister** to protect itself. #1191 The largest ball of hair in the world weighs over 75 kg and is 1.2 m high! #1192 The average head of human hair is strong enough to hold the weight of two adult **elephants**. #1193 Hair is made from keratin – the same stuff as your fingernails. #1194 The only part of your hair that isn't dead is the root inside your skin. #1195 A human has the same number of hairs on his or her body as a **chimpanzee**. #1196 In **Ancient Rome**, pigeon poo was used to dye hair blonde. #1197 A newborn baby poos out its own body weight every 60 hours. #1198 A baby will go through nearly 3,000 nappies a year. #1199 A newborn baby wees every 20 minutes. #1200 One in every 2,000 babies is born with **teeth**. #1201 **Penguins** vomit food back into their mouths to feed their chicks. #1202 Male **goats** wee on themselves to attract females. #1203 **Cows** often stick their tongues up their own noses to lick the salty mucus and keep flies away. #1204 Newborn **foals** eat their mother's poo. #1205 This gives them useful stomach bacteria which help them digest their food. #1206 A **dog's** sense of smell is up to

100,000 times better than a human's. #1207 Some dogs can smell dead bodies under water or detect cancer by smelling a person's breath. #1208 The wetness around a dog's nose is mucus. #1209 **Cats** swallow fur while licking themselves clean, then vomit it up as fur balls. #1210 Cats sometimes mark their territory by urinating. #1211 **Crocodiles** often rest with their jaws open because they sweat through their mouths. #1212 Crocodiles spin their prey around in a **'death roll'** to kill them. #1213 **Sharks** do bite humans, but it's usually by mistake. #1214 **Tigers** always attack their prey from behind. #1215 Some workers in **India** wear masks on the back of their heads to keep hungry tigers away. #1216 **Sperm whales** blast poo into the water as a defence, stirring it up into a brown cloud. #1217 Lots of **lizards** will drop off their tails to confuse attackers. #1218 The tail will keep wiggling for up to 10 minutes to distract the attacker while the lizard escapes. #1219 **Cuckoos** lay their eggs in other birds' nests. The cuckoo egg hatches first and throws other eggs or chicks out of the nest. #1220 **Polar bears**, **spiders**, **pigs** and **chimps** have been known to eat their own babies. #1221 The first **grey nurse shark** babies to hatch from their eggs will eat their brothers and sisters. #1222 **Ancient Egyptian** doctors recommended curing toothache by holding a freshly killed mouse onto the patient's gums. #1223 To make rotten teeth fall out during **Tudor** times, dentists used a mixture of poo and honey. #1224 In **1995** a nasal aspirator was invented to clean **snot** out of babies' noses, so that they could breathe more easily. #1225 In **2005**, scientists created a battery powered by urine. #1226 On an average day, you will inhale about 11 other people's fart gases. #1227 In **space**, poo has to be sucked away, freeze-dried and then stored to stop it floating around. #1228 Sometimes the bits of freeze-dried poo have floated free of the toilet. #1229 Astronauts have caught them in their mouths, thinking they were peanuts. #1230 The **kangaroo rat's** pee comes out in the form of paste, so it does not waste any water. #1231 Scientists who visit **Antarctica** have to take home all their rubbish, including wee and poo. #1232 When a passenger plane crashed in the **Andes** in **1972**, the survivors stayed alive by eating those who died. #1233 Some of the ice on **Mont Blanc** is so polluted by urine that it has turned yellow. #1234 If you **swallow** sea water, you'll also swallow

→ The scientific term for nose picking is **rhinotillexomania**. #1248

→ Snot is made of water, salt and a gluey sugary substance called mucin. #1249

→ A person swallows about a litre of snot a day without even realizing it! #1250

→ You don't sneeze in your sleep. #1251

→ The world sneezing record is held by British girl **Donna Griffiths**. She sneezed a million times in a row. #1252

→ Your snot looks more yellow when you have a cold because of all the white blood cells in it. #1253

→ Your snot protects you from germs and dirt in the air by catching them. #1254

→ If you've been hanging out in a dusty room, your snot will be grey. #1255

millions of viruses and bacteria. #1235 About 1 billion litres of raw sewage are dumped in the Ganges river in **India** every day. #1236 Many of the 420 million people who live near the Ganges rely on the water for washing and drinking. #1237 More than half of the world's 500 major rivers are polluted. #1238 If you wee in the River Nile in **Egypt**, parasitic worms could find their way into your body by following the warm pee trail. #1239 **New York City** is home to 8 million people and 250,000 rats. #1240 Approximately 500,000 people live in the city of San Pedro Sula in **Honduras**. In **2011** an average of three people were murdered there every day. #1241 Around 30 per cent of the drinking water in **Singapore** comes from recycled water, including some from toilets. #1242 About 6.3 billion kilograms of rubbish are dumped into Earth's oceans every year. #1243 In landfill, disposable **nappies** take around 800 years to completely biodegrade. #1244 Half of the 20 most polluted cities are in **India**. #1245 **Wembley Stadium** in England has 2,618 toilets. #1246 That's more than any other venue in the world! #1247

# 10 FACTS ABOUT LIFE IN SPACE

Russian cosmonaut Sergei Krikalev has spent **over two years** of his life in space. #1256

You get a little taller in space because there is **no gravity** to squash your bones. #1257

Astronauts living in space exercise for at least **two hours** each day so their muscles don't waste away. #1258

When in space, astronauts have to **strap themselves onto the toilet!** #1259

There are no washing machines in space so astronauts throw away dirty clothes. #1260

Astronauts on board space shuttles saw **16 sunrises** and **16 sunsets** a day because the shuttles orbited Earth 16 times in 24 hours. #1261

It takes a day to prepare for a **walk in space,** to allow the body to get used to the environment. #1262

Space-walking astronauts wear **adult-size nappies**. #1263

Astronauts use the **Vomit Comet,** which simulates weightlessness and encourages nausea, to prepare for zero gravity. #1264

The **Olympic torch** once flew on a space shuttle. #1265

**TELESCOPES** are a bit like **TIME MACHINES**.

The most powerful telescopes can look back in time, seeing stars as they were millions of years ago. #1266

# 10 FACTS ON THE ANCIENT ROMANS

A Roman **centurion** was in command of 80 men, divided up into 10 units of 8 men each. #1267

The Romans discovered **concrete**! They mixed lime, volcanic ash and water. #1268

Boys were **beaten** in Roman schools if they made mistakes! #1269

In Ancient Rome, urine was collected, and used for **tanning leather** and **cleaning togas**. #1270

The **Pantheon**, a temple to the gods, was built in AD 126. It is still the world's largest unreinforced concrete dome. #1271

Roman legions were named after their **qualities** or the **places** they served in. #1272

The Romans made **hamburgers** more than 2,000 years ago and ate **take-away food** from local bars. #1273

The world's **first fire engine** was invented by the engineer Hero, from Roman Egypt. #1274

The Romans heated their houses with the world's **first central heating system**, known as a hypocaust. #1275

While everyone else used scythes to cut corn, the Romans developed an early **combine harvester**! #1276

The Ancient Romans used guard dogs to guard their homes and, just like today, they even had **'BEWARE OF THE DOG'** signs. #1277

# 12 DOG
## FACTS

**Domestic dogs walk in a circle before they lie down, as their wild ancestors would have done, to flatten the ground.** #1279

Greyhounds have been recorded **running at 72 km/h** – that's nearly twice as fast as top human sprinters. #1281

All dogs have a see-through third eyelid that gives their eyes extra protection. #1282

Mongol ruler Kublai Khan kept **5,000** dogs. #1278

A Dalmatian puppy is born completely white. The first spots appear after about three weeks. #1280

**Puppies are born blind, deaf and toothless.** #1283

Dogs have up to
# 300 million
scent glands in their nose. #1285

A dog's wet nose traps chemicals in the air, helping it to smell them. #1284

**Dogs have 18 muscles in their ears.** #1286

Dogs drink water by forming the back of their tongue into a cup to scoop the water up. #1287

The tallest breed of dog is the Great Dane. The biggest of all, called Zeus, stood **1.12 m** from **paw to shoulder** – as tall as an average five-year-old child. #1288

About one third of all homes in the world have a pet dog. That's about
## half a billion
doggie homes. #1289

Many early canoes were hollowed-out logs called dugouts. #1290 Sails were first used around 7,000 years ago in **Mesopotamia** (an ancient region of Asia). #1291 The **Aborigines** arrived in Australia, by boat, at least 45,000 years ago. #1292 4,000 years ago **Ancient Egyptians** built ships more than 30 m long. #1293 Their sailing boats were called feluccas. #1294 Their triangular sails were called lateens. #1295 The sails were made from cotton and other natural fabrics like papyrus. #1296 They were the main mode of transport in Ancient Egypt. #1297 **Viking** ships were usually made of pine or oak. #1298 Their wooden frames were planked and held in place with iron rivets. #1299 Gaps were filled with animal hair mixed with tar to make the ship waterproof. #1300 Longships were the Vikings' fastest and largest ships. #1301 They measured up to 40 m long. #1302 They could carry up to 60 men and were used for pirating, exploration and combat. #1303 Vikings also used smaller ships called knarrs and karves. #1304 These were used for shorter journeys and transporting cargo. #1305 Dhows are wooden boats that have been used in the **Indian Ocean** and **Red Sea** for thousands of years. #1306 Dhows are made from teak and mango wood, then sewn together using coconut fibre. #1307 The first submersible boat, an early submarine, was built by **Magnus Pegel**. #1308 He built it in **1605**. #1309 The first workable submarine was built in **1620** by **Cornelius Drebbel**. #1310 The first military submarine was built in **1775**. #1311 It was called the *Turtle*. #1312 It was made of oak held together by iron rings. #1313 In **1864**, during the American Civil War, the *HL Hunley* was the first submarine to sink an enemy warship.

#1314 *HL Hunley* sank almost immediately after the successful attack. #1315 Its wreck was discovered in **1995** and recovered in **2000**. #1316 It is now on display in a museum in **South Carolina** in the United States. #1317 The first nuclear submarine, the *USS Nautilus*, was launched in **1954**. #1318 The first underwater circumnavigation of the world was by *USS Triton* in **1960**. #1319 Submarines are painted black to help them hide in the water. #1320 The British navy's *Astute* submarine can remain at sea for up to 25 years (if it needs to). #1321 It is also the quietest submarine in the world – which makes it perfect for surveillance missions. #1322 Boat passenger services were first introduced in **1844**. #1323 In **1839, Samuel Cunard**, **George Burns** and **David MacIver** set up a company called Cunard Line. #1324 Cunard Line pioneered the idea of a boat trip being a holiday in itself. #1325 *Allure of the Seas* is the world's largest cruise ship. #1326 It can hold around 6,300 passengers #1327 It has 2,384 crew onboard. #1328 Its top speed is 40 km/h. #1329 It cost around £1 billion to build. #1330 It has 24 lifts and 16 decks. #1331 The ship even boasts an outdoor park. #1332 The park contains 22,000 plants and trees. #1333 There are 20 restaurants and 20 pools. #1334 Passengers on a cruise ship called *The World* can live on it permanently. #1335 Between **2002** and **2014** *The World* visited over 900 ports worldwide. #1336 Many cruise ships don't have a deck number 13, as it is thought to be unlucky. #1337 **Christopher Cockerell** invented the hovercraft. #1338 He used a baked bean can and a firework to prove that a vehicle could float on air. #1339 The first commercial hovercraft crossed the English Channel in 1959. #1340 In the **1960s**, the US Navy began using hovercraft in the Vietnam War for patrol and rescue missions. #1341 Hovercraft are useful in combat because of their ability to travel over land, water and swamp ground.

# 80 facts on THINGS

# 20 TITANIC FACTS

The *Titanic* was a passenger ship that sank in **1912** after hitting an iceberg on its maiden voyage. `#1370` When it launched, the *Titanic* was the largest passenger ship ever built. `#1371` It measured 269 m in length and had 10 decks in total. `#1372` The ship's interior was based on the Ritz Hotel in London. `#1373` The grand staircase descended down seven decks. `#1374` The *Titanic* had a pool, a gym, a squash court and even a luxury kennel for first-class dogs. `#1375` 100,000 people attended the ship's launch in **1911**. `#1376` There were 885 crew members on board. `#1377` Only 23 of them were female. `#1378` The ship had its own newspaper called *The Atlantic Daily Bulletin*. `#1379` The richest passenger was **John Jacob Astor IV**. `#1380` The *Titanic*'s hull was torn open by an iceberg on **15 April 1912**. `#1381` There were only 20 lifeboats, not enough for everybody on board to escape. `#1382` Women and children were helped onto the lifeboats before men. `#1383` Musicians played for two hours while the ship sank. `#1384` Some passengers were reluctant to leave the *Titanic* as they believed it was unsinkable. `#1385` An estimated 705 survivors were rescued. `#1386` The survivors arrived in New York on the **18 April 1912**. `#1387` The wreck was discovered in **1985** off the coast of Newfoundland. `#1388` The bow had sunk 18 m into the seabed. `#1389`

`#1342` The fastest speed achieved by a hovercraft is 137.4 km/h. `#1343` It was driven by American **Bob Windt** at the **1995** World Hovercraft Championships. `#1344` A hovercraft is also known as an ACV – an air-cushion vehicle. `#1345` Hydrofoils are boats with hulls that lift up above the water when travelling at high speeds. `#1346` Only the foils, structures attached to the hull, dip into the water so there is less resistance and the boat can travel faster. `#1347` The first hydrofoil was built by Italian **Enrico Forlanini** in **1906.** `#1348` In **1918** the inventor of the telephone, **Alexander Graham Bell**, built a hydrofoil. `#1349` It broke the world water speed record at 114 km/h. `#1350` Hydrofoils are used as ferries in many countries in **Europe** and **Asia**, including **Hong Kong**. `#1351` **Billy Rossini** holds the record for the highest jump on a hydrofoil. `#1352` He jumped around 7 m in **2004**. `#1353` *The Prelude* is the world's largest floating structure. `#1354` It is as long as 10 Olympic-sized swimming pools. `#1355` It is the world's first floating liquified natural gas facility used to produce and export gas from the ocean. `#1356` **Ellen McArthur** sailed solo and non-stop around the world in **2005**. `#1357` She holds the fastest ever time for a woman – completing her trip in 71 days, 14 hours and 18 minutes. `#1358` In **2007 Francis Joyon** from **France** sailed around the world in 57 days, 13 hours and 34 minutes, the fastest time for a man. `#1359` The world's largest container ship is the *Mærsk Mc-Kinney Møller*. `#1360` Around 400 m in length, it was built in **2013**. `#1361` It can carry up to 18,270 containers. `#1362` Manned by a crew of 19, it can travel up to 23 knots. `#1363` Container ships transport many of the solids, liquids and gases that we use. `#1364` The **United States** has the largest navy in the world. `#1365` It also has the largest fleet of aircraft carriers. `#1366` It owns 3,700 aircraft. `#1367` One-third of its 291 battle force ships can be deployed at one time. `#1368` 325,000 United States servicemen were on active duty in 2014. `#1369`

# THAT FLOAT

Sometimes two **rainbows** will form at the same time. #1390 In the larger rainbow the colours will appear in reverse. #1391

There are basic weather records for the **UK** dating back to **55 BC**. #1392

The Met (Meteorological) Office in the UK uses one of the fastest **supercomputers** in the world. #1393

The Met Office's newest machine has as much computing power as 20,000 normal PC computers. #1394

The eye of a **hurricane** is at its centre, about which the winds rotate. #1395 It is the calmest section of the hurricane. #1396

Special aeroplanes fly directly into hurricanes to gather information. #1397 Weather forecasters then use the information to predict where the hurricanes will go, warning people of the danger. #1398

**Super Typhoon Tip** formed near **Japan** in October **1979**. #1399

Tip is the largest and most intense hurricane on record. It had wind speeds of up to 306 km/h and measured 2,220 km across. #1400

If you can hear **thunder**, you are within about 16 km of a storm. #1401

A roll of thunder can be up to 120 decibels, which is louder than a train speeding past! #1402

Thunder is one of nature's loudest sounds. #1403

There are about 16 million **lightning storms** around the world every year. #1404

That's about 100 lightning flashes happening every second. #1405

**Kifuka** in the **Democratic Republic of the Congo** gets more lightning strikes than anywhere else in the world. #1406

Kifuka gets hit with around 150 bolts a year per km$^2$ of land. #1407

A bolt of lightning is around 4 times hotter than the surface of the **Sun**. #1408

Sprites, Blue Jets and Elves are all types of lightning. #1409

If all the ice in the **Antarctic** melted, the world's oceans would rise by over 60 m, the height of a 20-storey building! #1410

**Antarctica** is one of the coldest and windiest places on the planet. #1411

Strong **Katabatic winds** in Antarctica form sheet-like rivers of snow that move at speeds of up to 200 km/h. #1412

The **Sun** has a surface temperature of around 5,700°C. #1413

The **foggiest** place on Earth is **Grand Banks**, on the Atlantic coast of Canada. #1414

One of the driest places on Earth is **Arica** in **Chile**. #1415

Less than 1 mm of **rain** falls in Arica every year. #1416

Every day 914 trillion litres of rain falls on Earth. #1417

*60 wacky*

92

# WEATHER facts

The record for the most rain to fall in a week was set in **2007** in **Réunion**, an island in the **Indian Ocean**. #1418

A powerful **storm** saw more than 5 m of rain fall on Réunion in just seven days – that's enough to leave a double-decker bus under water! #1419

**London, England**, gets less than 1 m of rain a year! #1421

The world's biggest **snowflake** was 38 cm wide and 20 cm thick. #1422

It fell in **Montana** in the United States in **1887**. #1423

In **Mawsynram** in **India** about 12 m of rain falls every year. It is known as 'the wettest place on Earth'. #1420

Many parts of the world experienced a cold period in the 17th and 18th centuries, known as the 'Little Ice Age'. #1424

The **River Thames** froze over in **England** and carnivals called 'frost fairs' were held on the ice. #1425

If 10 cm of **snow** melted in a glass, it would produce only about 1 cm of water. #1426

The tallest **snowman** in the world was actually a snow woman! #1427 She was 37 m tall. #1428

People from **Maine** in the United States spent one month building the snow woman in **2008**. #1429

**Snowflakes** can take as long as one hour to fall to the ground. #1430

In **1921** nearly 2 m of snow fell in just 24 hours in **Silver Lake, Colorado**, in the United States. This huge snowfall set a world record. #1431

56.7°C is the **hottest** temperature ever recorded on Earth. #1433

56.7°C was measured in **1911** at **Furnace Creek Ranch, California**, in the United States. #1434

The first weather satellite was sent into space in **1959**. #1432

There are 10 main types of **cloud**. #1435

There are **weather stations** set up all over the world. #1436

The highest weather station on land is on **Mount Everest**. #1437

The **highest** clouds are called cirrus clouds. They look like wispy curls of hair. #1438

The **Sahara Desert** gets very little rain. From **1973** to **1976** almost none fell at all! #1439

A **hailstone** the size of a bowling ball fell in South Dakota, in the United States, in 2010. #1440 Measuring around 20 cm in diameter, it is the largest hailstone ever recorded. #1441 Hailstones are most common during the summer, when there is more energy available, which makes bigger clouds. #1442 Hailstones are formed when water droplets fall and rise inside a cloud. #1443 When you cut a hailstone in half you can see rings of ice. #1444 The number of rings tells you how many times the hailstone has risen to the top of a cloud. #1445 Soft hailstones are called graupel and are small particles of snow with a crust of ice. #1446 Hailstones are usually between 5 and 200 mm in diameter. #1447 Hail Alley is an area in the United States where Colorado, Nebraska and Wyoming meet. On average it gets seven–nine days of hail a year. #1448 Hailstones that collide and stick together can be as heavy as 4 kg. #1449

# 10 SUPER-POWERED ANIMAL SENSES

Sharks can sense the **electrical signals** animals' bodies give off when they move. #1450

A male emperor moth can smell a female from **10 km away**. #1451

A **pit viper snake** has heat-sensing 'pits' on its face that allow it to detect its prey's body heat. #1452

A **rat's whiskers** are so sensitive, they can pick up sound vibrations in the air. #1453

**Giant pouched rats** can be trained to **sniff out** landmines and certain diseases. #1454

When **flies** land on food, they have a quick taste – using the tastebuds on their feet! #1455

**Camels** can close their **ears and noses** to protect themselves in a sandstorm. #1456

Some **butterflies** have **ears on their wings,** to listen out for bats that want to eat them. #1457

Octopuses can taste and smell with their **suckers**. #1458

A **chameleon** can point its eyes in **two different directions** at the same time. #1459

# 3 ODD ANIMAL FACTS

**Goats and sheep** have **rectangular pupils** to help them see sideways. #1460

The **shy-eye shark** covers its eyes with its fins when it sees a bright light. #1461

All **domestic dogs,** however different they are in size, belong to the **same animal species.** #1462

# 5 FACTS ABOUT OTTERS

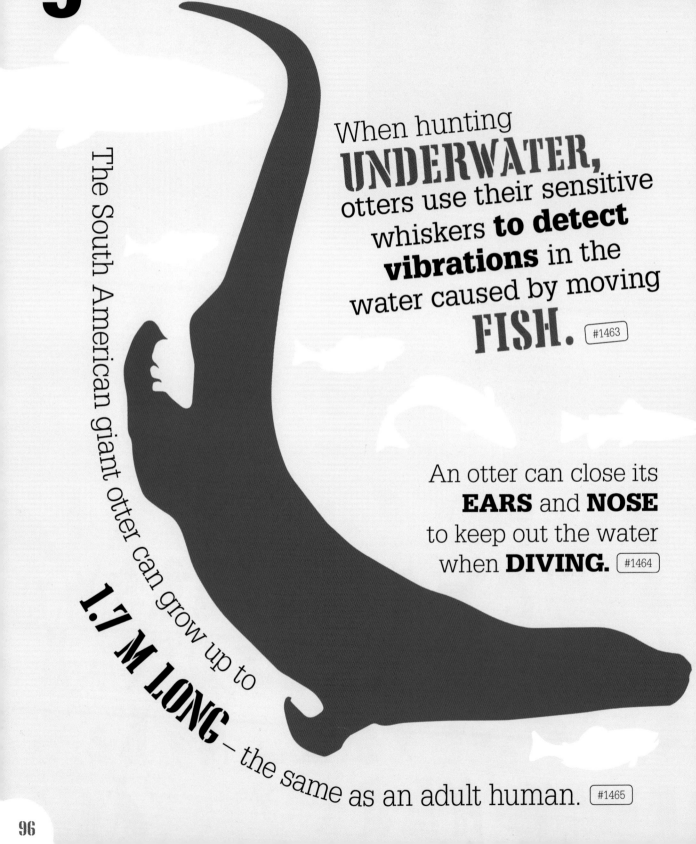

When hunting **UNDERWATER,** otters use their sensitive whiskers **to detect vibrations** in the water caused by moving **FISH.** #1463

An otter can close its **EARS** and **NOSE** to keep out the water when **DIVING.** #1464

The South American giant otter can grow up to **1.7 M LONG** – the same as an adult human. #1465

zZZZZZZZZZZZZZ

# Sea otters

sleep in the water. They often hold onto each other's paws so that they don't drift away. #1466

A sea otter has the **THICKEST fur of any animal.** It has as many hairs on **1 square centimetre** of its skin as we have on our **whole head** – **150,000.** #1467

# 4 LITTLE FACTS ABOUT LITTLE PEOPLE

More babies are born on a **TUESDAY** than on any other day. #1468

Babies start **dreaming** before birth. #1469

Babies are born with around **300 bones**, but by adulthood only 206 are left. #1470

Babies are born able to **swim** and to hold their breath underwater. #1471

An average human body contains enough:

## COPPER
to make
1 centimetre
of thin copper
wire #1473

## CARBON
to make
15,000 pencils #1474

## ALUMINIUM
to make
a piece of foil the size
of your palm #1476

## IRON
to make
a large nail #1472

## ARSENIC
to kill a rat #1475

# 69 dazzling DANCE facts

For thousands of years, dance has been an important part of ceremonies, rituals and celebrations. #1477 The **Dancing Plague** of 1518 lasted about a month. Hundreds of people took to the streets to dance. #1478 People danced uncontrollably until they collapsed. #1479 It killed dozens of people in Strasbourg in France through exhaustion or heart attack. #1480 **Capoeira** is a martial art that dates back to the 16th century. #1481 It was created by slaves brought to Brazil from Africa. #1482 They transformed their martial art and traditions into a dance form. #1483 The Chinese **lion dance** is performed to chase away ghosts and evil spirits. #1484 The lion dance combines art, history and kung fu moves. #1485 The **conga** is a dance where people move together in a long line. #1486 The longest conga on ice took place in London in 2013. #1487 353 dancing ice-skaters took part. #1488 The largest **maypole dance** took place in Canada in 2013. #1489 220 people joined in a traditional dance around the maypole. #1490 The largest **robot** dance in the world was at the University of Pittsburgh in the United States. #1491 2,524 dancers took part. #1492 A nightclub in Holland has a dance floor that is powered by energy created by people dancing on it. #1493 Before rugby matches, the New Zealand national team performs a dance of war called the **Haka.** #1494 **International Dance Day** was founded in 1982. #1495 It is celebrated on 29 April. #1496 **Ballroom dancing** dates back to the 17th century. #1497 Dances evolved from traditional **folk dances** and were performed at royal courts throughout Europe. #1498 All dances had to be performed facing royalty. #1499 It was forbidden to turn your back on a ruler. #1500 The **minuet** was made popular by the French King Louis XIV. #1501 King Louis XIV loved to dance and performed at court from a young age. #1502 He took daily dance lessons and dancing became an important accomplishment for gentlemen. #1503 In **1661** the king formed the first dance academy. #1504 As etiquette relaxed over the years, dancers started to dance in circles, squares or facing a partner. #1505 When the **Viennese waltz** emerged in the second half of the 18th century, it caused a great scandal. #1506 People were shocked by a dance where the man and woman danced in hold together. #1507 It eventually gained acceptance and became a popular dance among the upper class. #1508 The Viennese waltz is a different dance from the **waltz**. #1509 The Viennese waltz has about 180 beats to the minute. #1510 The waltz has just 90. #1511 The **tango** emerged from Argentina around 1880. #1512 The steps were created by people living in the lower-class areas of Buenos Aires. #1513 The **foxtrot** was invented by **Harry Fox** in 1914. #1514 There is more variety in the foxtrot than any other dance. #1515 This makes it one of the hardest to learn. #1516 The **quickstep**, **lindy hop** and **hustle** all developed from the foxtrot. #1517 **Irish dancing** dresses are based on the Irish peasant dress worn hundreds of years ago. #1518 It is an unusual type of dance that does not use the arms or hands. #1519 Since *Riverdance* was first performed in Dublin in **1995,** the show has played around 10,000 performances. #1520 1,500 Irish dancers have been in the shows, wearing out 14,000 dance shoes. #1521 **Tap** originated in the United States. #1522 It is a mixture of several cultures including African tribal dances, Irish and Scottish reels, and English clog dancing. #1523 In the late **1800s** dance competitions were the main showcase for tap dancers. #1524 In the early 20th century, Vaudeville variety shows were playing in theatres all over the United States, with many famous tap-dancing acts. #1525 Tap dancers originally wore normal shoes and banged their feet hard to make sounds, but in the **1920s** hard plates were added to their shoes to make their movements even louder. #1526 The plates were usually made of iron, but some were made of wood. #1527 Famous tap dancer **Fred Astaire** started his dancing career in a dancing act with his sister. #1528 He made over 30 films. #1529 His legs were insured for over £650,000. #1530 The most taps in one minute was 1,163. #1531

They were tapped by **Anthony Morigerato** in New York in 2011. #1532 **Flamenco** is a Spanish dance that is loud, fast and very colourful. #1533 The dancers move in time to the guitar music, clapping their hands and stamping their feet to the beat. #1534 Sometimes the dancers hold two pieces of wood, called castanets, in each hand that they click together in time to the music. #1535 Flamenco is made up of four elements: *cante* (voice), *baile* (dance), *toque* (guitar) and *jaleo* (hand clapping, foot stomping and shouts of encouragement). #1536 The most typical Spanish flamenco dress features a polka-dotted pattern. #1537 The female flamenco dancer normally appears with her hair in a bun, a mantle (similar to a shawl) on her shoulders and high heels. #1538 The Japanese love flamenco dancing and there are around 600 dance schools across Japan. #1539 **Breakdancing** grew up around hip hop music in the United States in the 1970s. #1540 The earliest moves were called the 'drop' and 'in-and-out'. #1541 Breakdancing moves slowly evolved into **freestyle** in which dancers would improvise their own moves. #1542 **Salsa** is a mixture of Cuban and African dances. #1543 Although it is a partner dance, it can also be danced in a line known as the *salsa suelta*. #1544 The largest salsa dance ever consisted of 1,686 dancers in Mexico in 2012. #1545

# 31 FACTS ABOUT BALLET

**Ballet** began in the 17th century in the royal courts of Europe. #1546 It was part of a flamboyant entertainment, to celebrate marriages or demonstrate wealth. #1547 The ballets were performed by the courtiers and royalty in their own palaces. #1548 The dances told the stories of Ancient Greek and Roman myths. #1549 Following the French Revolution in **1789,** women abandoned restrictive corsets for floating dresses, and ballet dancers followed. #1550 Looser dresses meant they could perform more movements. #1551 Dancers started to dance *en pointe* (on the tips of the toes) around **1800.** #1552 Ballet performances told the stories of ordinary, rather than mythical, heroes. #1553 Italian dancer **Carlo Blasis's** book *The Code of Terpsichore* was published in **1828.** #1554 Terpsichore was the Greek goddess of dance. #1555 The dance manual included many of the set exercises and steps that dancers still do in class today. #1556 It was Blasis who insisted on the 90-degree turnout from the hips. #1557 Until then, a 45-degree turnout had been the norm. #1558 Carlo Blasis was born in Naples in **1797.** #1559 He studied dance with the great 18th-century choreographer **Salvatore Vigano** and became the lead dancer in Milan. #1560 Blasis trained the most famous Italian dancers of the day, who went on to dance in St Petersburg, Paris and London. #1561

Blasis died in **1878** when he was 91 years old. #1562 Ballet composer **Pyotr Ilyich Tchaikovsky** was born in 1840, and began piano lessons when he was five years old. #1563 His family wanted him to be a civil servant, but he became a composer instead. #1564 *The Nutcracker* was first performed in 1892 but wasn't a success. #1565 Today it is one of the most commonly performed ballets – especially at Christmas. #1566 In 1995 **Matthew Bourne** replaced the traditional female ballet swans of *Swan Lake* with menacing male dancers. #1567 **Anna Pavlova,** born in 1881, was the first ballerina to tour ballet around the world. #1568 The famous Russian ballet star **Rudolf Nureyev** was born in 1938 on a train journey. #1569 In 1961 he moved to France where he became director of the Paris Opera Ballet. #1570 **George Balanchine** and **Lincoln Kirstein** co-founded the New York City Ballet in 1948. #1571 It can take up to 90 hours to make a professional tutu. #1572 A principal dancer (the highest-ranking dancer within a dance company) will often wear one new pair of shoes for every performance. #1573 Most professional dancers go through three or four pairs of ballet shoes a week. #1574 Young dancers must study ballet for four to five years before going *en pointe* – it requires a great deal of strength in the legs, ankles and feet. #1575 The amount of energy needed for performing a ballet is around the same amount as playing in two football matches. #1576

# 9 VENOMOUS snake facts

Venomous snakes have fangs like hypodermic needles.

#1577

The venom runs through the middle of the fang, and is delivered straight into the bloodstream of the victim.

#1578

Burrowing asps can move each fang separately as they bite their victims.

#1579

The bite of an inland taipan contains enough venom to kill **100 people.**

#1580

There are more than **10,000** Indian cobra attacks on humans every year in India.

#1581

In California, rattlesnakes bite people more than **800 times a year.**

#1582

The rattle in a rattlesnake's tail is made from skin from past moults.

#1583

Unless it is treated immediately, the bite from a black mamba is almost always fatal to humans.

#1584

Rather than hissing, the king cobra makes a growling sound.

#1585

# 10 FACTS ON THE HISTORY OF SCIENCE

Early doctors put **maggots** into wounds to eat decaying flesh, helping the wounds to heal. #1586

The Ancient Greeks thought a camel mating with a leopard produced the **giraffe**! #1587

Around 2,600 years ago, Buddhist philosophers suggested that all matter is made of **atoms.** Modern physics has reached the same conclusion. #1588

Centuries ago, doctors in India would let an **ant** bite through the edges of a wound, then snap off its head, leaving the jaws to act as a stitch. #1589

The first important **dinosaur fossils** were found in 1811 in Dorset, England. #1590

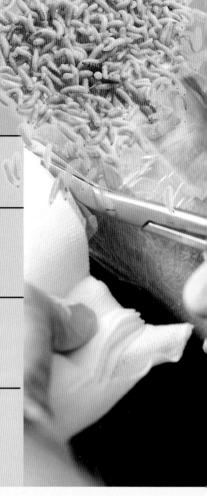

In 1947, an American engineer invented the **first microwave,** which was nearly 2 m tall! #1591

Scientist Robert Bunsen suffered **partial paralysis** and **lost an eye** in an explosion in 1840 when he was researching toxic and explosive compounds called cacodyls. #1592

In 1746, a scientist sent an electric charge along **1,500 m of wire,** held by 200 monks. All the monks yelled at the same time, showing electricity moves very quickly! #1593

The **giant squid** was thought to be legendary until it was photographed in 2004. #1594

A scientist trying to extract **gold from urine** discovered **phosphorus** by mistake in 1669. #1595

Forensic science can be used to help solve criminal cases. In the case of **FORENSIC ENTOMOLOGY,** scientists examine insects found in and around human remains to determine the time of death, or even if the body has been moved! #1596

# 5 FACTS ABOUT THE FASTEST FISH

The **sailfish** is the fastest animal in the sea, reaching speeds of

# 110 km/h

– as fast as a car on the motorway. #1597

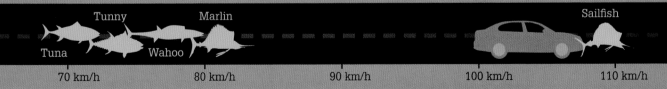

| Tunny | Marlin | | | Sailfish |
| Tuna | Wahoo | | | |
| 70 km/h | 80 km/h | 90 km/h | 100 km/h | 110 km/h |

Second-fastest is the **marlin** at 80 km/h. #1598
Third is the **wahoo** at 78 km/h. #1599
Fourth is the **tunny** at 74 km/h. #1600
Fifth is the **bluefin tuna** at 70 km/h. #1601

# 3 BLUEFIN TUNA FACTS

A bluefin tuna can **weigh** more than **500** kg – that's as **heavy** as a horse. #1602

Unusually for fish, the bluefin tuna is **WARM-BLOODED.** #1608

**When they are swimming at full SPEED,** tuna pull their fins tight to their sides to stay streamlined. #1604

# 84 fascinating facts on PREHISTORIC FOSSILS

We know everything we do about dinosaurs from fossils. #1605 Dinosaur fossils were formed when the dead dinosaur's bones became covered in mud and stones, and slowly turned into stone themselves. #1606 Dinosaur fossils have been found on every continent, including Antarctica. #1607 Hard tissues, such as shells, teeth and bones, are more likely to become fossils. #1608 Fossils can also be a trace of an animal, such as a trail and burrow, rather than of the animal itself. #1609 These are called **trace fossils.** #1610 Trace fossils also include such things as poo and footprints. #1611 As new fossils are discovered, the number of dinosaur species grows. #1612 The most dinosaur fossils and the greatest variety of species have been found in the deserts of the United States, China and Argentina. #1613 Desert environments make fossils easier to find. #1614 Drills, crowbars and dynamite are used to remove fossils from the ground. #1615 Delicate tools like toothbrushes are also used. #1616 The greatest variety of fossil species have been found in Dinosaur Provincial Park in Alberta, Canada. #1617 40 distinct species have been uncovered there. #1618 In the last 100 years many fossils have been discovered in China. #1619 The Liaoning province, north-east of Beijing, is a dinosaur fossil hotspot. #1620 Fossils found there have been amazingly well preserved under layers of volcanic ash, from volcanoes that erupted millions of years ago. #1621 In 1811 **Joseph Anning** discovered the skull of an **ichthyosaur** (a large marine reptile) on the south coast of England. #1622 About a year later, Joseph's sister **Mary Anning** found the rest of it. #1623 Mary was only a young girl at the time of her discovery, but she went on to discover many more important fossils. #1624 Her discoveries included the first two **plesiosaur** skeletons (a large marine reptile). #1625 Mary nearly lost her life in 1833 during a landslide that killed her dog Tray. #1626 She became well known all over the world, but she was poor and had to sell the fossils she found. #1627 As a woman, she was not eligible to join the Geological Society of London and did not always receive credit for her contributions. #1628 In 2010 the Royal Society included Mary in a list of the 10 British women who have most influenced the history of science. #1629

The first dinosaur to be described scientifically was **Megalosaurus** in 1824. #1630 The first dinosaur found was **Iguanodon** by **Gideon A Mantell** – he named and described it in 1825. #1631 It wasn't until later in the 19th century that dinosaur fossils were recognized as dinosaurs. #1632 **Richard Owen** came up with the name 'dinosaur' in 1842. #1633 In 1868 the first mounted dinosaur skeleton was created using bones found from a **Hadrosaurus**. #1634 US paleontologist **Joseph Leidy** reconstructed *Hadrosaurus* as a biped (walked on two legs), despite the view at the time that *Hadrosaurus* walked on four legs. #1635 Its skeleton was assembled by a team including English sculptor **Benjamin Hawkins** and was put on display at the Philadelphia Academy of Natural Sciences. #1636 In 1870, two of the greatest fossil hunters, **Edward Drinker Cope** and **Othniel Charles Marsh,** competed to find the most fossils – now referred to as the **'Bone Wars'.** #1637 Their feud started when Cope embarrassed Marsh by pointing out that he'd placed the skull of a dinosaur on the tail of the specimen, instead of the neck. #1638 The feud went on for years, and Cope requested that his brain be dissected by scientists, after he died, to prove it was bigger than Marsh's. #1639 This didn't happen and their achievements were measured by the number of new dinosaurs they discovered – Marsh around 80 and Cope around 56. #1640 Marsh named more dinosaurs than any other palaeontologist, including **Triceratops, Allosaurus** and **Stegosaurus.** #1641 Many fossils of *Stegosaurus* have been found in western United States, western Europe, southern India, China and southern Africa. #1642 The first *Stegosaurus* fossil was found in Colorado, United States, in 1876 by **M. P. Felch**. #1643 Marsh came up with the name *Stegosaurus* in 1877 using the Greek words *stegos* (roof) and *sauros* (lizard). #1644 In 1885 Felch also discovered a nearly complete *Stegosaurus* skeleton in Colorado. #1645 Fossils found of adult and baby *Stegosaurus* footprints together have led experts to believe *Stegosaurus* cared for their young. #1646 **Triceratops** was one of the last species of dinosaurs to evolve before the mass extinction in the Cretaceous Period. #1647

*Triceratops* fossils are rare and only found in the United States. #1648 The first *Triceratops* fossil was thought to be a species of buffalo. #1649 In 2008, a *Triceratops* skeleton called Cliff was bought at an auction and given to the Boston Museum of Science by an anonymous donor. #1650 *Triceratops* are often found together, suggesting they lived in herds. #1651 Fossils of **Spinosaurus** were found in Egypt around 1912 by German palaeontologist **Ernst Stromer**. #1652 These fossils were destroyed in a British bombing raid on Munich in 1944 during World War II. #1653 Based on fossils found in Morocco in 2008, experts believe *Spinosaurus* ate sharks and other large fish in the river it lived by. #1654 **Barnum Brown** was one of the greatest dinosaur fossil experts. #1655 He discovered the first **Tyrannosaurus rex** fossil in 1902. #1656 Only about 30 *Tyrannosaurus rex* fossils have ever been found. #1657 Most have been found in the United States. #1658 The world-famous fossil known as Sue is the largest and most complete *Tyrannosaurus rex* ever found. #1659 This 67-million-year-old skeleton was unveiled in 2000. #1660 Sue boasts 58 dagger-like teeth and is on display at the Field Museum in Chicago, United States. #1661 More than 16 million visitors have been to see her. #1662 Amazing dinosaur fossil beds were discovered on the border between Colorado and Utah in the United States in 1909. #1663 The discovery was made by **Earl Douglass**. #1664 **President Woodrow Wilson** proclaimed the dinosaur beds a Dinosaur National Monument in 1915. #1665 **Roy Chapman Andrews** was an explorer for the American Museum of Natural History in New York City. #1666 He began his career at the museum in 1906 by sweeping floors. #1667 By 1934 he had become the museum's director. #1668 From 1922 to 1930 Andrews and a team of scientists explored the Gobi Desert where they discovered the first nest of dinosaur eggs, fossils of early mammals that coexisted with dinosaurs and new species of dinosaurs. #1669 Andrews is said to have been the inspiration for the Hollywood character Indiana Jones. #1670 **Parasaurolophus** was first discovered in Canada around 1920. #1671 Fossils of its crest were observed to be different lengths. #1672 Experts believe that female *Parasaurolophus* had shorter crests than male ones. #1673 Following the discovery of **Psittacosaurus** fossils, it was named by **Henry Osborn** in 1923. #1674 The dinosaur **Carcharodontosaurus** was discovered when its skull and a few bones were found in North Africa in 1927. #1675 After studying fossils in the 1960s, **John H. Ostrom** caused an outcry when he proposed that birds had descended from dinosaurs, which changed the way the world looked at dinosaur evolution. #1676 One of the most amazing fossils ever discovered is of two fighting dinosaurs, locked together. #1677 The fossil was discovered in Mongolia around 1972. #1678 The fossil is the joint remains of a **Velociraptor** and a **Protoceratops,** which lived during the Cretaceous period. #1679 Some experts believe the dinosaurs died from their battle injuries. #1680 Other scientists think they could have been killed and buried under a collapsing sand dune, during battle. #1681 In 2009, huge **sauropod** (long-necked, plant-eating dinosaur) fossil footprints were discovered in France. #1682 The imprints measured up to 1.5 m long. #1683 Experts believe that these footprints prove that sauropods, like **Diplodocus,** moved in herds. #1684 Other fossil discoveries show that *Diplodocus*' skin was covered in small scales. #1685 Its fossils also tell us that its tail was made up of around 80 vertebrae (the bones that make the spine). #1686 Feathered dinosaur fossils have recently been found preserved in rocks in Liaoning, China. #1687 The important dinosaur discoveries in this area are helping to solve the mysteries of the evolution of dinosaurs and the origin of birds. #1688

# 13 FACTS ON POO

Fossil poos are called coprolites. #1689 A scientist who studies dinosaur poo is called a **palaeoscatologist.** #1690 Dinosaur poo ranges in size from a few millimetres to over 60 cm – as long as your arm! #1691 Some coprolites can tell us which food types a dinosaur may have eaten. #1692 **Sauropods** produced up to 1,000 kg of poo every day (that's a pile of poo as heavy as a polar bear). #1693 **Meat-eating dinosaurs'** dung was more likely to become fossilized because meat decomposes more slowly than plants. #1694 Some coprolites have been found inside dinosaur skeletons. #1695 Some dinosaurs might have mistaken coprolites for stones and unknowingly swallowed the fossilized poo to help digest their dinner. #1696 One discovery of **Tyrannosaurus rex's** poo contained bones in it. #1697 This suggests that whatever the *Tyrannosaurus rex* ate didn't remain in its digestive system long enough for it to break down. #1698 Dinosaur poo belonging to the plant-eater **Titanosaurus** was stolen from the Natural History Museum in London in 2006. #1699 If sold at auction, dinosaur poo attracts huge sums of money, sometimes thousands of pounds. #1700 Some **ichthyosaur** poos are black with the ink from squid-like animals that they had swallowed. #1701

# 7 DEER FACTS

The smallest species of deer, the **South American pudu,** stands less than **40 cm tall** – about the height of a wine bottle.
#1702

The **Chinese water deer** does not have antlers. The males grow **TUSKS** instead. #1703

The largest deer is the elk (also known as a moose). It stands up to 2 m tall. #1704

Male deer use their bony antlers to fight one another over the **FEMALES.** This is called **RUTTING.**

#1705

A deer's antlers fall off every year, and the deer **grows a new set.** #1706

The only female deer to grow antlers are **reindeer. They use them to clear away the snow** when feeding in winter.
#1707

**Reindeer migrate further** than any other land mammal, travelling up to **5,000 KM** a year in search of **FRESH PASTURES.**
#1708

The **gerenuk** is an **antelope** with an extra-flexible hip joint. This allows it to **stand straight upright** on its rear legs to reach leaves high above it. #1709

111

# 43 top TV facts

The abbreviation of television is TV. #1710 A video camera converts images into **electrical impulses**. #1711 These are sent by radio waves, satellite or cable to a TV receiver, where they are turned back into pictures. #1712 **Radio waves** travel in straight lines and cannot bend around the world. #1713 Earth-orbiting communication **satellites** are like giant mirrors – they can bounce waves back to Earth, extending their travel distance. #1714 Thousands of tiny dots or stripes of light are used to make a full picture on our TV screens. #1715 The picture is usually made of three primary colours of light – red, green and blue. #1716 By using these three colours in different combinations, our televisions can make any colour. #1717 Originally many televisions used a cathode-ray tube, which shoots rays of energy (electrons) at the back of TV screens. #1718 These rays can hit just one tiny red, green or blue point on the screen. #1719 When they hit, a small part of the TV screen shines as one of those colours. #1720 The rays light up different colours faster than our brains can notice – we just see a full picture on the TV screen. #1721 Plasma screens use tiny compartments filled with gas. Electricity charges the gas,

The images on a TV screen refresh so quickly, that it looks like smooth motion to the human eye. #1722

lighting up red, green or blue spots on the screen. #1723 The invention of the TV was the result of work by many inventors, scientists and engineers in the late **1800s** and early **1900s**. #1724 The first electromechanical TV was proposed and patented by **Paul Julius Gottlieb Nipkow**. #1725 Nipkow did not build a working model of his TV. #1726 **John Logie Baird** built and presented the world's first working TV system in **1926**. #1728 The first flat plasma display panel (PDP) was invented by **Donald Bitzer**, **Gene Slottow** and **Robert Willson** in **1964**. #1729 Early TV was displayed in black and white. #1730 Most people dream in colour, but those who grew up watching black and white TV often dream in black and white. #1731 Although the technology was developed earlier, colour TV sets didn't become widespread until the **1970s**. #1732 The **1980s** saw the arrival of remote controls. #1733 One of the first original TV shows in the United States was *The Television Ghost* in **1931**. #1734 It featured an actor who dressed up as dead people and told the stories of their murders. #1735 John

Televisions first went on sale in the late **1920s**. #1727

The first televised **Queen's** speech was in **1952**.
#1737

Logie Baird convinced the BBC (British Broadcasting Corporation) to lend him one of their transmitters – he used it to transmit the first TV broadcast in the UK. #1736 One of his transmissions was a play that featured just three actors and not a lot of movement. #1738 In **1932** the BBC took over control of the programmes and in **1936** launched a regular service. #1739 The longest-running children's TV show is *Sooty*, which started in **1955** and is still on TV today. #1740 The BBC Television Centre in London officially opened in **1960**. #1741 In **1969** Fuji Television broadcast a cartoon called *Sazae-san*. #1742 It is still on air today, making it the longest-running cartoon series in the world. #1743 The most-watched TV broadcasts are usually global sporting events such as the Olympics and football World Cup. #1744 British TV show *Top Gear* is the most watched factual programme in the world. #1745 It has an estimated 350 million weekly viewers in 170 countries. #1746 In the **1970s** there were no TV broadcasts in Iceland on Thursdays or for the entire month of July. 1747 In **1987** a man hijacked a TV station during an episode of *Dr Who* and still hasn't been caught. #1748 **Earl Wild** was the first person to give a live piano recital on US TV. #1749 He was also the first pianist to stream a performance on the Internet, 60 years later in **1997**. #1750

# 7 FACTS ABOUT JOHN LOGIE BAIRD

→ John Logie Baird was born in **1888** in Scotland. #1752

→ Like many scientists, he wanted to create a TV and in **1924** managed to transmit a few flickering images a small distance. #1753

→ In **1926** he gave the world's first demonstration of a TV before 50 scientists in London. #1754

→ In **1927** his TV was demonstrated over a telephone wire between London and Glasgow. #1755

→ His system was eventually replaced by the BBC for the more technically advanced one created by Marconi-EMI. #1756

→ His other inventions met with less success – including inflatable shoes that burst and a glass razor that shattered. #1757

→ Australia's TV Week Logie Awards (television industry awards) were named in his honour. #1758

The average person in the UK watches just over 4 hours of TV a day.
#1751

In **2010** the number of TV sets in the USA overtook the number of people.
#1759

# 3 BODY FACTS

Everyone has their own **smell** (except identical twins, who share a smell). #1760

Humans are the only animals known to **cry** when they are sad. #1762

# 5 MAGNIFICENT MUSCLE FACTS

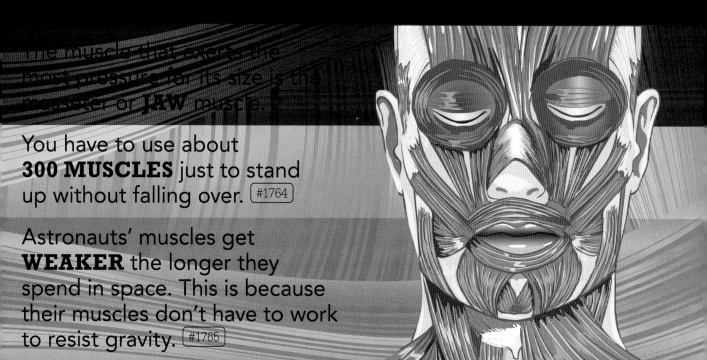

The muscle that exerts the most pressure for its size is the MASSETER, or **JAW** muscle.

You have to use about **300 MUSCLES** just to stand up without falling over. #1764

Astronauts' muscles get **WEAKER** the longer they spend in space. This is because their muscles don't have to work to resist gravity. #1765

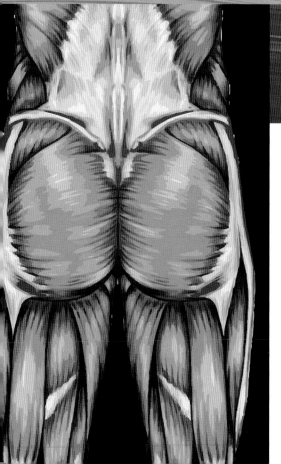

The biggest muscle in the body is the **GLUTEUS MAXIMUS,** or **BUTTOCK.** #1766

**DIMPLES** are caused by muscles pulling on the skin of your face. #1767

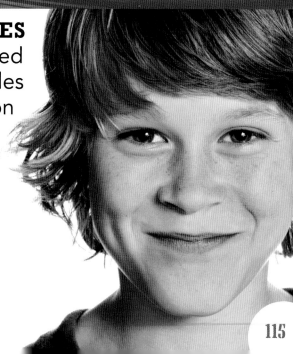

# 9 MEERKAT

FACTS

A group of meerkats is called a **mob,** and can include as many as **40 animals**. #1768

In a mob, just one dominant pair breeds. The dominant pair is called the **alpha pair**. #1769

The dark patches around a meerkat's eyes lessen the glare of the Sun. #1770

Meerkats can eat poisonous scorpions. They pluck off the stinger quickly before tucking in. #1771

Young meerkats are taught how to do this by the adults. #1772

As they forage, the meerkats take turns to be sentries. The sentries keep watch, standing on their hind legs to look out for eagles and other predators. #1773

When the sentries call out, the meerkats run for their burrows. #1774

One mob may have up to five different burrows. #1775

Adults take it in turns to stay in the burrows looking after the newborn pups. #1776

Mercury's atmosphere is so thin that if all of it was collected it wouldn't fill a **party balloon.** #1777

Mercury and Venus are the only planets that have **no moons.** #1778

The weight of Venus's atmosphere would **crush you instantly.** #1779

A **day** on Venus lasts longer than its **year.** #1780

Venus is called **'Earth's evil twin'**, because it is a similar size but hostile to life. #1781

Olympus Mons on Mars is the **tallest volcano in the solar system.** It stands three times the height of Mount Everest. #1782

The surface of Mars is icy cold, with temperatures that rarely rise above **freezing**, even in summer. #1783

The Grand Canyon on Mars is **20 times wider** than the Grand Canyon in Arizona, USA. #1784

Earth is the **only planet** we know of in our solar system that humans can live on. #1785

About **71 per cent** of Earth's surface is covered by water. #1786

# 10 WOW FACTS ABOUT INNER PLANETS

The **longest eclipse of the Sun** lasts no more than seven and a half minutes. #1787

Stars are **different colours** depending on how hot they are. The hottest stars are blue, medium ones like our Sun are yellow, cooler stars are red. #1788

In space, **blood rushes to your head,** making your face appear puffy. #1789

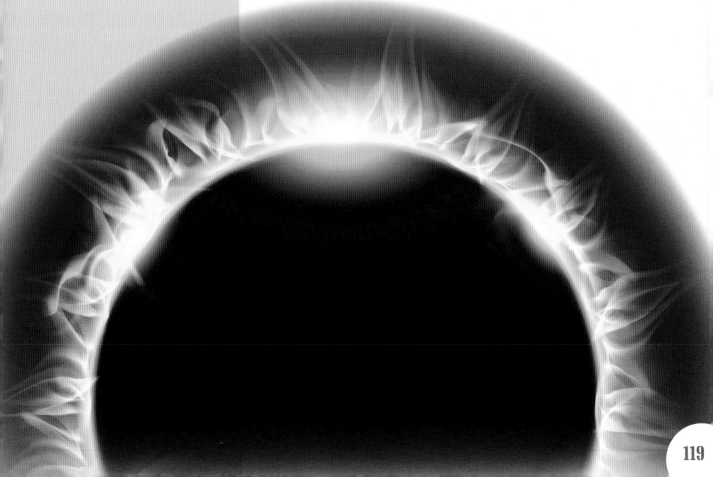

# 3 FACTS ABOUT THE INSPIRATIONAL INCAS

The Incas of South America could not read or write, so they used lengths of knotted, coloured strings called **quipus** to keep records. #1790

The Incas built around **40,000 kilometres** of **roads.** Messengers ran along them day and night carrying messages for the emperor. #1791

The Incas cut and fitted together **stone bricks** so perfectly that their walls didn't need any mortar to hold them in place. #1792

# 10 FACTS ABOUT RUTHLESS RULERS

In 1258, the Mongol army attacked Baghdad and killed at least **200,000 of its 1 million people**. #1793

When an Iranian city rebelled against his high taxes in the 1400s, Central Asian conqueror Timur **killed all 70,000 inhabitants**. #1794

The Aztecs of Central America **sacrificed humans to satisfy their gods**! #1795

As a child, Russian ruler Ivan the Terrible was known to have **tortured animals**. #1796

Kaiser Wilhelm II of Germany abdicated in 1918 after almost **13 million soldiers** died during World War I between 1914 and 1918. #1797

During **Pol Pot's** rule of Cambodia, between 1975 and 1979, about **2 million** people were killed – a third of the population. #1798

In the 540s BC, **King Nabonidus of Babylon** ate **grass** and thought he was a **goat**! #1799

When feared dictator **Joseph Stalin** had a stroke in 1953, his ministers and police were too scared to call a doctor for him! #1800

**Idi Amin,** president of Uganda from 1971 to 1979, killed up to 500,000 opponents. #1801

In 1976, **President Jean-Bédel Bokassa,** military ruler of the Central African Republic, declared himself **emperor**! #1802

# 4 DEEP-SEA MONSTER FACTS

The **gulper** **eel's** HUGE MOUTH allows it to swallow prey that is BIGGER than itself.

#1803

The **vampire squid** has the **largest eyes** of any animal compared to its body size.

#1804

The **anglerfish** makes its own light, which it uses to tempt fish near enough for it to strike.

#1805

The **giant squid** grows up to **14 m** in length – longer than a bus.

#1806

# 4 GIANT CLAM FACTS

**Giant clams** can weigh up to **200** kg – nearly as much as three adult humans. #1807

They can measure **1.2 m across**. #1808

Giant clams are **hermaphrodites,** meaning that they are both

## MALE AND FEMALE. #1809

A **giant clam** can live for up to 150 years. #1810

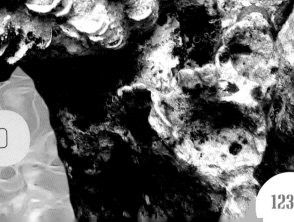

# 65 magnificent

There are around 40 reigning monarchs in the world today. [#1811] Some monarchs, like those of **Saudi Arabia**, **Kuwait**, **Jordan** and **Qatar**, rule absolutely. Some just have ceremonial powers. [#1812] In **1235 Henry III** of **England** received three leopards as a wedding gift. [#1813] He collected more exotic animals and created a zoo at the Tower of London. [#1814] The Tower of London remained a zoo for 600 years. [#1815] **Japan's** Yamato dynasty can be traced back to **AD 660**. [#1816] It is the oldest continuous monarchy in the world. [#1817] Equal female succession is when the crown is passed down to the oldest heir, regardless of their gender. [#1818] **Sweden** was the first country to allow equal female succession to its throne. [#1819] In 2015 a few other countries allow equal female succession – they include the **UK**, **Holland**, **Belgium** and **Denmark**. [#1820] In **1995 King Oya** became the youngest monarch in the world. [#1821] At just three years of age he became the ruler of the Toro Kingdom in **Uganda**. [#1822] In Japan only the imperial family are allowed to travel in a maroon car. [#1823] **King Constantine** of Greece won a gold medal in yachting in the **1960 Olympics**. [#1824] **Bhumibol Adulyadej** (the King of Thailand) is the richest monarch in the world. [#1825] He has a fortune of £18 billion. [#1826] **Richard III** was crowned king of England in **1483**. [#1827] He became king after **Edward V**, his 13-year-old nephew, had his right to the throne overturned. [#1828] Edward V and his brother then disappeared. [#1829] Many believe that Richard III murdered them. [#1830] The **Dutch Royal Family** is the most expensive in the world. [#1831] The Dutch Royal Family costs the Dutch people around £31 million a year. [#1832] The **British Royal Family** costs around £29 million a year. [#1833] **Henry VIII** was the first English king to be called 'your majesty'. [#1834] Henry VIII reigned from **1509** to **1547**. [#1835] He had six wives – **Catherine of Aragon**, **Anne Boleyn**, **Jane Seymour**, **Anne of Cleves**, **Catherine Howard** and **Catherine Parr**. [#1836] A good way to remember the fates of Henry's wives is the rhyme divorced, beheaded, died, divorced, beheaded, survived. [#1837] During his reign he had more than 70,000 people executed. [#1838] **King Alexander** of Greece married a commoner (someone who is not royalty) in **1919**. [#1839] This caused a scandal and the couple had to leave Greece for several months. [#1840] He died in **1920** after being bitten by a pet monkey. [#1841] Henry VIII's son, **Edward VI**, ruled England for six years from **1547** to **1553**. [#1842] He became king when he was 9 years old and died when he was just 15. [#1843] Edward's half-sister **Mary** ruled for the next five years. [#1844] **Elizabeth I** became queen in **1558** and ruled for 45 years. [#1845] Many people tried to kill Elizabeth during her reign, including her cousin **Mary Queen of Scots**. [#1846] Elizabeth had Mary captured and killed. [#1847] To protect herself, Elizabeth set up a network of spies across England. [#1848] In **1547 Ivan IV** was the first ruler to be crowned **Tsar of Russia**. [#1849] Also known as Ivan the Terrible, he killed his son in a fit of rage. [#1850] **Nicholas II** was the last Tsar of Russia and in **1917** was executed in the Russian Revolution. [#1851] **James I** was the first king to rule both England and **Scotland**; he ruled from **1603** to **1625**. [#1852] In **1605** a group of men tried to assassinate him by blowing up Parliament. [#1853] The plot failed but is remembered in the UK on 5 November each year with bonfires and fireworks. [#1854] James I's son, **Charles I**, became king in **1625**. [#1855] He disagreed with Parliament and ruled for 12 years without them. [#1856] This eventually led to civil war and Charles being tried for treason. [#1857] In **1649** Charles was beheaded. [#1858] **King Louis XIV** ruled **France** from **1774** to **1792**. [#1859] He married **Marie Antoinette** when he was just 15 years old. [#1860] He was executed for treason in **1793**. [#1861] Marie Antoinette was executed nine months later. [#1862] **Charles VI** of France and his wife **Isabella** of Bavaria had 12 children. [#1863] The Danish monarchy can be traced back over 1,000 years. [#1864] **George I**, who became king of Great Britain and Ireland in **1714**, objected to medals being awarded to people in the Royal Navy. [#1865] No sailor received a medal during his reign. [#1866] **Catherine the Great** of Russia ruled from

# MONARCHS facts

**1762** to **1796**. #1867 Her real name was Sophie. #1868 She became leader of Russia after removing her husband, **Peter III**, from power. #1869 The **Pope** is considered the monarch of **Vatican City**, in **Italy**. #1870 Vatican City has a population of about 800 people in total. #1871 The Pope has been protected by the Swiss Guard since **1506**. #1872 Richard III of England was killed in battle after being on the throne for only two years. #1873 He was the last English king to die in battle. #1874 His remains were discovered buried under a car park in **Leicester**, England, in 2012. #1875

## 14 FACTS ABOUT QUEEN VICTORIA

**Victoria** was Queen of the United Kingdom and Ireland from **1837** to **1901**. #1876 Her full name was Alexandrina Victoria. #1877 She ruled for 64 years, longer than any other British monarch. #1878 However, if Queen Elizabeth II is on the throne on 9 September 2015 she will become the longest-reigning British monarch. #1879 Victoria was also the Empress of India. #1880 When she was 21 years old Victoria married her cousin Albert, a German prince. #1881 They had 9 children, 40 grandchildren and 37 great-grandchildren. #1882 As a child Victoria was never allowed out of sight of an adult, not even at night. #1883 Queen Victoria's family nickname was Drina. #1884 Her first language was German. #1885 By the time she was three years old she could also speak English and French. #1886 She later learned to speak Hindustani. #1887 She was the first monarch to live at Buckingham Palace. #1888 Queen Victoria survived seven assassination attempts. #1889

## 21 FACTS ON QUEEN ELIZABETH II

**Elizabeth II** became queen of the **United Kingdom** and Northern Ireland in **1952**. #1890 She is also the monarch of another 15 of the 53 Commonwealth countries. #1891 The Queen never went to school; instead she was taught at home with her sister Margaret. #1892 Her family nickname was Lilibet, because she couldn't pronounce Elizabeth. #1893 She became a Girl Guide when she was 11 years old. #1894 The Queen has travelled more kilometres than any other king or queen in history. #1895 She was born in **1926**, and has become the oldest person ever to be a British monarch. #1896 She married Prince Philip, Duke of Edinburgh, in **1947**. #1897 Queen Elizabeth has owned more than 30 corgis. #1898 The first was called Susan and was an 18th birthday present. #1899 Her robes were so heavy at her **Coronation** that she asked the Archbishop of Canterbury to give her a push, saying, 'Get me started'. #1900 The Queen watched England win the 1966 football World Cup final at **Wembley Stadium** in **London**. #1901 Her collections of art, furniture, jewels and horses are thought to be worth around £70 million. #1902 There is a cash machine at Buckingham Palace. #1903 The Queen owns several racehorses. #1904 She is the only person in Britain who can drive a car without a driving licence. #1905 Queen Elizabeth celebrates two birthdays each year. #1906 Her official birthday is on a Saturday in June. #1907 Historically a monarch has their official birthday in the summer, in the hope of better weather for the official birthday parade, called Trooping the Colour. #1908 The Queen's real birthday is on 21 April. #1909 She has given out more than 80,000 Christmas puddings as presents to staff over the years. #1910

# 50 facts on TREES

There are over 300,000 identified plant species and the list is growing all the time. [#1911]

Humans use around 2,000 different types of plants to make food. [#1912]

Some plants are carnivorous – they eat insects and spiders. [#1913]

A **Venus flytrap** lures small insects in with sweet-smelling nectar, then snaps its leaves shut to trap its prey. [#1914]

**Bamboo** plants can grow almost 1 m in just one day. [#1915]

In Ancient Rome people used **roses** to decorate their rooms. [#1916]

Anything said under the rose was deemed to be a secret. [#1917]

Some people believe that different-coloured roses symbolize different things – red means love, orange means desire and yellow means joy. [#1918]

**Sunflowers** can grow to around 3.7 m tall in just six months. [#1919] Sunflowers can be used to extract toxins, such as lead, arsenic and uranium, from contaminated soil. [#1920]

The tallest known sunflower grew to 7.76 m high. That's about as tall as four men standing on each other's heads. [#1921]

During the 1600s, **tulips** were so valuable in Holland that their bulbs were worth more than gold. [#1922]

This craze was called tulip mania, or tulipomania, and caused the crash of the Dutch economy. [#1923]

The **titan arum**, or corpse flower, has one of the largest unbranched flowers in the world. [#1924] Its bloom produces a smell like that of rotting meat, hence its common name. [#1925] It developed its scent so it could be pollinated by flies; as it couldn't compete with other blooms for butterflies and hummingbirds. [#1926]

All parts of the **oleander**, a native Mediterranean flowering shrub, are poisonous. [#1927]

If you squeeze the sides of a **snapdragon** flower, it looks like a dragon's mouth opening and closing. [#1928]

The **marcgravia evenia** depends on bat pollination, and has evolved a special leaf that acts like a satellite dish for bats' hearing. [#1929]

Flowers did not always exist; the earliest evidence of flowers is 240 million-year-old pollen. [#1930] Before that, **ferns** and **cone-bearing trees** dominated Earth. [#1931]

Lots of plants are used as dyes – you can colour cloth with dye made of stewed onion skin, tea bags or walnut juice. [#1932] One of the oldest blue dyes comes from a plant called **woad** – it has been used since Neolithic times, more than 6,000 years ago. [#1933]

# FLOWERS and PLANTS

**Seaweed** contains a kind of gloopy jelly that helps it hold on to water. [#1934]

A head of **Broccoli** is actually a head of flower buds. [#1935]

All **carrots** were originally white or purple, but now they come in a range of colours. [#1936]

White and yellow carrots come from Europe, and purple carrots come from the Middle East. [#1937]

Some plant roots are so tough that they can break through concrete. [#1938]

Giant Amazon **water lily pads** are strong enough for a child to stand on. [#1939]

The **bee orchid** flower looks like a real bee. [#1940]

**Fungi** can grow in soil, on old wood, around baths and even on your feet and toenails. [#1941]

Just one **mushroom** can release billions of spores (tiny fungus seeds). [#1942]

Some mushrooms, such as **stinkhorns**, smell of rotting meat or even poo. [#1943] The smell attracts flies, which then spread their spores. [#1944]

**Caterpillar fungus** invades a caterpillar's body in winter (so the fungus looks like a worm), then grows out of its brain in summer (so it looks like grass). [#1945]

When a **squirting cucumber** explodes, it shoots seeds and slime up to 6 m into the air. [#1946]

**Pebble plants** in the desert hide from hungry animals by looking exactly like stones. [#1947]

The **castor oil plant** makes a poison so deadly that one teaspoon of it could kill hundreds of people. [#1948]

The meat-eating giant **pitcher plant** has traps so large it can swallow and eat a rat. [#1949]

85 per cent of plant life is found in the ocean. [#1950]

## TREE OF KNOWLEDGE

The **dwarf willow** is the tiniest tree in the world – it grows to about 6 cm in height. [#1951] One large tree can provide a day's supply of oxygen for up to four people. [#1952] Trees trap the Sun's energy – they act like big batteries to power our planet. [#1953] Britain is thought to have the largest population of 'ancient' trees in Europe. [#1954] Britain's oldest tree is probably the **Fortingall Yew** in Perthshire, Scotland. It is believed to be over 3,000 years old. [#1955] The trunk of a **banyan tree** is made up of a mass of aerial roots that have grown into each other. [#1956] It could take 10 minutes to walk around the trunk of a giant banyan tree. [#1957] When **maple trees** are attacked by insects, they release chemicals into the air to warn other trees. [#1958] A **bristlecone pine tree** in California, United States, is thought to be around 4,800 years old. [#1959] Giant **redwoods** are the world's tallest trees, reaching 115 m high, with trunks 5 m across. [#1960]

# 10 **TUATARA** FACTS

Tuataras are **'LIVING FOSSILS'** – they have hardly changed since their nearest relatives died out **60 MILLION YEARS AGO**. #1961

Tuataras are only found in **New Zealand**. #1962

They became **extinct** on the main islands of New Zealand about 200 years ago, and survive only on the smaller islands. #1963

The name **'TUATARA'** comes from a Maori word meaning **'SPINY BACK'**. #1964

In 2009, a male tuatara called Henry, kept at Southland Museum in New Zealand, became a father at the age of **111.** #1965

Tuataras are active at night, but their hatchlings are active during the day, probably in order to avoid the adults, which are known to eat the hatchlings. #1966

## BABY TUATARAS
have a 'third eye' on the tops of their heads. Scientists are not sure what it's for. #1967

Tuataras do not have true teeth, but instead sharp projections of jaw bone – **A FEATURE NOT SEEN IN ANY OTHER REPTILE.**
#1968

As they get older, the points on their **jaw bones** wear away, and their diet changes from geckos and skinks to **softer prey** such as worms and slugs. #1969

Air temperatures of more than 28°C can be fatal to tuataras because they have a **lower body temperature** than most other reptiles. #1970

# 10 FACTS ABOUT WHAT GOES IN... AND WHAT COMES OUT

A human consumes as much food and drink in a lifetime as the weight of **one medium-sized blue whale.** #1971

If your **intestines** were stretched out, they would be more than four times as long as your body. #1972

You can eat upside down, as **special muscles** squeeze food towards your stomach. #1973

**Eating snot** can be good for you – it teaches your body to fight off germs! #1974

If you lose part of your **liver,** it can regrow itself. #1975

You can live without a **stomach.** #1976

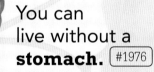

The **stomach** secretes about 1.5 litres of acid a day. #1977

The average person **farts 14 times** a day. #1978

You have **billions of bacteria** living in your intestines. They help you digest food. #1979

Your stomach avoids **eating itself** by coating its own inside with thick mucus! #1980

# 4 BIZARRE BODY FACTS

Your brain is made up of **85 PER CENT WATER** – the same as a **CABBAGE!** #1981

If you wear **headphones,** your ears make extra **earwax.** #1982

Most people sweat about **two teacups of liquid** per day, but it can be as much as a small bucketful! #1983

Your saliva (spit), tears, earwax, snot and sweat all contain **chemicals that kill germs.** #1984

# 7 FACTS ABOUT OCTOPUSES

An octopus has **three hearts**.

#1985

Octopuses swim by **squirting jets of water** behind them. This propels them forwards.

#1986

The **female octopus** does not eat while she guards her eggs. She takes care of them for several weeks until they hatch, then **dies of exhaustion**.

#1987

Octopuses have big brains, and can work out how to use tools in the wild. #1988

Each octopus arm contains about **50 million brain cells.** The arms do their own thinking. #1989

When threatened, octopuses squirt **black ink** at their enemies. #1990

Octopuses have soft bodies, and can squeeze through tiny gaps just a **few millimetres wide**. #1991

# 5 facts about the
# COLOURFUL CUTTLEFISH

A cuttlefish's eyes have 'W'-shaped pupils. #1992

A cuttlefish can look to the front or behind without moving its head. #1993

Cuttlefish can change the colour of their skin to any pattern they want in less than a second. #1994

Although it can change into any colour, a cuttlefish is probably colour-blind. #1995

Cuttlefish have green blood. #1996

# 25 TALL TOWERS and BIG BUILDINGS facts

The **Transamerica Pyramid** in San Francisco was built from **1969-1976**. #1997 Its pyramid shape allows natural light down to the streets below. #1998

The **Eiffel Tower** in Paris was the tallest building in the world when it was completed in **1889**. #1999 It is around 324 m tall. #2000 It is repainted every seven years. #2001 There are 1,665 steps to the top. #2002 Its design has been copied around the world, including the Tokyo Tower in Japan, which is 333 m tall. #2003

The **Burj Khalifa** in Dubai is the tallest building in the world. #2004 It is 828 m tall. #2005 It has 58 lifts and 2,957 parking spaces. #2006

The **Empire State Building** in New York is 443 m tall. #2007 It cost over £26 million to build. #2008 It took one year and 45 days to complete. #2009 It is designed to be a lightning rod and is struck by lightning about 100 times a year. #2010

**The Shard** in London is 310 m tall. #2011 It is the tallest building in Europe. #2012 It has 11,000 glass panels, 44 lifts and 306 flights of stairs. #2013 Architect **Renzo Piano** made the first rough sketch of the building on the back of a restaurant menu in **2000**. #2014 Its viewing floor is twice as high as any other viewing platform in London. #2015

The **Petronas Towers** in Kuala Lumpar, Malaysia, are the tallest twin towers in the world. #2016 The towers are connected by a sky bridge and are 452 m tall. #2017

**Makkah Royal Clock Tower Hotel** in Saudi Arabia is the world's tallest hotel and clock tower. #2018 It is around 600 m tall and has the world's largest clock face. #2019

The **Bitexco Financial Tower** in Vietnam was built in 2010 and is 262 m tall. #2020 It has a helipad on the 52nd floor that juts out 22 m. #2021

An ichthyosaur

**Pliosaurs**, **ichthyosaurs** and **plesiosaurs** were prehistoric marine reptiles. #2022 They lived millions of years ago, at the same time as the dinosaurs. #2023

A plesiosaur

Plesiosaurs lived in the oceans but breathed air. #2024 They probably laid eggs on sandy beaches, just as sea turtles do. #2025 The largest known plesiosaur was the **Elasmosaurus**. #2026 It measured 15 m from head to tail. #2027 Half of its body length was made up by its neck, which had over 70 bones in it. #2028 Its long neck helped it catch passing fish or even a pterosaur (flying reptile) flying just above the sea. #2029 A typical ichthyosaur looked like a fish or a dolphin, but was a reptile. #2030 It had huge eyes and a swimming speed of around 36 km/h. #2031 The largest known ichthyosaur was the **Shastasaurus**. #2032 It was around 21 m long. #2033 It lived during the Triassic period, around 220 to 210 million years ago. #2034

Pliosaurs were a type of short-necked plesiosaur. #2035 One study estimated that some pliosaurs could swim at almost 10 km/h. #2036 They were predators that hunted fish, molluscs and other marine reptiles. #2037 They had four flippers and pointed tails. #2038 They paddled with all four flippers as they swam, like turtles. #2039 A pliosaur called **Liopleurodon** lived in the Jurassic period, between 165 and 150 million years ago. #2040 It was about 7 m long. #2041 It was found in the UK, France, Chile and Russia. #2042 It fed on ichthyosaurs and plesiosaurs. #2043 The pliosaur **Kronosaurus** lived in the Cretaceous period, around 121 to 112 million years ago. #2044 It was found in Australia and Colombia. #2045 It was around 10 m long. #2046

A pliosaur

In **1488 Leonardo Da Vinci** designed an ornithopter after studying the flight of birds. [#2047] He also came up with designs for a helicopter, and a flying machine that was also a boat. [#2048] **The Wright brothers**, Orville and Wilbur, built the world's first successful aeroplane in **1903**. [#2049]

It was called the *Flyer*. [#2050] The brothers were bicycle makers from Ohio in the United States. [#2051] Their experience with bikes helped them when designing their planes. [#2052] Many early planes lacked control, but the Wright brothers used wires to warp (twist) the wings, which controlled the plane. [#2053] The first historic flight only lasted 12 seconds. [#2054] The *Flyer* travelled 37 m in this time. [#2055] The first jet engines were built in the **1930s** by two different people in two different countries. [#2056] **Hans von Ohain** in Germany and **Frank Whittle** in Britain both created an engine without knowing of the other's work. [#2057] Jet engines work by pushing a jet of exhaust gas out of the back. [#2058] The exhaust gas hits the air so fast that it forces the plane forward, like a deflating balloon. [#2059] In a typical turbojet, exhaust gases are pushed out at over 1,600 km/h. [#2060] Supersonic planes travel faster than the speed of sound. [#2061] That's about 1,000 km/h at around 12,000 m up. [#2062]

A Mach number is the speed of the plane divided by the speed of sound at the plane's altitude. [#2063] **Chuck Yeager** made the first supersonic flight in **1947**. [#2064] He made the flight in a Bell X-1 plane. [#2065] He was in the United States Air Force. [#2066] **Concorde** was the longest-running commercial supersonic aircraft. [#2067] Its fastest journey was in **1986**. [#2068] It took just under three hours to fly from London to New York. [#2069] A plane is controlled by the hinged flaps on its wings and tail. [#2070] When a plane goes nose-up to climb, or nose-down to dive, it is called changing **pitch**. [#2071] The **elevator** (horizontal flap on the tail) controls the pitch. [#2072] When a pilot steers a plane right or left, it is called changing **yaw**. [#2073] The **rudder** (vertical flap on the tail) controls the yaw. [#2074] When a plane dips its wings to roll to one side, it is called changing **roll**. [#2075] The **ailerons** (horizontal flaps on the wings) control the roll. [#2076] Planes take off when air is moving fast enough over the wing to provide enough lift. [#2077] **Microlights** are very small, lightweight aircraft. [#2078] They are also known as ultralights. [#2079] The first microlight was a hang-glider with a chainsaw motor. [#2080] It was built by the American **Bill Bennett** in **1973**. [#2081] Some microlights have flexible wings made from fabric. [#2082] Others have fixed wings with flaps so they can be steered. [#2083] **Jacques Garnerin** was the first human to do a **parachute** jump. [#2084] He jumped out of a balloon over Paris in **1797**. [#2085] Early parachutes were made of canvas. [#2086] Later materials included silk and nylon. [#2087] Parachutes used to be shaped like umbrellas. [#2088] They're now shaped liked wings. [#2089] Jet planes and high-speed cars use funnel-shaped parachutes to slow them down. [#2090] They are called drogues. [#2091] In **2012** Austrian skydiver **Felix Baumgartner** became the first human to break the sound barrier without any form of engine power. [#2092] He flew 39 km into the stratosphere over the

# 111
# HIGH-FLYING
## facts

United States in a helium balloon before freefalling, then parachuting back to Earth. #2093 His descent took around 10 minutes. #2094 He broke the record for the highest manned-balloon flight. #2095 He also broke the record for the highest-altitude jump. #2096 The two rotating blades on a **helicopter** provide the lift and thrust. #2097 In **1907 Paul Comu** flew the first **helicopter**. #2098 It had two sets of rotors. #2099 His flight lasted 20 seconds. #2100 The fastest helicopter is the Westland Lynx. #2101 It can fly around 400 km/h. #2102 **Igor Sikorsky** crafted his first working helicopter in **1939**. #2103 It pioneered the way helicopters have rotors today. #2104 In **1942** his Sikorsky R-4 became the world's first mass-produced helicopter. #2105 It also became the first service helicopter for the United States Army Air Forces. #2106 Airbus Helicopters makes the most helicopters in the world. #2107 It employs around 22,000 people globally. #2108 **Hot air balloons** are bags filled with hot air. #2109 They have a burner that heats the air inside the balloon to keep it afloat. #2110 Balloons are normally launched at dawn or dusk, when the air is calm. #2111 To descend quickly, a cord can be pulled to let air out through a vent at the top of the balloon. #2112 The first flight in a hot air balloon was in **1783**. #2113 It was by French scientist **Jean-Francois Pilatre de Rozier**. #2114 His balloon was made by the **Montgolfier** brothers. #2115 In recognition of their work, their father **Pierre Montgolfier** was elevated to nobility by **King Louis XVI** of France. #2116 The first people to fly around the world non-stop in a hot air balloon were **Bertrand Piccard** and **Brian Jones**. #2117 They completed their journey in **1999**. #2118 Their balloon was called the *Breitling Orbiter 3*. #2119 It was 55 m tall when fully inflated. #2120 The total distance was 42,810 km. #2121 It took almost 20 days to complete the journey. #2122 They actually flew further than they needed to. #2123 They took off from Switzerland and landed in Egypt. #2124 In **1852** French engineer **Henri Giffard** made a balloon **airbus** that could be steered. #2125

It was filled with the light gas hydrogen. #2126 Giffard powered it with a steam-driven propeller with a rudder. #2127 In **1909 Count Ferdinand von Zeppelin** set up the world's first airline. #2128 It was called DELAG. #2129 This was short for Deutsche Luftschiffahrts-Aktien-gesellschaft (German Airship Travel Corporation). #2130 Its airships were 148 m long. #2131 They carried around 34,000 passengers in the airline's first 14 years. #2132 By the **1920s**, huge airships were carrying people across the Atlantic in luxury. #2133 In **1937** the *Hindenburg* airship caught fire as it docked in the United States. #2134 35 people were killed. #2135 It marked the end of airship travel. #2136 **Rockets** work by burning fuel. #2137 As the fuel burns and swells out behind, the swelling pushes the rocket forward. #2138 The Chinese experimented with gunpowder-filled tubes around **AD 850**. #2139 They discovered a rocket could launch itself by the power produced by the escaping gas. #2140 In **1686 Isaac Newton** presented his laws of motion. #2141 These were later applied by scientists in the development of rockets. #2142 In **1898** school teacher **Konstantin Tsiolkovsky** came up with the idea of space travel by rocket. #2143 He wrote science-fiction books about space travel before moving on to write scientific papers on space travel. #2144 In the early **1900s** he published a rocket equation in a Russian aviation magazine. #2145 It was called the Tsiolkovsky formula. #2146 It established the relationship between rocket speed, the gas at exit and the mass of the rocket. #2147 This paved the way for space exploration. #2148 Tsiolkovsky died in **1935.** #2149 A crater on the Moon was named after him. #2150 **Robert Goddard** conducted many rocket experiments. #2151 In **1926** he invented a liquid-fuelled rocket. #2152 Both the Americans and Russians realized the potential of using rockets as military weapons and for space travel. #2153 They competed in their development of space and arms programmes. #2154 This contributed to hostilities during the Cold War. #2155 The Cold War was a period of hostility between the Soviet bloc and the West, notably the Americans. #2156 It lasted from 1945 to 1990. #2157

# 4 FACTS ABOUT YOUR INSIDES

Sometimes if a patient is given a **FAKE MEDICINE**,it can affect them like a real drug because they believe they will get better – it's called the 'placebo effect'. #2158

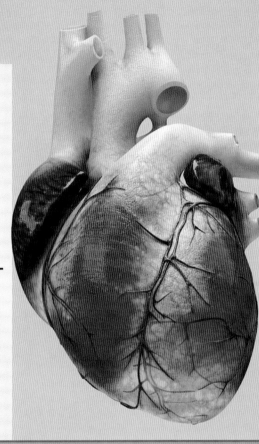

You can have a heart, lungs, kidney, liver, hand or even face **TRANSPLANTED** from another person. #2159

Before anaesthetics, people having a limb amputated would **bite down on a piece of leather** to help deal with the pain. #2160

**Cola** drinks and **tomato ketchup** were once sold as **medicines**. #2161

medicine

# 10 FACTS ABOUT YOUR OUTSIDES

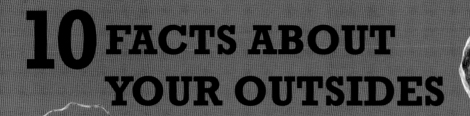

Your skin makes up around 16 per cent of your body weight. #2162

Your skin is as heavy as wearing **four winter coats**. #2163

Every day, you shed about **40 million** dead skin cells. #2164

**Dust** is mainly dead skin cells. #2165

In a lifetime, you'll leave up to **20 kilograms** of dead skin lying around. #2166

Tiny dust mites live in your house and eat your dead skin. #2167

Your **nose gets runny** on a cold day because your nose is trying to warm up the air you breathe. #2168

Xie Qiuping of China holds the record for the longest hair in the world, at **5.6 metres**. #2169

She has not had a haircut since **1973**! #2170

Humans have been decorating their nails for more than **5,000 years**. #2171

# 8 FACTS ABOUT
# Hornbills

The rhinoceros hornbill's casque (crest) curves like the shape of a **rhino's horn**.

#2172

A **hornbill's casque** acts like a **sound chamber,** to make its calls much louder.

#2173

A hornbill has **EYELASHES MADE FROM MODIFIED FEATHERS,** which shade its eyes from the Sun.

#2175

## Hornbills
can live for up to
## 70 YEARS.

#2174

**GROUND HORNBILL** pairs need the help of at least **two relatives** to rear their young. Hornbills spend several years helping other birds before they have their own chicks.

#2176

When nesting, female hornbills **wall themselves up inside tree trunks** where they will stay with their chicks **for four months.**

#2177

The chicks stay with their parents for **SIX MONTHS** after leaving the nest.

#2179

While they are inside the nest, the female and her chicks are **fed through a narrow slit in the wall** by the male.

#2178

# 5 FACTS ABOUT TOUCANS

A toucan's tongue is up to 15 cm long. #2180

It uses its bill to reach for fruit, **search holes** in tree trunks and steal food from other birds' nests. #2181

Its bill measures half the bird's entire body length. #2182

A toucan's **HUGE BILL** is **HOLLOW** AND **LIGHT.** #2183

The bill is **serrated,** which helps it to hold on to **PREY** such as a small lizard. #2184

# 11 CHAMELEON
## FACTS

There are **80** different species of chameleon. Half of these live on the **island of Madagascar.**

#2185

Chameleons **change colour** depending on their mood or temperature.

#2186

**Male chameleons are usually more colourful than females.**

#2187

The feet of a chameleon are shaped like tongs, or pincers, allowing them to grip firmly onto the branches of trees. #2188

A chameleon's eyes can swivel 180 degrees in any direction. #2189

The **Brookesia micra chameleon** is less than 3 cm long. #2190

That's small enough to stand on the head of a match! #2191

Chameleons have no ears, but they can still sense vibrations in the air. #2192

The egg of a Parson's chameleon can take up to two years to hatch. #2193

**A chameleon's tongue can be up to twice as long as its body.** #2194

In less than a tenth of a second, a chameleon's tongue can shoot out and snare a buzzing insect. #2195

# 42 facts about our CHANGING EARTH

Earth has changed significantly since it was first formed. #2196

It is thought that Earth was originally made up of molten rock, like the lava found in volcanoes. #2197

Earth's early atmosphere was probably formed from the gases given out by the volcanic activity. #2198

This early atmosphere would probably be toxic to humans, with little or no oxygen. #2199

It also contained carbon dioxide, and small amounts of water vapour and methane. #2200

Carbon dioxide levels were around five times higher than they are now. #2201

As Earth cooled down it formed three layers – core, mantle and crust. #2202

This led to the formation of tectonic plates (areas of Earth's crust which fit together, much like a jigsaw puzzle). #2203

There was just one ocean, known as Panthalassa. #2204

Between 300 million and 100 million years ago a supercontinent called Pangaea existed. #2205

All land was attached as one large mass, you could have walked from South America to Africa! #2206

The environment was very different. Antarctica was once a rainforest. #2207

Over millions of years the movement of Earth's plates caused Pangaea to slowly divide. #2208

The area that is now India broke away from Africa and slowly pressed up against Asia, creating the Himalayas (a vast mountain range). #2209

This movement of Earth's plates is known as continental drift. #2210

Continental drift continues today, so Earth's land will change shape. #2211

Some scientists predict that a new supercontinent will form, millions of years in the future. #2212

North America and Europe are drifting apart at a rate of around 2.5 cm a year. #2213

Seafloor spreading is the process of new crust forming where two plates are moving apart. #2214

This is a very slow process. #2215

Other natural processes have changed Earth and its climate, including volcanoes, the energy output of the Sun and ice ages. #2216

Ice ages are extended periods of extreme cooling of Earth's surface and atmosphere. #2217

During an ice age, glacial sheets and polar caps expand to cover large areas of land. #2218

We are currently living in a warmer period, also known as an interglacial period. #2219

Planet Earth has warmed and cooled in cyclical patterns for millions of years, but around 11,000 years ago the pattern changed. #2220

Some scientists believe it changed because humans began to farm and rear animals. #2221

This produced more greenhouse gases like carbon dioxide and methane. #2222

These gases in the atmosphere stopped temperatures falling as they had in the past. #2223

This change in temperature is known as global climate change or global warming. #2224

Today, other human activities such as burning coal and driving cars add greenhouse gases to the ones naturally present in the atmosphere. #2225

Global sea levels rose by around 17 cm in the last century. #2226

However, the speed at which the sea level is rising has increased – since 1990 it has risen by approximately 6 cm. #2227

Scientists do not know for sure why sea levels are

rising. #2228
Many cities are at risk of being submerged if the sea levels continue to rise. #2229
These include New York City, Venice and Shanghai. #2230
The warmest years recorded since **1900** all occurred after **1980**. #2231
The warmest decade on record is **2001–2010**. #2232
Since the start of the Industrial Revolution in the **1800s** acidity in the oceans has increased by around 30 per cent. #2233
This acidity is harmful to marine life. #2234
The temperature of our oceans has increased by around 0.1°C in the past century. #2235
Higher temperatures can cause more powerful storms to form at sea. #2236
Some experts believe that global climate change could cause around 25 per cent of Earth's species to be extinct (die out) by **2115**. #2237

# 10 FACTS ABOUT ANIMAL LIFE AND EXTINCTION

➡ When Earth first formed no life was able to survive on its surface. #2238

➡ Around 540 million years ago shrimps and snails evolved in the oceans, followed by fish. #2239

➡ Over time, plants started to grow on land, and over millions of years, fish evolved the ability to survive out of water. #2240

➡ Amphibians, insects, reptiles and mammals then evolved over millions of years. #2241

➡ Many animals are now extinct, their species killed off by each other, nature or humans. #2242

➡ Woolly mammoths survived the ice age but became extinct because they couldn't adapt to warmer climates. #2243

➡ Dodos (flightless birds) became extinct in the late 17th century. #2244

➡ They died out less than a century after they were discovered. It is thought they became extinct due to human involvement and disturbance. #2245

➡ The quagga, which died out around **1883**, looked like a zebra but only had stripes on one half of its body. #2246

➡ The Amur Leopard, Black Rhino, Mountain Gorilla, Siberian Tiger and Borneo Pygmy Elephant are all endangered species, which means they are at risk of extinction. #2247

# The planet Saturn is so light, it would **FLOAT ON WATER.** #2248

# 5 HOT FACTS ABOUT THE SUN

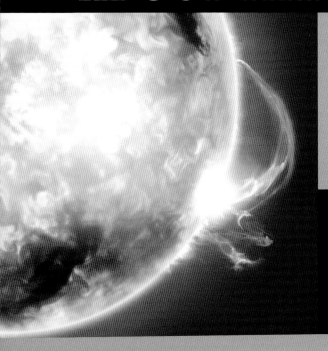

Sunlight travels at 300,000 kilometres per second. This is known as **THE SPEED OF LIGHT**. #2249

Fountains of flame **LARGER THAN EARTH** shoot from the surface of the Sun. #2250

Dark spots on the Sun called **SUNSPOTS** can measure 80,000 kilometres across – larger than the planet Uranus. #2251

The temperature at the centre of the Sun is **150,000 TIMES HOTTER** than boiling water. #2252

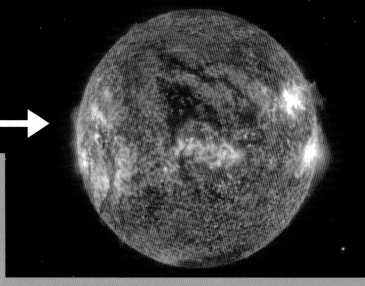

The Sun contains **99.8 PER CENT** of all the matter in the solar system. #2253

# 50 facts on WORLD WAR I

World War I (WWI) is also called the Great War. #2254 It started in **1914**. #2255 The **Allied Powers** (Britain, France and Russia) fought against the **Central Powers** (Germany and Austria-Hungary). Other countries were also involved. #2256 The United States did not initially join the war, but joined the Allied powers in **1917** after American merchant ships were attacked. #2257 There were a number of reasons why war broke out. One was the assassination of the heir to the throne of Austria-Hungary, Archduke **Franz Ferdinand**. #2258 WWI was the first war in which aeroplanes and tanks were used. #2259 At the Western Front (in Belgium and France) much of the war was fought from **trenches** (connected ditches). #2260 The battling armies barely moved as as they fired at each other across **No Man's Land** – the narrow strip of land between the two sides. #2261 British soldiers had to be 18 years old. #2262 Many boys lied about their age. Around 250,000 underage soldiers served in WWI. #2263 The youngest was just 12 years old! #2264 By **1915** nearly 2.5 million men had signed up to fight. #2265 In **1916** conscription (a British law stating that all 18–41-year olds had to join the army) was introduced. #2266 There were 16,000 **conscientious objectors** (those who refused to fight) in Britain. #2267 Some were given white feathers as a sign of cowardice. #2268 Some conscientious objectors were given non-combat roles in the war. #2269 Others were sentenced to time in prison. #2270 Average life expectancy in the trenches was just six weeks. #2271 Over time the amount of food given to soldiers (rations) was reduced. #2272 The war claimed the lives of around 6,000 soldiers a day. #2273 More than 9 million people died fighting overall. #2274 Around 65 million people fought in total. #2275 German trenches were often very well built. #2276 Some even had windows and doorbells. #2277 At Christmas **1914** an unofficial ceasefire broke out along parts of the Western Front. #2278 German and Allied troops gave gifts to each other and exchanged prisoners. #2279 60 per cent of all **casualties** were caused by shellfire (bombing). #2280 There were 80,000 reported cases of shell shock (an illness caused by the stress of a warzone). #2281 The French first introduced metal helmets in **1915**. #2282 The world's first large scale tank battle was fought in **1917**. #2283 It was called the **Battle of Cambrai**. #2284 The most famous tank involved was called the **Mark IV**. #2285 Disease caused around one third of deaths. #2286 Over 300 British soldiers were sentenced to **execution** during WWI. #2287 This was the punishment for deserting your post in battle. #2288 Most would have been killed by firing squad. #2289 In **1917** anti-German feelings led to **King George V** changing the Royal Family's surname. #2290 He changed it from Saxe-Coburg-Gotha to Windsor. #2291 The Victoria Cross is a British medal to award bravery. #2292 It was awarded 628 times during WWI. #2293 At the **Battle of Messines** in **Belgium** 19 mines were detonated by the British. #2294 The blast could be heard in London! #2295 100,000 homing pigeons were used to send messages. #2296 In **1918** a pigeon saved 200 US soldiers by delivering a message, despite having been injured by a bullet. #2297 The British Army had around 870,000 horses. #2298 They were mostly used to transport supplies and carry soldiers. #2299 **Edward Harrison** invented the first gas mask. #2300 12 million letters were delivered to the Western Front every week. #2301 The Allied Powers won the war in **1918**. #2302 WWI officially ended at 11am on the 11 November **1918**. #2303

# 51 FIGHTING FACTS ON WORLD WAR II

World War II involved 61 countries and 1.7 billion people. #2304 World War II began on 3 September **1939**. #2305 Russia had the most casualties in World War II, losing over 21 million people. #2306 **Britain** and **France** declared war on **Germany**, following the German invasion of Poland. #2307 **Queen Elizabeth II** grew up during the war. She was 13 when it started and 19 by its end. #2308 She did her bit to help out and served as a mechanic and driver. #2309 America entered the war in **1941** after Japan attacked US warships at Pearl Harbor in Hawaii. #2310 In a two-hour attack the Japanese sank 18 warships and destroyed 164 aircraft. #2311 Over 2,400 servicemen and civilians lost their lives. #2312 After the United States declared war on Japan its allies, Germany and Italy, declared war on the United States. #2313 Nearly 40 per cent of US servicemen and women were volunteers. #2314 'The Blitz' was a term used to describe the heavy bombing of London and other British cities by the German Luftwaffe (air force). #2315 The word 'Blitz' comes from the German word *blitzkrieg*, meaning lightning war. #2316 The bombings started in September **1940** and didn't end until May **1941**. #2317 During one stage, London was bombed for 57 nights in a row. #2318 When the bombers were on their way a loud siren was started. #2319 It made a very loud wailing noise and was nicknamed the Moaning Minnie. #2320 The London Underground was used as a bomb shelter during raids. #2321 Around 30,000 people were killed during the Blitz. #2322 Around 60 per cent of London's buildings were damaged or destroyed. #2323 The longest battle of WWII was the Battle of the Atlantic, which lasted from **1939** to **1945**. #2324 **Winston Churchill**, who became Prime Minister during WWII, later admitted that the only thing that really frightened him during the war was the U-boat peril. #2325 Germany realized that if they could cut off Britain's supplies coming across the Atlantic they could win the war. #2326 The Germans produced around 20 U-boats a month to attack ships carrying British supplies. #2327 The U-boats would hunt in groups called wolf packs. #2328 At the height of the war, more than 100 ships were being sunk each month. #2329 US General **Dwight D. Eisenhower** was Supreme Commander of the Allied Forces in Europe. #2330 He was in charge of over 5 million soldiers. #2331 Eisenhower went on to become US president. #2332 He ruled for two terms from **1953** to **1961**. #2333 On 6 June **1944** the Allies invaded Normandy in France. #2334 It was the largest seaborne invasion in history. #2335 Its codename was Operation Overlord. #2336 The invasion happened a day later than planned, due to bad weather. #2337 Nearly 2 million servicemen were involved in the operation. #2338 The German city of Konstanz was not bombed during Allied raids because it left all its lights on. #2339 This led the bombers to think it was a Swiss city, so they left it alone. #2340 Nutella was invented during World War II as an alternative to chocolate, as cocoa powder was in short supply. #2341 The most famous British planes during the war were the Spitfire and Hurricane. #2342 The fastest American fighter plane was the P-51 Mustang. #2343 It could reach speeds of over 700 km/h. #2344 More than 50,000 M4 Sherman tanks were produced during the war. #2345 Around 40,000 Soviet T-34 tanks were made. #2346 The Soviet T-34 was one of the most powerful tanks during the war; variants of it are still in service around the world today. #2347 The Night Witches were a Soviet squadron of female fighter pilots who flew night raids on Germany. #2348 40 planes, each crewed by two women, would fly eight or more missions a night. #2349 Adolf Hitler committed suicide at the end of the war in **1945**. #2350 On 7 May **1945** Germany signed an unconditional surrender. Japan fought on, finally surrendering on 2 September **1945**. #2351 At the end of the war, Germany was split in half. #2352 The western half was controlled by the western Allies and the eastern half by the Soviet Union. #2353 Germany wasn't reunited until **1990**. #2354

# 10 SMASHING FACTS ABOUT METEORS

Over a **million meteors** (shooting stars) will burn up in Earth's atmosphere today. #2355

Rock from a **meteorite** sells for as much as gold. #2356

A meteorite that fell 65 million years ago probably caused the **extinction of the dinosaurs.** #2357

Some scientists believe **life arrived on Earth** on a meteorite. #2358

Asteroids are **giant space rocks**. The largest, Ceres, is 950 kilometres across. #2359

Over **40,000 shooting stars** fell in 20 minutes during a meteor shower in 1966. #2360

In 1954, an American woman was seriously injured when a meteorite **crashed through her roof.** #2361

An **Egyptian dog was killed** when it was struck by a meteorite in 1911. #2362

In 1908, a meteorite broke up, causing a **gigantic fireball** that flattened 80 million trees. #2363

Earth is **getting heavier each year,** because of the meteorites and other space debris that crash here. #2364

# 4 LOST FACTS ABOUT BLACK HOLES

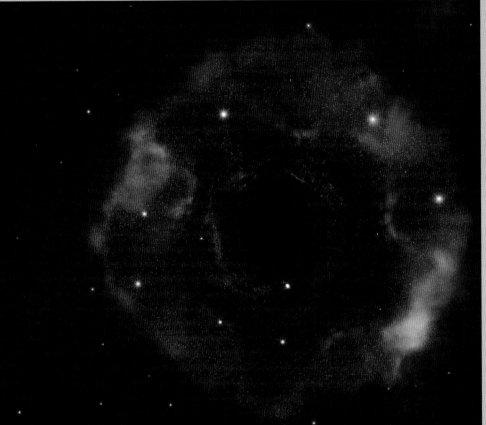

A black hole is born when a dying star collapses in an **EXPLOSION** called a **SUPERNOVA**. #2365

A black hole **sucks everything nearby into it.** Nothing can escape from a black hole, not even light. #2366

In a black hole, **time virtually stops**. That's because time goes more slowly as gravity increases. #2367

If you fell into a black hole, your **BODY** would be **STRETCHED LIKE SPAGHETTI**. #2368

151

# 11 FACTS ABOUT

# SHARKS

Sharks can detect a single drop of **blood** in an Olympic-sized swimming pool full of **water**. #2369

The smallest shark is the **dwarf lanternshark.** It is just **20 cm** long. #2370

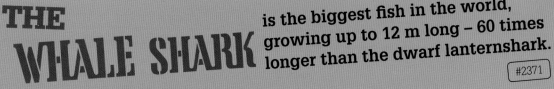

**THE WHALE SHARK** is the biggest fish in the world, growing up to 12 m long – 60 times longer than the dwarf lanternshark. #2371

A shark's **skeleton** is made of **bendy cartilage** (the same stuff your nose is made from), **not bone**. #2372

If a shark **stops** swimming, it **sinks,** as it does not have a swim bladder to help with buoyancy. #2373

**SHARKS** have been swimming in the oceans for **400 MILLION** years – since before the dinosaurs. #2374

A **GREAT HAMMERHEAD** shark's eyes are **1 m** apart. #2375

A great white's bite is **three times** more **powerful** than the bite of a **lion**.

#2376

**On average,** fewer than **ten people** a year are killed by great whites... but more than **1,000 people** a year are killed by **bees**.

#2377

#2378

A **GREAT WHITE** shark needs to eat **11 TONNES** of food a year – equivalent in weight to 150 people.

#2379

# 5 DRAMATIC FACTS ABOUT DESERTS

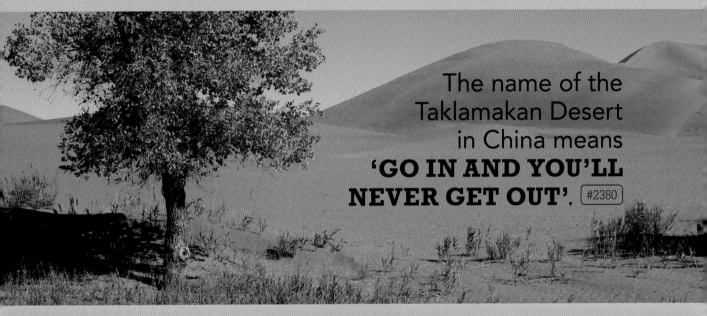

The name of the Taklamakan Desert in China means **'GO IN AND YOU'LL NEVER GET OUT'**. #2380

The Sahara Desert, **EARTH'S BIGGEST DESERT,** covers an area about the size of the United States. #02381

It is still getting bigger – growing **50 KILOMETRES** south every year. #2382

Despite being covered in ice, **ANTARCTICA** is actually classed as a desert because it hardly ever snows! #2383

In 1913, the temperature at Furnace Creek in Death Valley, USA, hit a sizzling **56°C** – the highest on record in the country. #2384

# 4 EARTH-SHATTERING EARTHQUAKE AND AVALANCHE FACTS

In 1970, an **earthquake** in Peru triggered an avalanche that buried the town of Yungay and its 20,000 inhabitants. #2385

A cliff collapse in northern England in 1993 sent a **HOTEL TUMBLING INTO THE SEA**. #2386

The cliffs of Holderness in Britain are moving **1 TO 2 METRES INLAND** each year as they are eaten away by the sea. #2387

In 1916, **avalanches** in the Alps killed 10,000 soldiers fighting in World War I. #2388

The world's longest tunnel is the Thirlmere Aqueduct, a 155-kilometre water tunnel under the north of England. #2389

# 10 POPULAR FACTS ABOUT POPULATIONS

The world's **population** is over **7 billion** and rising fast. #2390

In **1960**, the population of the world was **3 billion** people. #2391

During 2011, about **135 million** people were born in the world... #2392

The world's population is increasing by **2.4 people a second.** #2393

... and **57 million** died. That's an increase of 78 million people in just one year. #2394

252 babies are born in the world every minute, or **4.2 births a second.** #2395

107 people die in the world every minute, or **1.8 deaths a second**. #2396

Japan's population is shrinking. There are more deaths than births in the country. #2397

More than **60 per cent** of the world's population live in **Asia.** #2398

On 29 May 2007, for the first time in human history, more people lived in **cities and towns** than in the countryside! #2399

The first humans lived in Africa, about **2 million years ago,** then spread across the world. #2400 Early explorers went out in search of food and places to live. #2401 Millions of years ago people could walk from country to country, where seas and oceans now lie. #2402 During his lifetime, the **14th century** explorer **Ibn Battuta** travelled 120,000 km by foot, camel and ship – as far as three times around the world. #2403 In **1862**, British explorer **John Speke** became temporarily deaf after a beetle crawled into his ear and he tried to remove it with a knife. #2404 In **1860** **Robert Burke** and **William Wills** walked across Australia in search of an inland sea. They discovered there was no sea and died on the journey home. #2405 Instead of using maps, Indigenous Australians sang songs about landmarks to help them remember paths across the continent. #2406 The largest-ever empire was the **British Empire,** which peaked in **1922** when it covered a fifth of the world's lands. #2407 The **Roman Empire** included millions of people living over a large area. The Romans would count all the people to keep track of who lived where. #2408 The **Chinese Empire** was the longest-lasting empire and lasted over 2,000 years. #2409 Today, Japan is the only country that calls itself an empire and has an emperor. #2410 The ancient **Polynesian people** had no navigation but sailed across vast distances of open sea using only their senses. #2411 Polynesian explorers would also watch the stars, feel the motion of the waves, listen to wildlife and follow weather signs. #2412 **Zheng He** was a great Chinese explorer who established Chinese trade in new areas. #2413 Zheng He's first expedition in **1405** visited Vietnam, Thailand and India. #2414 VIKING FACTS The **Vikings** were brave sailors and explorers from Denmark, Norway and Sweden. #2415 In the late **700s** they risked their lives to go on journeys to find new lands. #2416 The Vikings traded all over Europe and as far east as Central Asia. #2417 Everywhere they went they bought and sold spices, jewellery, pottery, wool, iron, fur, fish and slaves. #2418 The name 'Viking' means 'pirate raid'. #2419 Viking longboats were designed to sail in shallow waters, so the Vikings could get close to land and jump out quickly to begin their raid. #2420 Vikings raided treasures and art from churches, monasteries and homes in England and Scotland. #2421 They also raided Ireland, where they founded the city of Dublin. #2422 Wealthy Viking warriors were buried or burned in their ships as they believed these would carry them into the next world. #2423 EUROPEAN EXPLORERS In **1271**, an Italian called **Marco Polo** began a 24-year trek across Asia, to find out what was there. #2424 When he returned he fought in a war, was captured and sent to prison for several years. #2425 He used his time in jail to write about his travels. #2426 Marco Polo introduced paper money to Europeans, something he had seen in China for the first time. #2427 Marco Polo was a major influence on other explorers, such as **Christopher Columbus**. #2428 In **1488, Bartolomeu Dias**, the Portuguese navigator, was the first European to sail around the Cape of Good Hope at the tip of Africa. #2429 In **1492** Christopher Columbus sailed across the Atlantic Ocean, looking for a new route to Asia. #2430 When Columbus arrived in the Bahamas he thought he was in Asia. He had actually discovered the New World. #2431 Even though Christopher Columbus was Italian, his discovery was claimed by Spain, because the Spanish king had funded his trip. #2432 Columbus took three ships on his expedition, the *Santa María*, the *Pinta* and the *Niña*. #2433 Columbus wasn't the first European to have sailed across the Atlantic – the Vikings had done so before him. #2434 Columbus's discovery opened up the Americas to European colonization. #2435 Spanish explorers and soldiers, called **Conquistadors**, soon followed to claim new lands for Spain and open up new trading routes. #2436 The Conquistadors sailed across the Atlantic in ships called Spanish galleons. #2437 The most common gun used on board a galleon was called a demi-culverin; it could fire shots around 500 m. #2438 Conquistadors stole lots of gold and treasures from the people and lands they discovered and sent it home in ships to Spain. Lots of these ships were stolen by enemies or sunk in storms. #2439 In **2007** gold and silver coins worth £300 million were discovered in a shipwreck off the coast of Portugal. #2440 El Dorado is the mythical land in South America said to be rich in gold beyond all dreams. Explorers have been looking for it for centuries but have yet to find it. #2441 In **1497** an Italian explorer called **John Cabot** wanted to find a new route to Asia. Supported by the English **King Henry VII**, Cabot discovered Canada and called it New-found-land. #2442 In the same year, Portuguese explorer **Vasco de Gama** was the first person to sail directly from Europe to India. #2443 In **1519**, Ferdinand Magellan from Portugal led the first fleet of ships to sail around the world. Sadly he didn't survive his heroic trip. #2444 Also in **1519**, the famous Spanish explorer **Hernando Cortes** kidnapped the Aztec **Emperor Montezuma** and looted lots of gold from Mexico. #2445 **Sir Francis Drake** was the first British man to sail around the world. He set off on his voyage in **1577.** #2446 It took him three years to get back home, but he returned with rich spices and treasures. #2447 **Queen Elizabeth I** was so pleased with all the presents he brought back for her, she made him a knight. #2448 Drake later set sail again and stole Spanish treasure from colonies along the coast of Florida and in the West Indies. #2449 The king of Spain put a bounty on Drake's head of 20,000 ducats. That's millions of pounds in today's money. #2450 Drake died in **1596** of dysentery (a disease that killed a lot of sailors) off the coast of Panama in South America. #2451 In **1578** British explorer **Sir Walter Raleigh** set sail to explore America and brought back the first potatoes to Britain. #2652 Raleigh became a favourite of Queen Elizabeth I, but when she found out he had married one of her maids, she sent him and his wife to the Tower of London. #2453 Raleigh was later released but was executed in **1618** by **King James I**, after defying the king's orders and attacking the Spanish. #2454 In **1642**, **Abel Tasman** from Holland was the first European to sail around Australia and found Tasmania, New Zealand and other Pacific islands. #2455 Tasman failed to realize that Australia was there though! #2456 **James Cook** was a British explorer who sailed and mapped much of the South Pacific. #2457 Cook set off on his first journey in **1768**, hoping to work out the distance from Earth to the Sun, by looking at the planet Venus, and discover new lands too. #2458 Cook's ship was called the *Endeavour*. It wasn't fast but could carry lots of supplies. #2459 Cook discovered the east coast of Australia, claimed it for Britain and called it New South Wales. #2460 Cook explored many other parts of the world and was killed by natives in Hawaii in **1779**. #2461 In **1841**, a British explorer called **Dr Livingstone** began to explore Africa, determined to free its people from slavery and introduce them to Christianity. #2462 In **1856** Dr Livingstone became the first person to cross the width of southern Africa. #2463 THE POLES The Norwegian explorer **Roald Amundsen** was the first man to reach the South Pole in **1911**. #2464 In **1887** he was first mate on a ship called *Belgica*, which was the first expedition to ever survive a winter in the Arctic. #2465 Amundsen learned valuable lessons on this expedition, such as that animal skins were warmer to wear than animal furs. #2466 In **1903** he discovered the Northwest Passage from the Atlantic Ocean to the Pacific Ocean, a passage that had been searched for over many centuries. #2467 In **1911**, he raced British explorer **Captain Scott** to the South Pole. #2468 Amundsen's team consisted of five men who all made it back alive. #2469 Captain Scott's expedition made it to the South Pole 35 days later. Unfortunately they didn't make it back alive; they were found frozen to death. #2470 In **1926** Amundsen flew over the North Pole in an airship. #2471 Amundsen was the first person to reach both the North and South Poles. #2472 SPACE In **1942**, the German V2 was the first rocket to reach 100 km from Earth's surface, into Space. #2473 The rocket was designed by **Wernher von Braun**, who later worked with NASA to design the rockets that went to the Moon. #2474 In **1947** the US launched fruit flies into space, on a V2 rocket, to study the effect of space on animals. #2475 Russian **Yuri Gagarin**, the first man to travel in space, took 108 minutes to orbit Earth in 1961 in his spacecraft *Vostok 1*. #2476 Yuri became an instant celebrity and travelled the world to promote his successful mission. #2477 Yuri sadly died in 1968 on a routine training flight. #2478 In **1962**, the first American, **John Glenn**, orbited Earth. #2479 He circled the globe three times in just under five hours. #2480 **Valentina Tereshkova**, the first woman in space, has a crater on the Moon named after her. #2481 The first US mission to land on the Moon was manned by three astronauts. #2482 Only two of those astronauts, **Neil Armstrong** and **Buzz Aldrin**, got to walk on the Moon. The third, **Michael Collins**, had to remain onboard to control the command module. #2483 Neil Armstrong said the famous words 'That's one small step for man, one giant leap for mankind.' #2484 In **1973** Russian space probe *Mars II* explored Mars taking and sending photos of Mars back to Earth. #2485 In **1986** the construction of a space station called MIR began. It took 10 years to build and was the first consistently inhabited space station. #2486 MIR was destroyed in 2001 when it burned up as it crashed back to Earth. #2487 In **1991 Helen Sharman** became the first British astronaut in space when she responded to an advertisement on the radio which said, 'Astronaut wanted, no experience necessary.' #2488 Before she became an astronaut, Helen worked for the chocolate company that made Mars bars. #2489 The first piece of the International Space Station (ISS) was launched in **1998**. #2490 The ISS took two years to build and has science labs from the US, Russia, Japan and Europe. #2491 American millionaire **Dennis Tito** became the first space tourist in **2001** when he paid around 20 million US dollars for a ride on a Russian spacecraft. #2492 OCEAN EXPLORATION Earth's deepest spot, the Mariana Trench, was discovered in **1875** by *HMS Challenger* using sound equipment during a global circumnavigation. #2493 The trench's depth has been measured at 11,034 m. #2494 It is found in the western Pacific Ocean. #2495 The deepest part of the trench is called the Challenger Deep. #2496 The Mariana Trench is 2,550 km long, five times the length of the Grand Canyon. #2497 In **2012**, film director **James Cameron** became one of only three people to successfully dive to the Earth's deepest point in the Mariana Trench. #2498 Explorers have discovered all kinds of life in the trench, including the snail fish, which has been found 7,700 m below sea level. #2499

# 50 ANCIENT GREECE

The first Ancient Greek civilization was formed about 3,500 years ago by people we call the **Mycenaeans**. #2500 The Ancient Greek civilization lasted till **146 BC** when the Romans invaded. #2501 The Ancient Greeks lived in mainland Greece and on islands in the Aegean Sea. #2502 Ancient Greece was made up of city-states, each with its own ruler. #2503 The two most important city-states in Ancient Greece were **Athens** and **Sparta**. #2504 They often fought each other but would join forces when threatened by foreign invaders. #2505 Their biggest enemy was **Persia**, which wanted the Greeks to become part of the Persian Empire. #2506 The wars with Persia went on for years. #2507 They finally ended when **Alexander the Great** led the Ancient Greeks to defeat Persia in **330 BC**. #2508

Athens was the richest city-state because it controlled an area called Attica, which had a lot of silver, lead and marble. #2509 Athens also had the biggest navy in Ancient Greece. #2510 In **621 BC** Athens was ruled by **Draco**. #2511 His laws were very harsh, which is where the word 'draconian' (meaning harsh or severe) comes from. #2512 Under Draco's rule, stealing bread or fruit was punishable by death. #2513 Athens's most famous building was a temple called the **Parthenon**. #2514 It was built on a rocky hill called the **Acropolis**, a Greek word meaning 'upper city'. #2515 Inside the Parthenon were lots of treasures including a statue of the city's protector, the goddess **Athena**. #2516 It was made of gold and ivory, and was 12 m high. #2517 The Ancient Greeks invented democracy – the word means 'rule by the people'. #2518 Only men were allowed to vote. #2519 The first two letters of the Ancient Greek alphabet – **alpha** and **beta** – have given us the word 'alphabet'. #2520 Ancient Greeks also invented the theatre. #2521 Most cities had an open-air theatre that could hold hundreds or thousands of spectators. #2522 Only men and boys were allowed to be actors. #2523 The highest mountain in Greece is **Mount Olympus**. #2524 It has over 50 peaks, with the highest reaching 2,917 m. #2525 The Ancient Greeks believed their 12 most important gods and goddesses lived at the top of Mount Olympus. #2526

# facts

The most powerful god was **Zeus** who was the god of the sky and ruler of all other gods. #2527 The first **Olympic games** were held in the city of Olympia in **776 BC**. #2528 The Olympic games were held every four years at Olympia. #2529 Events at the Olympic games included wrestling, boxing, long jump, javelin, discus and chariot racing. #2530 Those taking part in the wrestling event had to be the toughest, as there were hardly any rules and they had to compete naked. #2531 Thousands of people from all over the Greek world came to watch the games and the main stadium held about 45,000 people. #2532 Married women were prohibited from watching the games under penalty of death. #2533 There were no gold, silver or bronze awards in the Greek Olympics. Winners were awarded palm branches and olive wreaths. #2534

Ancient Greece was home to many famous writers and thinkers, such as **Socrates**, **Plato** and **Aristotle**. #2535 Students came to Athens to study at two famous schools – Plato's Academy and Aristotle's Lyceum. #2536 These philosophers' ideas challenged existing beliefs of the time. #2537 Socrates was accused by the Ancient Greek authorities of corrupting the young so was sentenced to death. #2538 He was killed by drinking poison made from the hemlock plant. #2539 Some Ancient Greeks wouldn't eat beans as they thought they contained the souls of the dead. #2540 Ancient Greek men wore a tunic called a chiton. #2541 Poor male slaves had to make do with a loincloth (a small strip of cloth wrapped around the waist). #2542 Slaves were very important to Ancient Greek daily life. #2543 Slaves did all kinds of jobs, from cleaning and teaching to working in mines and quarries. #2544 The Ancient Greeks grew olives, grapes, figs and wheat to eat. #2545 Ancient Greek city-states had law courts with trial by jury. #2546 Juries were made up of up to 500 people, but there were no lawyers. #2547 According to a famous legend, in **1180 BC** the Ancient Greeks conquered the city of **Troy**. #2548 They left a giant wooden horse (with their soldiers hidden inside) outside Troy's city walls and, thinking it a gift, the people of Troy wheeled the horse inside, only for the soldiers to creep out and take over the city. #2549

# 6
## FACTS
## ABOUT KANGAROOS

The red kangaroo is the
# LARGEST SPECIES
of kangaroo. It can weigh more than
# 100 KG
– as much as a baby elephant. #2550

Kangaroos can't hop
## <<< BACKWARDS
because their large, muscular tails are in the way. #2551

A red kangaroo can leap a distance of 9 m in a **single hop.** #2552

Male kangaroos fight each other in 'boxing matches'. They stand on their hind legs and try to push each other over.

#2559

Kangaroos can jump to a height of more than 2 m. #2554

Although they have been known to ATTACK PEOPLE, there is only one recorded human death caused by a kangaroo.

#2555

# 10 AMAZING BODY NUMBERS

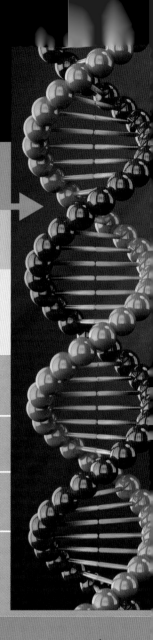

If all the **DNA** in your body was unravelled and stretched out, it could reach to the **Sun and back**. #2556

Frenchwoman Jeanne Calment lived to be **122 years old**, longer than anyone else on record. #2557

A Russian woman, Mrs Vassilyev, is thought to have had **69 children** – 32 twins, 21 triplets and 16 quadruplets. #2558

Every human started off as **one cell**, for about the first half hour that they existed. #2559

A sneeze zooms out of your nose and mouth at around **145 km/h**. #2560

Robert Wadlow, the **tallest person ever**, measured **2.7 m** and had **size 37 feet**. #2561

Lucia Zarate, the **smallest person ever**, was **50cm** tall and weighed 2 kg. #2562

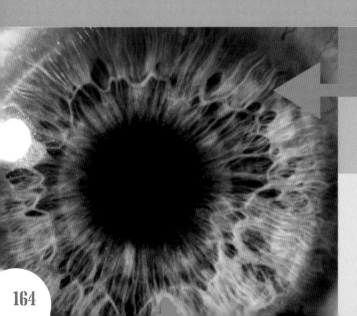

The **human eye** can see stars that are **millions of miles away**. #2563

Park Ranger **Roy Sullivan** survived being struck by lightning **seven times**. #2564

Charles Osborne of Iowa **hiccupped** non-stop for 68 years. #2565

Because you blink around

**15 TIMES A MINUTE...**

... you actually spend two years of your waking life with your **EYES SHUT.** #2566

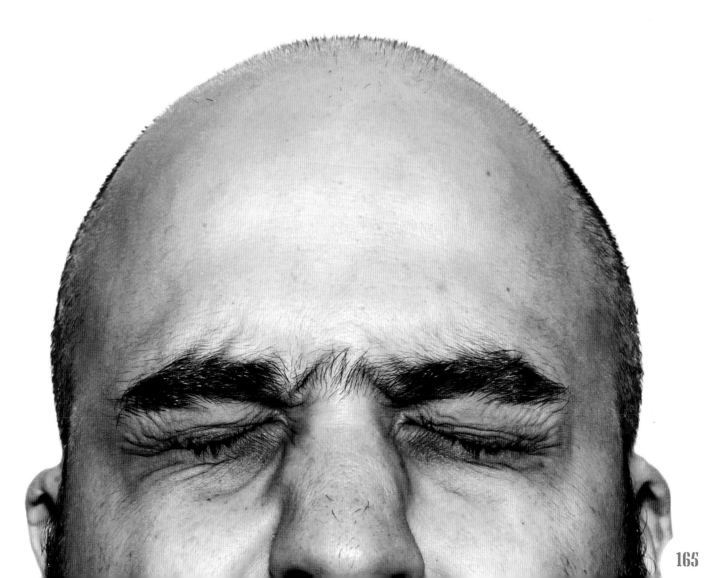

Amphibians were the first animals to live on land. #2567 A group of **toads** is called a knot. #2568 Toads have shorter legs than frogs, so they walk instead of hopping. #2569 Toads do not have teeth, but most frogs do. #2570 Most toads burrow beneath the ground in the daytime and come out at night to feed on insects. #2571 A toad's bumpy skin helps it blend into the environment around it. #2572 Many countries have built toad tunnels under roads, so that toads can cross safely. #2573 The wart-like glands behind a toad's ears are dangerous – they squirt poison at predators. #2574 There are about 550 species of **salamander**. #2575 Most salamanders have gills and lungs. #2576 One type of salamander has gills but no lungs, so that when it is on land, it breathes through its skin. #2577 Male salamanders become a brighter colour during the mating season, in order to attract females. #2578 Each individual **spotted salamander** has its own unique pattern of spots. #2579 The **Chinese giant salamander** is the largest salamander in the world. #2580 It can weigh up to 65 kg – the same weight as an average woman. #2581 It can grow up to 1.8 m long – the height of a tall man. #2582 The **olm** is a blind and transparent salamander. #2583 It can survive up to 10 years without food. #2584 The **axolotl** is a unique salamander which keeps its juvenile appearance. #2585 Roasted axolotl is considered a delicacy in Mexico. #2586 It is only found in Lake Xochimilco and surrounding canals in Mexico City. #2587 An axolotl can regrow its limbs and tail, but it can also regenerate damaged parts of its brain and other organs. #2588 Larger axolotls sometimes eat smaller ones. #2589 Similar-sized axolotls eat each other's limbs. #2590 **Newts** spend their lives on land, returning to the water to breed. #2591 Newts can grow new limbs, eyes, hearts and jaws. #2592 The **great crested newt** is the UK's largest newt species. #2593 The great crested newt is a protected species in the UK, and you need a licence to handle one. #2594 During mating season, the male great crested newt develops a large wavy crest on his back. #2595 Newts can mate without touching each other. #2596 When newts come out of water after breeding, they can travel up to 1 km on land, looking for food, such as worms and beetles. #2597 Most newts have poisonous skin to protect them from predators. #2598 The **Japanese fire belly newt** can regenerate its eye lens up to 18 times during its lifetime. #2599 **Palmate newts** got their name because their feet look like human hands. #2600 The **rough-skinned newt** produces enough poison to kill a human, but it would only be harmful if the newt was eaten. #2601 A **caecilian** is often confused with a worm, but it's actually a kind of amphibian. #2602 Its skin is made up of ring-shaped segments that encircle its entire body. #2603 Unlike a worm, it has a skull and a backbone. #2604 Some species of caecilian have no lungs and breathe through their skin. #2605 They have a pair of tentacles on their face that can sniff out food. #2606 Like other amphibians, the caecilian releases toxins to deter predators. #2607 A mother feeds her babies by allowing them to scrape skin off her body and eat it. #2608 The **Sagalla caecilian** feels it way around using the tentacles on the side of its head. #2609 Most amphibians lay eggs in clusters called spawn. #2610 Toads lay spawn in strings up to 1 m long. #2611 One frogspawn contains about 2,000 eggs. #2612 A female newt lays one egg at a time on a piece of pond plant. #2613 After laying the egg, she closes the leaf around it to protect the egg. #2614 Frogs, toads and salamanders start life as **tadpoles**. #2615 Tadpoles live in water and breathe using gills. #2616 A tadpole begins as a dot-shaped embryo inside an egg. #2617 As it grows, the tadpole eats its way through the egg jelly. #2618 After 21 days, the tadpole leaves the jelly, complete with gills and a long tail. #2619 In medieval times, tadpoles were called porwiggles or pollywogs. #2620 As they grow, tadpoles absorb their tails into their body. #2621 Tadpoles can survive for some

# AMPHIBIAN facts

time out of water, so long as they remain moist. #2622 As they grow, tadpoles develop lungs and eventually leave the water. #2623 Amphibians have many enemies, but their biggest threat is often pollution because they absorb harmful toxins through their skin. #2624

## 44 FASCINATING FROG FACTS

Frogs don't drink water! #2625 They absorb it through their skin. #2626 Every frog call is unique to its species. Some sound like a croak, others like a whistle or the chirp of a bird. #2627 A group of frogs is called an army. #2628 When a frog hibernates, its bones grow a new layer. #2629 You can tell how old a frog is by counting the layers in its bones. #2630 Some frogs can jump 20 times their body length! #2631 When a frog swallows its prey, it blinks; this pushes its eyeball down on top of its mouth to help push the food down. #2632 A tornado can suck water high into the air. If that water contains frogs, it may rain frogs some time later! #2633 The frog catches its prey with its long tongue. When it's not needed, the tongue stays rolled up inside the frog's mouth. #2634 **Tree frogs** keep moist by sitting in pools of water on leaves. #2635 Rather than webbed feet, like other frogs, tree frogs have sticky pads on their feet for climbing. #2636 The **White's tree frog** has a tendency to get fat, so is also known as the dumpy frog. #2637 The **waxy monkey leaf frog** is covered in a sticky substance to stop its body from drying out in the high trees of the Amazon. #2638 Its skin contains a powerful drug, used by Amazonian tribes in rituals, that makes people see things that are not there. #2639 Some Australian frogs create their own insect repellent, which smells like rotten meat. #2640 The **golden poison dart frog** is one of the most toxic animals on Earth. #2641 It contains enough poison to kill 10 adults. #2642 But the fire-bellied snake can eat the golden poison dart frog – it is immune to its poison. #2643 The **blue-jeans poison dart frog** has a red body with blue legs. It looks like it's wearing blue jeans, hence its name. #2644 Poisonous frogs get much of their poison from the alkaline-rich ants and other bugs they eat. #2645 The world's largest frog is the **goliath frog**, which lives in Western Africa. #2646 It can grow up to 33 cm and weigh as much as a small baby! #2647 The goliath frog can jump more than 3 m. #2648 The smallest frog in the Northern Hemisphere is the ***Eleutherodactylus iberia***, which is less than 10 mm long. #2649 It is only found in Cuba. #2650 The smallest frog in the Southern Hemisphere is the ***Paedophryne amauensis*** from Papua New Guinea, which is less than 8 mm long. #2651 The **wood frog** freezes solid during the winter, but survives and thaws out again in spring. #2652 **Horned frogs** have a projecting flap, or horn, of skin above each eye. #2653 **Banded bullfrogs** are the same colour as the bark of the tree they cling to, making them almost impossible to see. #2654 To confuse predators, some frogs have stripes on their backs that appear to split the frog in two when seen from above. #2655 The **glass frog** has transparent skin. #2656 You can see its heart beating and its stomach digesting food. #2657 Male frogs are often more colourful than females – they use their appearance to attract mates. #2658 The **large four-eyed frog** has a pair of eyespot marks on its backside that are actually poison glands. #2659 Some frogs feed their tadpoles unfertilized eggs, if there is no other food available. #2660 The **waxy monkey leaf frog** lays its eggs in a jelly-like substance rolled up in a leaf. #2661 When the tadpoles emerge, they drop off the leaf into the water below. #2862 The male **Darwin's frog** carries fertilized eggs in his vocal pouch. #2663 The tadpoles develop in the pouch and, when they are tiny froglets, hop out and swim away. #2664 If you show pet frogs dripping water, it might help them reproduce as they will think it's the rainy season, which is when frogs reproduce in the wild. #2665 The extinct **gastric brooding frog** looked after its young in its stomach. #2666 When they were ready, the young froglets hopped out of their mother's mouth. #2667 Some frogs' eggs hatch into frogs with tails, bypassing the tadpole stage. #2668

# 10 SPARKLING ICE FACTS

Antarctica holds **70 per cent of Earth's freshwater**, locked up in ice. #2669

To be called an **iceberg**, the height of the ice must be at least 4 metres above sea level. #2670

The **tallest iceberg** ever spotted was a 167-metre whopper floating off Greenland. #2671

The Sahara Desert was covered by **glaciers** 450 million years ago. #2672

In 1991, the **5,000-year-old** preserved body of a huntsman was found in a glacier in the Alps. #2673

In 1848, ice blocked **Niagara Falls** for nearly two days, so people explored the dry river bed. #2674

The largest iceberg ever seen was the size of **Jamaica**! #2675

It broke away from Antarctica. #2676

In 1829, a chunk of ice weighing 2 kilograms **inexplicably fell** on the town of Córdoba in Spain. #2677

The South Pole is covered by a sheet of ice **2,700 metres** thick. #2678

In 1859, a shower of fish fell on Glamorgan in Wales when a strong updraught of wind sucked them out of the sea and dropped them inland. #2679

169

# 10 TONGUE-TWISTING FACTS ON LANGUAGES

The most commonly spoken language in the world is **Mandarin Chinese**, spoken by **845 million people.** #2680

The United Nations recognizes **six official world languages:** Mandarin Chinese, Spanish, English, Arabic, Russian and French. #2681

Around the world, people speak about **6,500 different languages**. #2682

Approximately 83 of these are spoken by **80 per cent of the world's population.** #2683

Approximately 473 of the world's languages are **almost extinct** and spoken only by a few people. #2684

Approximately one language dies out in the world **every two weeks,** when its last speaker dies. #2685

The **Sumerian language** of the Middle East is one of the earliest on record, dating back to around **2900 BC**. #2686

Most **European languages** are closely related to each other, such as German and Dutch. #2687

However, **Euskara,** the language of the Basque people in northern Spain, is **unrelated to any other known language** in the world. #2688

In 1825, blind Frenchman **Louis Braille** developed a language that could be read by blind people by feeling a series of bumps on paper. #2689

# 3 BOREDOM-BUSTING BOOK FACTS

The world's **longest novel** is Marcel Proust's *A la recherche du temps perdu* (In Search of Lost Time), which has more than **1.5 million words** and was originally published in seven volumes. #2690

The **oldest printed book** is the *Diamond Sutra*, a Buddhist religious text printed in China in AD 868. #2691

In 1969, the French writer Georges Perec wrote *La disparition* (The Void) **without using the letter 'e'.** He followed that up in 1972 with *Les revenentes* (The Ghosts) in which **'e' is the only vowel used.** #2692

# 14 facts about CORAL REEFS

## and the fish that live in them

Coral looks like a plant, but is actually a simple kind of animal.
#2693

**Reefs build up over time from the hard skeletons of dead coral.**
#2694

Reefs grow a few centimetres each year. Some of the largest began growing **50 million years ago**.
#2695

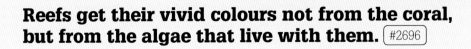

**Reefs get their vivid colours not from the coral, but from the algae that live with them.** #2696

**Coral likes water that is 26–27°C.** If the water is warmer than this, the coral dies. Global warming is a danger to many reefs.
#2697

# Coral Reef Creatures

When threatened, a puffer fish will fill itself with water, and balloon up to several times its normal size.
#2698

**When a starfish loses one of its arms, it grows a new one.** #2699

After mating, the male seahorse carries the eggs in a special pouch until they are ready to hatch. #2700

**Clownfish** live alongside anemones in coral reefs. The anemone provides the fish with food, while the fish protects the anemone from predators.
#2701

**Coral is very sensitive to pollution. Dirty water kills it.**
#2702

# The Great Barrier Reef

**It contains 2,900 individual reefs.** #2703

It contains more than 900 islands. #2704

**Over 1,500 different species of fish live there.** #2705

Around 215 species of birds visit the reef to nest or roost on the islands. #2706

# 88 facts on PEOPLE
## WHO CHANGED THE WORLD

➔**Leonardo da Vinci** was born in **1452**. #2707 His journals were filled with over 13,000 pages of his inventions and ideas. #2708 He wrote backwards to keep his ideas secret. #2709

Leonardo da Vinci

➔**Galileo Galilei** was born in **1564** in Pisa, Italy. #2710 At first he wanted to become a doctor, so started to study medicine in **1581**, but then he left to be a teacher. #2711 In **1609** he built his own telescope. #2712 He discovered four large moons around Jupiter. #2713 He also discovered the phases of the planet Venus. #2714 He learned that the Moon was not smooth, but was covered with craters. #2715 In **1632** he wrote a book on his belief that Earth and the other planets orbited the Sun. #2716 He questioned the existing ideas of how things worked, which was not popular at the time. #2717 The Catholic Church thought he was against them so put him in prison. #2718

Galileo Galilei

➔During his lifetime, **Sir Isaac Newton** developed the theory of gravity, discovered the laws of motion and made a breakthrough in optics (telescopes). #2719 He was born in Woolsthorpe, England, in **1643**. #2720 In **1661** he went to Cambridge University. #2721 During the plague, the university was shut down and Isaac was sent home. #2722 He used this time to invent a new type of maths called calculus. #2723 He became a professor of mathematics and a Fellow of the Royal Society. #2724 He was knighted by **Queen Anne** in **1705**. #2725 He had two nervous breakdowns, which might have been caused by chemical poisoning from his experiments. #2726

Sir Isaac Newton

➔**Thomas Jefferson** was born in **1743** in the British colony of Virginia to wealthy landowners. #2727 He had nine siblings. #2728 He became the third president of the United States in **1801**. #2729

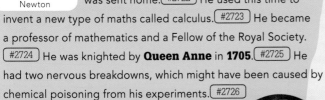

Thomas Jefferson

Before he became president, he was a lawyer and a farmer. #2730 Jefferson drafted the *Declaration of Independence*, helped by **John Adams** and **Benjamin Franklin** in **1776**. #2731 The Declaration stated that the 13 American colonies considered themselves free from British rule and were willing to fight for that freedom. #2732 The colonies went on to fight for their freedom from Britain, and the United States was born. #2733 Jefferson liked to write and wrote about 19,000 letters during his lifetime. #2734 He also liked birds and kept mockingbirds as pets. #2735

➔**Napoleon Bonaparte** was born in **1769** in Corsica, an island belonging to France. #2736 When the French Revolution happened, Napoleon joined a radical group of the French revolutionaries called the Jacobins. #2737 In **1796** Napoleon was given command of the French army. In **1804** he was crowned Emperor of the French. #2738 Napoleon wasn't just a soldier, he also wrote a romance novel called *Clisson and Eugenie*. #2739

Napoleon Bonaparte

➔**Charles Darwin** was an English naturalist who came up with the theory that animals and humans shared a common ancestry. #2740 He was born in **1809** on the same day as **Abraham Lincoln**. #2741 At 22 years of age he sailed around the world. #2742 His ship was called the *Beagle*. #2743 He travelled for five years to places such as the Brazilian jungles, Australia and the Galapagos Islands. #2744 He married his cousin and they had 10 children. #2745

Charles Darwin

➔**Marie Curie** was born in **1867** in Poland. #2746 In **1891** she went to Sorbonne University, where she got a degree in physics. #2747 Marie and her husband discovered two new elements for the periodic table. #2748 In **1903** they won the Nobel Prize in Physics. #2749 In **1911** Marie won the Nobel Prize in Chemistry, making her the first person to win two. #2750 During WWI,

Marie Curie

she put together a fleet of vehicles to carry X-ray machines around the war zones, to help wounded soldiers. #2751

➜**Albert Einstein** was born in Germany in **1879**. #2752 He became a theoretical physicist, using maths to explain scientific theory. #2753 Einstein developed the general theory of relativity. #2754 This remains one of the key theories of modern physics. #2755 He recieved the Nobel Prize in Physics in **1921**. #2756

Albert Einstein

➜**Mother Teresa** was born in Macedonia in **1910**. #2757 She became a nun and missionary, and spent her entire life helping the poor and needy. #2758 She formed the Missionaries of Charity with just 13 members. #2759 It now has over 4,000 nuns who care for people all over the world. #2760 Mother Teresa won the Nobel Peace Prize in **1979**. #2761 She once travelled through a war zone to rescue children. #2762

Mother Teresa

➜**Martin Luther King** was a civil rights activist in the **1950s** and **1960s**. #2763 He led non-violent protests to fight for the rights of all people, including African Americans. #2764 He was so clever that he skipped two years in secondary school. #2765 He started his college education at the age of 15, got two degrees and became a doctor of theology. #2766 In **1963** Martin Luther King helped to organize a famous civil rights march in Washington, D.C. #2767 Over 250,000 people attended the march. #2768 In **1964**, he was awarded the Nobel Peace Prize. #2769 In **1968** he was assassinated. #2770 There are over 730 streets in the United States named after him. #2771

Martin Luther King

➜**Nelson Mandela**'s real name was Rolihlahla Mandela. #2772 His school teacher gave him the name Nelson, as it was easier to say. #2773 Mandela was sent to prison for 27 years by the South African government, who saw him as a terrorist. #2774 He was released from prison in **1990**. #2775 Thanks to all his hard work in the fight against apartheid, all races were allowed to vote in the **1994** election, which he won. #2776 He was awarded the Nobel Peace Prize in **1993**. #2777 One of his favourite foods was tripe. #2778

Nelson Mandela

➜**Neil Armstrong** was born in **1930** in Ohio. #2779 At the age of 15, he got his pilot's licence. #2780 Neil joined the Navy and became a fighter pilot. #2781 He fought in the Korean War where he flew fighters from aircraft carriers. #2782 Armstrong applied to become an astronaut, and in **1962** he was selected for the NASA Astronaut Corps. #2783 Armstrong's first trip into space was on board the *Gemini 8*. #2784 In **1968** Armstrong was offered the command of the *Apollo 11* and in **1969** was the first man to walk on the Moon. #2785

Neil Armstrong

➜**Mikhail Gorbachev** was born in Stavropol, Russia in **1931**. #2786 His parents both worked in agriculture. #2787 Gorbachev also worked in agriculture while he was at school. #2788 In **1980** he was selected to be a member of the Politburo, the most powerful group in the Communist Party. #2789 He was the youngest member of the Politburo, and by **1985** he had become leader of the Soviet Union. #2790 He helped bring an end to the Cold War, and in **1990** won a Nobel Peace Prize. #2791

Mikhail Gorbachev

➜**Tim Berners-Lee** was born in London in **1955**. #2792 Both his parents worked on one of the first computers – the Feranti Mark I. #2793 In **1989** he invented the World Wide Web. #2794 He once admitted that the slashes in web addresses aren't really necessary. #2795

Tim Berners-Lee

# 13 FACTS ON WINSTON CHURCHILL

➜**Winston Churchill** was born in **1874** at Blenheim Palace in England. #2796 His parents were wealthy aristocrats. #2797 His father **Lord Randolph Churchill** was a politician who held many high offices in the British government. #2798 Churchill went to the Royal Military College, then joined the British cavalry. #2799 He travelled to many places while with the military. #2800 He also worked as a journalist, writing reports about battles. #2801 While in South Africa during the Second Boer War, Churchill was captured and became a prisoner of war. #2802 He escaped from prison and travelled nearly 500 km to be rescued. #2803 In **1900** Churchill was elected to Parliament. #2804 He held many roles up to the outbreak of World War II, when he became First Lord of the Admiralty in command of the Royal Navy. #2805 He didn't become prime minister until **1940**, after World War II had started. #2806 He was famous for popularizing the 'V for Victory' sign. #2807 While leading the country, he suffered a heart attack and pneumonia but kept going to help Great Britain defeat Germany. #2808

Winston Churchill

# 50 facts about WONDERS

The **Salar de Uyuni** in Bolivia is the world's largest salt flat. [#2809] It covers an area of around 10,500 km². [#2810] Once a lake, the water evaporated and left a thick salt crust. [#2811] The flat, white landscape causes optical illusions and reflects colours. [#2812] Locals have built hotels made entirely of salt for the tourists. [#2813]

The **Ngorongoro Crater** in Africa was created when a huge volcano exploded 2–3 million years ago. [#2814] The 300 km² area is home to around 25,000 animals including lions, rhinos and leopards. [#2815]

The highest uninterrupted waterfall in the world is **Angel Falls** in Venezuela. [#2820] The waterfall has a height of 979 m. [#2821] That's nearly 20 times taller than Niagara Falls. [#2822] It is named after Jimmie Angel, an aviator from the United States. [#2823] He was the first person to fly over the falls, in 1930. [#2824]

Uluru, or **Ayers Rock**, in Australia, is 348 m high and over 9 km in circumference. [#2816] The rock is a sacred place for the Aboriginal people who have lived there for thousands of years. [#2817] It's around 600 million years old and would have originally sat at the bottom of the sea. [#2818] Its orange colour is made by the oxidation of the iron in the rock. [#2819]

The **Grand Canyon** is 433 km in length. [#2825] At its widest point it stretches 29 km across. [#2826] It is around 1,800 m deep. [#2827] The Colorado River runs through the canyon. [#2828] The rock found at the bottom of the canyon is around 2 billion years old. [#2829] It became a National Park in 1919. [#2830] Almost 5 million people visit every year. [#2831]

# OF THE WORLD

The aurora borealis, or **northern lights**, is an amazing natural light display that can be seen from areas near the North Pole. #2832 The lights are caused by charged particles that come from the Sun and hit air molecules in the upper atmosphere. #2833 We are usually protected from these particles by Earth's magnetic field, but there are weak spots near the polar regions. #2834 In these areas, the charged particles react with particles in the air and become visible. #2835

One of the world's largest bays is the **Guanabara Bay** in Brazil. #2836 It measures 28 km from east to west. #2837 It is 30 km from north to south. #2838 It has 80 km of beaches. #2839 Within the harbour are around 130 islands. #2840 The bay is surrounded by tall granite mountains. #2841 On top of Corcovado is a statue of Jesus Christ. #2842 The statue is almost 40 m tall. #2843

The **Great Barrier Reef** is the largest coral reef system in the world. #2844 It is 2,300 km long. #2845 It covers an area larger than Italy. #2846 Astronauts can see it from space. #2847 2 million people visit every year. #2848

The **Galapágos Islands** in the Pacific Ocean span across the equator line. #2849 They are an offshore territory of Ecuador and are over 900 km off its coast. #2850 There are 18 main islands, 3 smaller ones and 107 islets or rocks. #2851 The largest island is Isabela. #2852 The oldest island is more than 4 million years old. #2853 The younger islands are still being formed. #2854 Over 25,000 people live there. #2855 There are a huge number of endemic species on the island (that only live there), including the marine iguana, flightless cormorant, blue-footed booby and the Galapágos tortoises the island is named after. #2856 These giant tortoises have slightly different features, depending on which island they live on. #2857 **Charles Darwin** visited in **1835** and his findings there helped him come up with his theory of evolution. #2858

# 8 EEL FACTS

The electric eel isn't a real eel at all. It is a kind of fish called a knifefish. #2859

There are more than **400** different species of eel. #2860

A moray eel ties its body into a knot to anchor itself to one place while it eats. #2861

**Moray eels** can grow up to 3 m long. #2862

A moray eel must open its mouth in order to breathe – this forces water over its gills. #2863

The **European eel** migrates **5,000 km** to the Sargasso Sea to spawn.
#2864

Europe

Sargasso Sea

Eel larvae float back to Europe from the Sargasso Sea on ocean currents. #2865

**Eels can travel distances of up to 100 m over wet land,** by slithering through grass, and digging through wet sand.
#2866

# 5 SUPER-SMART ROCKET SCIENCE FACTS

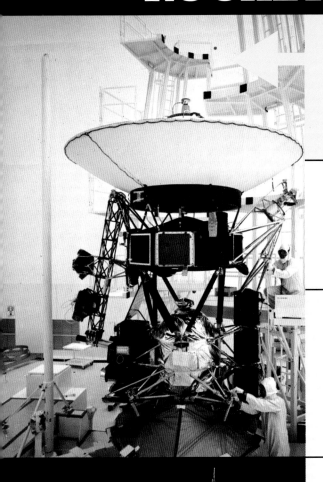

Since 1977, the unmanned spaceships **VOYAGER 1 AND 2** have been heading into outer space carrying a message for any aliens they meet. #2867

If you could convert the heat energy from a space shuttle's **ROCKET BOOSTERS** to electric power, two minutes could supply all the power needed by 87,000 homes for a day. #2868

The spacecraft **ROSETTA** landed on a comet in 2014. It weighs 100 kilograms on Earth, but low gravity on the comet will reduce its weight to a **SHEET OF PAPER**. #2869

The USSR put an unmanned lander on **VENUS** in 1970. The USA has still not landed a craft on the planet. #2870

There are **170,000 KILOGRAMS** of human junk on the Moon, including abandoned and crashed spacecraft and two golf balls left by an astronaut. #2871

Americans make up **5%** of the world's population but use **25%** of the world's energy. #2872

Beam bridges, suspension bridges, cantilever bridges and cable-stayed bridges are common types of bridge. #2873 Bridges were used in ancient times but originally spanned short distances. #2874 The Romans developed new ways of building longer and stronger bridges. #2875 The oldest bridge in Rome is the **Pons Fabricius** in Italy. #2876 It was built around **62 BC**. #2877 Built around **AD 600**, the **Zhaozhou Bridge** is the oldest bridge in China. #2878 It is also the world's oldest stone-arched bridge. #2879 The Incas in South America made use of rope bridges in the Andes Mountains. #2880 While they were strong and reliable, repairing the bridges was a dangerous job that often ended in death. #2881 During the Industrial Revolution of the 19th century, wrought iron was introduced into the design of large bridges. #2882 Wrought iron was later replaced by steel. #2883 The first welded road bridge was designed by Polish engineer **Stefan Bryla** in **1927**. #2884 The **Rialto Bridge** is the oldest bridge across the Grand Canal in Venice, Italy. #2885 Until **1854**, the Rialto Bridge was the only place where you could cross the canal on foot. #2886 The bridge was built to provide access to the main financial and commercial centre of Venice. #2887 The history of the Rialto Bridge is full of collapses. #2888 In **1444** it collapsed under the weight of a crowd watching a boat parade. #2889 It collapsed again in **1524** for the final time. #2890 In **1524** many famous artists and architects, including Michelangelo, submitted designs for a new bridge. #2891 In **1588**, the commission was awarded to Swiss engineer **Antonio da Ponte** who built the bridge in marble. #2892 It took three years to construct the new bridge and was completed in **1591**. #2893 The Rialto Bridge also has shops on it. #2894

The **Brooklyn Bridge** in New York, USA, joins Manhattan and Brooklyn over the East River. #2895 When completed in **1883** it was the longest suspension bridge in the world. #2896 It was also the first steel-wire suspension bridge. #2897 It contains around 21,000 wires that, if combined, would have a total length of around 22,000 km. #2898 It cost nearly £10 million to build. #2899 On its first day of opening to the public, 1,800 vehicles and 150,300 people crossed it. #2900 In **1883** a rumour that the bridge was collapsing spread through the crowds who were on it, causing a stampede. #2901 At least 12 people were killed in the panic. #2902 Conman **William McCloundy** was sentenced to two and a half years in prison for selling the Brooklyn Bridge to a tourist in **1901**. #2903 On average, 145,000 vehicles cross it each day. #2904 It has six lanes of traffic. #2905 **Tower Bridge** is a bascule bridge across the River Thames. #2906 Over 50 designs were originally submitted for consideration. #2907 In **1884 Horace Jones** and **John Wolfe Barry** came up with the chosen design. #2908 The total length of Tower Bridge is 244 m. #2909 It took eight years, five major contractors and the labour of 432 construction workers to complete it in **1894**. #2910 The bascules (moving sections) of Tower Bridge were initially powered by energy created from steam. #2911 Since **1976** oil and electricity have been used to produce the energy. #2912 In **1952** the bridge began to open while a bus was still on it. #2913 The bus had to leap across the gap in the middle. #2914 The bridge was painted red, white and blue in **1977** as part of the **Queen's** Silver Jubilee celebrations. #2915 In **1994** Tower Bridge became available for party hire. #2916 The **Golden Gate Bridge** in San Francisco, USA, is a suspension bridge. #2917

# 81 facts on brilliant BRIDGES

It was built in **1937**. #2918 It has a total length of 1,280 m and features 129,000 km of wire in its two main cables. #2919 It took just over four years to build. #2920 Eleven men died during its construction. #2921 There are approximately 600,000 rivets in each tower of the bridge. #2922 It is named after the Golden Gate Strait, which is the entrance to the San Francisco Bay from the Pacific Ocean. #2923 Painting the Golden Gate Bridge is an ongoing task. #2924 Hong Kong's **Tsing Ma Bridge** is the world's largest suspension bridge to feature two decks and carry both rail and road traffic. #2925 It opened in **1997**. #2926 There are no walkways on the bridge. #2927 The **Confederation Bridge** in Canada is the world's longest bridge that spans ice. #2928 The 12.9 km beam bridge opened in **1997**. #2929 The bridge rests on 62 piers and takes around 12 minutes to cross. #2930 The longest suspension bridge in the world is the **Akashi Kaikyo Bridge** in Kobe, Japan. #2931 It opened in **1998** and its central span is an incredible 1,991 m. #2932 It is also known as the Pearl Bridge. #2933 The Akashi Kaikyo Bridge can expand in the heat by up to 2 m a day. #2934 The bridge has a total of 1,737 lights. #2935 Some bridges, like the **Millau Viaduct** in France, cross land not water. #2936 Completed in **2004**, the Millau Viaduct is 270 m high. #2937 It is the tallest bridge in the world. #2938 At its tallest point it is slightly taller than the Eiffel Tower. #2939 You cannot walk across the bridge. #2940 You also cannot look down, as the road edge is too far from the edge of the bridge. #2941 Of the ten longest bridges in the world, seven are in China. #2942 The world's longest bridge is the **Danyang-Kunshan Grand Bridge** in China. #2943 The rail bridge has a length of 164.8 km. #2944 It was constructed in **2010**. #2945 The world's longest sea bridge is also in China. #2946 The bridge spans 42.4 km and has an undersea tunnel. #2947 The bridge is supported by more than 5,200 pillars. #2948 The **Helix Bridge** in Singapore was inspired by the double helix structure of DNA. #2949 Completed in **2010**, it is 280 m long. #2950 The **Evergreen Point Floating Bridge**, in Washington, USA, spans water too deep for a conventional bridge design, so it floats on the water instead. #2951 It is 4,750 m long. #2952 Its 2,310 m floating section makes it the longest floating bridge in the world. #2953

# 20 FACTS ABOUT SYDNEY HARBOUR BRIDGE

The **Sydney Harbour Bridge** in Australia is the world's largest steel arch bridge. #2954 It is 1,149 m long. #2955 It was first opened in **1932**. #2956 Before it opened, 96 steam trains were positioned in various ways to test its load capacity. #2957 The bridge contains 6 million hand-driven metal bolts. #2958 The bridge can rise or fall up to 18 cm depending on the temperature, due to the steel expanding or contracting. #2959 79 per cent of the steel used to build it came from England. #2960 21 per cent came from Australia. #2961 272,000 litres of paint were needed to give the bridge its initial three coats. #2962 It took 1,400 men eight years to build. #2963 Sixteen people died during construction. #2964 The bridge is grey because that was the only paint colour available (in the quantities needed) to cover it at the time. #2965 The bridge wasn't paid for until almost 60 years after it was built. #2966 Around 160,000 vehicles cross the bridge each day. #2967 Before BridgeClimb (a company allowing people to climb the bridge) opened in **1998**, people climbed it illegally. #2968 Since BridgeClimb opened, the most frequent climber is an 83-year-old who has climbed it over 40 times. #2969 It takes around four hours to climb up and down. #2970 Around 3 million people have climbed the bridge. #2971 Around 5,000 marriage proposals have been made during climbs. #2972 During World War II, a pilot flew a US Kittyhawk plane under the bridge as a stunt. #2973

# 10 PENGUIN FACTS

Penguins in **Antarctica** are easy to film. They have no predators on land, so they are not afraid of humans. 2974

**All penguins live in the southern hemisphere.** #2975

Most penguins live in cold places, but the **Galapagos penguin** lives near the equator. #2976

As they swim, penguins leap out of the water in arcs – an action called **porpoising**. #2977

**Rather than walk, penguins slide down icy hills on their bellies.** #2978

Antarctica

Emperor penguins can stay underwater for **18 minutes**, and dive to depths of

# 535 m.

#2979

The emperor penguin breeds in the Antarctic winter. The females leave the eggs with the males, who huddle together in their thousands in **temperatures of**

# –50°C.

#2980

The males incubate the eggs by **balancing them on their feet for 64 days.**

#2981

By the time the egg hatches, the male has not eaten for **115 days.**

#2983

The emperor penguin stands 1.2 m tall, and weighs up to 45 kg. It is the largest species of penguin.

#2982

185

# 3 SHOCKING ELECTRICITY FACTS

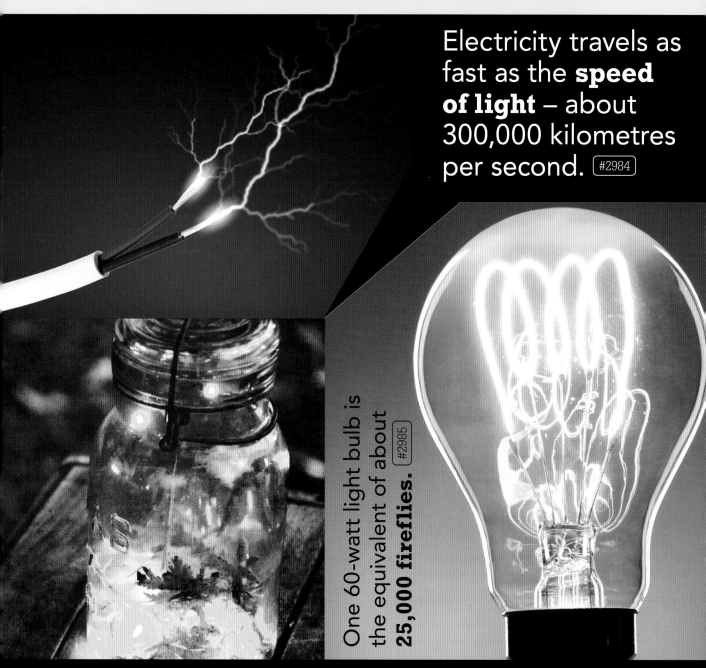

Electricity travels as fast as the **speed of light** – about 300,000 kilometres per second. #2984

One 60-watt light bulb is the equivalent of about **25,000 fireflies.** #2985

An **electric eel** can produce an electric shock strong enough to **kill an adult human.** #2986

# 5 PLANT BIOLOGY FACTS TO GROW YOUR MIND

Gregor Mendel, a scentist in the 1800s, came up with some of the first ideas on genetics (how traits are passed from one generation to the next) by looking at **PEA PODS AND THEIR FLOWERS**. #2987

The **SMALLEST FLOWERING PLANT,** *Wolffia angusta*, is so tiny that two plants in flower would fit inside this letter 'o'. #2988

The 'desert onion' Onyanga grows in the Namibia desert in Angola. It's a shrub that can live for up to **2,000 YEARS**. #2989

A mushroom in Africa, called 'Lady in the veil', can be heard cracking as it grows by a **CENTIMETRE A MINUTE**. #2990

African bugleweed contains a chemical that affects caterpillars so that they turn into **BUTTERFLIES WITH TWO HEADS**. #2991

# 10 MIND-BOGGLING MATHS FACTS

If you put a single **grain of rice** on the first square of a chessboard, then two on the next square, then four, and kept on **doubling** the rice, for the last square you would need enough rice to cover India to a depth of 1 metre. #2992

The Pirahã tribe in Brazil have words for only 'one', 'two' and 'many' so can't count **three or more objects.** #2993

Our system of 60 seconds in a minute and 60 minutes in an hour comes from the **Babylonian counting system** devised 4,000 years ago. #2994

$12 + 3 - 4 + 5 + 67 + 8 + 9 = 100$
and
$1 + 2 + 34 - 5 + 67 - 8 + 9 = 100.$
There are at least nine more sums like this. #2995

You can turn a strip of paper into a **shape with only one surface** by twisting it once and gluing the ends together. #2996

There is an infinite number of infinities. 1, 2, 3...; –1, –2, –3...; 0.1, 0.11, 0.111...; 0.1, 0.12, 0.13...; 0.1, 0.01, 0.001... #2997

A **googol** is $10^{100}$, which is 1 followed by 100 zeroes. This is **larger than any number that needs to be counted.** #2998

A **googolplex** is $10^{googol}$. It would take longer than the Universe has existed (around 13 billion years) to write this number out in full. #2999

The pattern of seeds in a sunflower head, the shape of a nautilus seashell and the arrangement of leaves around a plant all follow the same spiral pattern, called the **golden spiral.** #3000

The mathematician Descartes invented the system we use for drawing graphs, using x and y axes, after watching a **fly crawl over the ceiling** as he lay in bed. #3001

More than

# 99.9%

of all species of plants and animals that have ever existed are now **EXTINCT**.

#3002

SEED FERN

CAPE LION

TASMANIAN WOLF

DODO

# ARCHITECTURE

The **Colosseum** (an amphitheatre) in Rome, Italy, was built around **AD 72**. #3003 It was built by **Emperor Vespasian** for **Titus**, his successor. #3004 It had about 80 entrances to accommodate the 50,000 spectators it could hold. #3005 It has been the inspiration for many modern-day stadiums. #3006 British architect **Christopher Wren** took 10 years to finalize his design for **St Paul's Cathedral** in London, England. #3007 Its famous dome measures around 111 m high. #3008 The original church on the site was founded in **AD 604**. #3009 Work on the present church began in the 17th century after the Great Fire of London. #3010 Construction took 40 years. #3011 The **Leaning Tower of Pisa**, in Italy, is famous for its tilt. #3012 The tower began to lean soon after construction – the soft ground on one side was unable to support it. #3013 Building work began on the tower in **1173** and went on for 199 years. #3014 Japan is full of temples and one of its most famous is **The Temple of the Golden Pavilion** in Kyoto. #3015 It was built in **1397** as a home for the shogun (Japan's military leader) **Ashikaga Yoshimitsu** and became a temple after his death. #3016 The upper two levels are covered in real gold, inside and out. #3017 In **1955** the temple had to be rebuilt after it burned down. #3018 **St Basil's Cathedral** in Moscow, Russia, was built in **1555**. #3019 It was commissioned by **Tsar Ivan the Terrible**. #3020 The colour and detail added to its domes were added 200 years after its construction. #3021 The **Blue Mosque** in Istanbul, Turkey, was built by **Sultan Ahmed I** from **1609** to **1616**. #3022 He wanted to build an Islamic place of worship that could compete with **Hagia Sophia**, which stands next to it. #3023 It gets its name from the 20,000 blue tiles that line the mosque's high ceiling. #3024 The **Taj Mahal** in Agra, India, was built by **Emperor Sha Jahan**. #3025 Often mistaken for a palace, it was actually built as a tomb for the emperor's wife. #3026 Construction began in **1632** and was completed in **1648**. #3027 It took around 3,000 workers to create the **Palace of Versailles** in France. #3028 It was built in the late 17th century for **King Louis XIV** #3029 The palace cost over £1.3 billion in today's money. #3030 It contains over 700 rooms, 60 staircases and more than 1,200 fireplaces. #3031 The Hall of Mirrors is the most spectacular room in the palace. #3032 It was originally lit with 3,000 candles. #3033 The Treaty of Versailles, officially ending World War I, was signed in this room in **1919**. #3034 Irish architect **James Hoban**

## 14 FACTS ON ARCHITECTURE THROUGH THE AGES

The first known small buildings were built around **7,000 BC** in western Asia. #3035 Larger buildings started to appear around **3,000 BC**. #3036 These were ziggurats (temples) in Asia and the pyramids in Egypt. #3037 **Alexander the Great** spread Greek architecture all over his empire. #3038 Theatres, gymnasia and temples were built wherever he fought. #3039 The Romans brought new ideas to building works under the influence of their empire. #3040 They built with bricks and concrete. #3041 They also incorporated the arch, the barrel vault and the dome in their designs. #3042 The conversion of the Roman Empire to Christianity around **AD 400** also inspired the Romans to build a lot of churches. #3043 Most large buildings being built around the world at this time were churches or temples, built by rulers to celebrate their gods. #3044 From **AD 1100** to **AD 1450** Gothic architecture gave rise to cathedrals like Notre Dame with pointed arches and flying buttresses. #3045 Much of the architecture during the Renaissance was influenced by Ancient Rome and Greece with pillars, arches and grand domes. #3046 Around **1840** the Art Noveau style spread to architecture and furniture and featured asymmetrical shapes, arches and plant-like designs. #3047 In the **1920s** the era of Art Deco celebrated and embraced new technologies and materials, and created a modern and decorative style. #3048

designed the **White House**, in Washington DC, USA. #3049 Construction began in **1792** and the mansion has been home to every US leader since the country's second president **John Adams**. #3050 The mansion contains 132 rooms, 35 bathrooms and 6 levels. #3051 There are also 412 doors, 147 windows, 28 fireplaces, 8 staircases and 3 lifts. #3052 The building has been known as the 'president's palace' and the 'president's house'. #3053 **President Roosevelt** gave the White House its current name in **1901**. #3054 **Big Ben** clock tower in London, England, was built between **1843** and **1858**. #3055 Big Ben is actually the name of the bell that chimes within the clock tower. #3056 The clock tower is called the Elizabeth Tower, named in **2012** to celebrate the **Queen**'s Diamond Jubilee. #3057 Each dial on the clock is over 7 m in diameter. #3058 The eye-catching **Flatiron Building** in New York, USA, was designed by **Daniel Burnham**. #3059 Its distinctive flat shape was created to fit a space on Fifth Avenue and Broadway in **1902**. #3060 During the 20th century, architects everywhere strove to build the world's tallest building. #3061 The **Chrysler Building** in New York, USA, was built in **1930**. #3062 Its spire (which was constructed in secret) enabled it to take the title of the world's tallest building for 11 months, before being beaten to the top spot by the **Empire State Building**. #3063 **Fallingwater** is a famous private home by the American architect **Frank Lloyd Wright**. #3064 Designed in **1934**, the building looks as if it hovers above a waterfall. #3065 The innovative design captured the world's attention. #3066 The **Atomium** in Brussels, Belgium, was constructed in **1958**. #3067 It was designed by engineer **André Waterkeyn** and architects **André and Jean Polak**. #3068 It stands 102 m tall. #3069 Its nine stainless steel-clad spheres are connected to create the shape of a unit cell of iron crystal, as if it were magnified 165 billion times. #3070 The innovative design of the **Sydney Opera House,** in Australia, was created by **Jorn Utzon** from Denmark. #3071 The architect won an international competition in **1957** to design an opera house in Sydney. #3072 He beat 232 other entrants. #3073 Work started in **1959**. #3074 The Sydney Opera House is a venue performing arts centre. #3075 The futuristic **Space Needle** observation tower in Seattle, USA, was built in **1962**. #3076 It was built in just one year. #3077 25 lightning rods are on its roof to withstand lightning strikes. #3078 Its lifts travel at the same speed that a raindrop takes to fall to Earth. #3079 The **Lloyd's Building** in London, England,

was built between **1978** and **1986**. #3080 It was designed by the architect **Richard Rogers**. #3081 It is known as the inside-out building because it has its services, including water pipes, lifts and staircases, on the outside. #3082 The **Guggenheim Museum Bilbao**, a museum of modern art in Spain, was designed by American architect **Frank Gehry**. #3083 It is covered in a shiny metal called titanium. #3084 It has all kinds of exhibitions inside, from modern art to architecture. #3085 Outside the museum sits the world's biggest sculpture of a puppy, which is as tall as a house and covered in flowers. #3086 **One World Trade Center** in New York, USA, is the fourth tallest skyscraper in the world. #3087 It stands at a symbolic height of 1,776 feet (541 m), reflecting the year of the US Declaration of Independence (**1776**). #3088

# 13 GREAT GAUDI FACTS

The **Sagrada Familia** church is one of Spain's most famous buildings. #3089 The iconic church is in the centre of Barcelona, the second biggest city in Spain, and millions of people visit it every year. #3090 So far it has taken more than 100 years to build and it still isn't finished. #3091 It was started in **1882** and in **1883 Antoni Gaudí**, a famous Spanish architect, was put in charge. #3092 He dedicated his life to designing and building the church. #3093 He worked on it until his death in **1926** and since then, other architects and builders have continued Gaudí's work, using his plans to try and finish the church as Gaudí had planned. #3094 Gaudí was born in **1852** and you can see his work and influence all over the city of Barcelona, where he studied and lived. #3095 Gaudí used lots of different crafts in his designs, like ceramics, stained glass and ironwork, and his work was influenced by nature and religion. #3096 This can be seen in his other unusual designs, like **Casa Milà (La Pedrera)**, a building that Gaudí designed to reflect nature. #3097 As there are no straight lines in nature, Gaudí made his building curvy. #3098 His design of the house **Casa Batlló** was inspired by sea life, with quirky bone-shaped pillars and coral-coloured walls. #3099 Gaudí also created the amazing **Park Güell**. #3100 He made it a magical and fun place with a huge curvy seat covered in bright mosaic tiles, interesting sculptures and a dragon fountain. #3101

# 101 facts on
# WORLD TREASURES

➜ **Machu Picchu** was built by the Inca Empire around **1450**. #3102 It was abandoned around **1572** after the Spanish arrived in Peru. #3103 Some believe it was built for use as a royal estate. #3104 It is located 2,330 m above sea level. #3105 American explorer **Hiram Bingham III** discovered the site in **1911**. #3106 Since then, around 30 per cent has been reconstructed and restoration is still ongoing. #3107 The Incas built a road to the site and today tourists can trek the Inca Trail to reach Machu Picchu. #3108 It is one of the most famous archaeological sites in the world today. #3109 Machu Picchu means 'Old Peak' or 'Old Mountain'. #3110

➜ **Monticello** was the home of US **President Thomas Jefferson**. #3111 Jefferson designed the house himself – it took from **1768** to **1809** build it. #3112 The house is located in Virginia, USA. #3113 The name Monticello means 'Little Mountain' in Italian. #3114 The house has 43 rooms. #3115 A picture of the house has appeared on US currency and postage stamps. #3116 Today it is owned by the Thomas Jefferson Foundation and is a tourist attraction. #3117

➜ A collection of stone objects called the **Elgin Marbles** got their name from **Thomas Bruce**, the 7th Earl of Elgin, who took them from Greece. #3118 He removed them while working as Ambassador to the Ottoman Empire in **1801**. #3119 The marbles include sculptures from the Parthenon (a former Ancient Greek temple). #3120 They are displayed in the British Museum in London, England, but the New Acropolis Museum in Athens, Greece, has a space waiting for their display, should they ever be returned. #3121

➜ The **Statue of Liberty** was a gift from France to celebrate America's Declaration of Independence. #3122 It was designed by French sculptor **Frederic Auguste Bartholdi**. #3123 It was officially dedicated by **President Grover Cleveland** in **1886**. #3124 It represents the goddess of liberty. #3125 A broken chain lies at the feet of the statue. #3126 The statue is 93 m from the ground to the torch at the top. #3127

➜ **Kakadu rock art** paintings are up to 20,000 years old. #3128 They provide a record of Aboriginal life in Australia over thousands of years. #3129 The local Aboriginal word for rock art is 'gunbim'. #3130 The colours in the art came from naturally occurring minerals. #3131 Paint brushes were made from hair, chewed sticks and feathers. #3132 The Aborigines also blew paint around objects, which they used like stencils. #3133

➜ Built around the late 12th century, the **Bayon Temple** is a richly decorated temple in Cambodia. #3134 It was the official state temple of Mahayana Buddhist **King Jayavarman VII**. #3135 On many of the temple's towers are stone faces. #3136 They face outwards, keeping watch at each compass point. #3137 The temple is surrounded by two long walls with scenes of historical events. #3138 There are more than 11,000 figures carved over 1.2 km of wall, representing historical and mythical scenes. #3139

➜ The **Crown Jewels of the United Kingdom** are on display at the Tower of London. #3140 The jewel house at the Tower has been used since the 14th century to guard precious ceremonial objects, also known as the crown jewels. #3141 At the heart of the collection are the 'regalia' – objects associated with the coronation of kings and queens. #3142 The oldest item is the 12th-century Gold Anointing Spoon. #3143 It was used to anoint sovereigns with holy water. #3144 This is the only piece to have survived the destruction of the pre-Civil War regalia in **1649**. #3145 The destruction was ordered by **Oliver Cromwell** after **Charles I** was executed. #3146 The treasures were melted down and turned into gold coins. #3147 When the monarchy was restored, **Charles II** ordered new regalia to be made. #3148 The most famous crown is the Imperial State crown. #3149 It was made for the **Queen**'s father **King George VI** in **1937** and has over 3,300 gems. #3150 The crown is worn for the State Opening of Parliament. #3151

➡ The **Great Wall of China** is made up of a number of sections, built mostly during the **Qin dynasty** and the **Ming dynasty**. #3152 The first parts of the wall were built 2,000 years ago. #3153 Its main purpose was to defend China against attacks from the north. #3154 It stretches 6,300 km. #3155 The widest section is around 9 m. #3156 The highest section is around 8 m tall. #3157 There are over 7,000 lookout towers along the wall. #3158 It is the longest structure built by humans in the world. #3159

➡ The **Terracotta Army** was discovered by farmers who were digging a well in **1974**. #3160 Terracotta is a common type of clay. #3161 Four main pits house the life sized clay statues. #3162 The pits are around 6 m deep. #3163 Most of the statues were found broken into many pieces. #3164 Archaeologists have been carefully putting the pieces back together for many years. #3165 They found over 40,000 real weapons, including crossbows, spears and swords. #3166 The bronze weapons were found in excellent condition. #3167 They estimate that over 700,000 craftsmen worked on the project for several years. #3168

➡ **Petra** is an ancient city in Jordan. #3169 It is thought to have been established around **312 BC**. #3170 The city is half

built by humans and half carved into the rock. #3171 It has around 800 carved tombs. #3172 It had an impressive water channel system and was a centre of trade. #3173 Petra is the Greek word for rock. #3174 Under Roman rule, the city declined and was abandoned around **AD 550**. #3175

➡ People have lived in **Cappadocia** in Turkey for thousands of years. #3176 The unique landscape was formed by the erosion of volcanoes. #3177 There are around 40 underground cities there and more are being discovered. #3178 They were built to protect people from invaders. #3179 The underground cities had churches, animal pens

and wine cellars. #3180 Cappadocia means 'land of the beautiful horses'. #3181

➡ The prehistoric circle of stones in England called **Stonehenge** was built around 5,000 years ago. #3182 It's older than the Egyptian pyramids. #3183 Nobody is really sure what it is, but it could have been a burial ground or a calendar. #3184 The monument is made of two stone types, sarsens and bluestones, which had to be transported many miles. #3185 The circle is in line with the midsummer sunrise. #3186

➡ **Mount Rushmore National Memorial** is a huge sculpture carved into the side of Mount Rushmore, USA. #3187 Local historian **Doane Robinson** came up with the idea in **1923** to promote tourism in South Dakota. #3188 It took 14 years and 400 workers to complete. #3189 Sculptor **Gutzon Borglum** died during the creation of the monument in **1941**. #3190 His son **Lincoln Borglum** continued his work, finishing it a year later. #3191 The memorial shows four presidents: **George Washington**, **Thomas Jefferson**, **Theodore Roosevelt** and **Abraham Lincoln**. #3192 Dynamite was used to carve out the rock. #3193 The monument is 18 m high. #3194 Each president's head is the size of a six-storey building. #3195

➡ The **Bayeux Tapestry** tells the story of events leading up to and including the Battle of Hastings in **1066**. #3196 It is kept in Bayeux in France. #3197 **King William I's** half-brother, **Odo**, **Bishop of Bayeux**, ordered the tapestry to be made. #3198 He did so to honour William's victory against the English. #3199 The tapestry is about 70 m long. #3200 It's the longest piece of embroidery in the world. #3201 It is thought to have been made in England. #3202

# 5 FACTS ABOUT RATS

Rats can tread **WATER** for three days. #3203

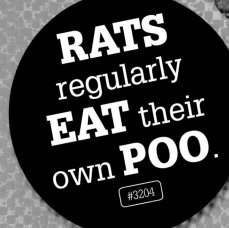

**RATS** regularly **EAT** their own **POO**. #3204

A rat can survive being washed **down a sewer**. #3205

There are **as many RATS AS PEOPLE** in the USA. #3206

A **rat can fall** from a height of **15 m** – about the height of a three-storey building – and still land safely. #3207

# 4 FACTS ABOUT **BEAVERS**

Beavers can **gnaw through tree trunks** up to **1 m** in diameter.

#3208

**A beaver's home** is called a **lodge.** Beavers build their lodges in lakes, and the lodge can only be **entered from underwater**.

#3209

A beaver has a **FLAT TAIL** that acts like a rudder, helping it to **steer as it swims**.

#3210

Beavers often create their own lakes by **damming streams.** The longest beaver dam ever found was **850 m long**.

#3211

Havergal Brian's Symphony No 1, the *Gothic Symphony*, is the **LARGEST ORCHESTRAL PIECE OF MUSIC** ever written. It needs:

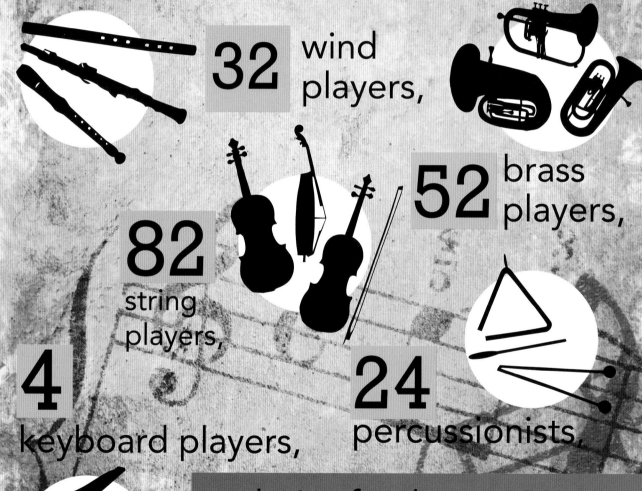

**32** wind players,

**52** brass players,

**82** string players,

**4** keyboard players,

**24** percussionists,

a choir of at least 600, a children's choir of 100 and four soloists. #3212

# 10 TOE-TAPPING MUSICAL FACTS

The **best-selling pop single** of all time is 'White Christmas', released by Bing Crosby in 1942. #3213

The **best-selling album** of all time is *Thriller*, released by Michael Jackson in 1982. #3214

The **biggest-ever choir**, with 121,440 singers, sang at an event organised by **The Art of Living** in India in 2011. #3215

The **saxophone** is named after its inventor, Adolphe Sax, and the **sousaphone** is named after the American composer John Philip Sousa. #3216

The earliest evidence for the existence of **bagpipes** is in ancient engravings dating back to biblical times. #3217

Wolfgang Amadeus Mozart, born in Austria in 1756, started composing at just **five years old!** #3218

**Bagpipes** arrived in Scotland in the 1300s and developed into the highland pipes we recognize today. #3219

On the US Billboard chart, the **Beatles** hold the record for **the most Number One hit singles – 20!** #3220

John Cage composed **4'33"** in 1952. Instruments play **no notes at all** during its four-minute, 33-second length! #3221

George Beauchamp designed the **first electric guitar** prototype in 1931. It was nicknamed the 'Frying Pan' because of its shape! #3222

# 3 DOLPHIN FACTS

Dolphins put only half of their **brain to sleep at a time**.

This allows them to keep swimming and stops them from drowning. #3223

The **Ganges river dolphin** is almost blind. It lives in muddy rivers, where eyesight is not much use. #3224

7 m

**Some dolphins** can jump **7 m** out of the water. **They could jump right over an adult giraffe.** #3225

# 4 facts about the
# KILLER WHALE

Despite its **name,** the killer whale is actually a **species** of
# dolphin.

#3226

Killer whales eat more than
# 50 kg
of food a day. #3227

A killer whale's brain is **five times larger** than a human
# BRAIN. #3228

Killer whales live in **family groups** that contain four different generations – from youngsters to their great-grandmothers.

#3229

## 22 FACTS ABOUT RIVERS AND LAKES

A lake is a body of water surrounded by land. #3230 Lagoons and estuaries are bodies of water connected to oceans or seas. #3231 Water also collects below Earth's surface and forms underground lakes. #3232 A lake usually contains fresh water, but some contain higher concentrations of salt (these are known as salt lakes). #3233 Most freshwater lakes are found in the northern hemisphere. #3234 The five **Great Lakes** in the United States contain about 20 per cent of the world's fresh water supply. #3235 **Lake Superior** is the largest of the Great Lakes. #3236 It has the largest surface area of any freshwater lake in the world. #3237 Canada has around two million lakes. #3238 Finland has over 187,000 lakes. #3239 A river is fresh water flowing across the surface of land, usually into the sea. #3240 The longest river in the world is the **Nile**. #3241 It runs for around 6,650 km. #3242 The **Amazon**, **Yangtze** and **Mississippi-Missouri** rivers are all over 6,000 km long. #3243 Most of the world's major cities are located on or near a river. #3244 In **2009** an aeroplane landed on the Hudson River in New York City. #3245 Only four out of the ten longest rivers in the world flow north. #3246 The world's deepest river is the **Congo** in Africa. #3247 At its deepest, darkest point it is around 220 m deep. #3248 The **River Thames** is around 346 km long. #3249 There are more than 200 bridges over the River Thames. #3250 The River Thames is also home to over 25 species of fish. #3251

Our planet contains over a billion trillion litres of water. #3252 Very little of it is safe to drink. #3253 This is because over 97 per cent of the water on our planet is salt water. #3254 The average person uses 3,400 lt of water every day. #3255 Most comes from hidden water usage, such as growing the food we eat. #3256 The **Pacific Ocean** is the largest ocean in the world. #3257 It is also the deepest ocean. #3258 The Pacific Ocean covers around 30 per cent of Earth's surface. #3259 This is a larger surface area than all Earth's areas of land combined! #3260 It was named by the Portuguese explorer **Ferdinand Magellan**. #3261 In Portuguese, *Mar Pacifico* means peaceful sea. #3262 The International Date Line passes through the Pacific Ocean. #3263 When you cross it, you move forward or backward by a day. #3264 Most of the world's fish are caught in the Pacific Ocean. #3265 The **Atlantic Ocean** is the youngest of the world's oceans. #3266 The North Atlantic formed during the Jurassic Period. #3267 The Atlantic Ocean is one of the busiest sea routes. #3268 The first person to fly non-stop across it was Charles Lindbergh in 1927. #3269 He took 33.5 hours to fly from the United States to France. #3270 The Atlantic Ocean is also the world's saltiest ocean. #3271 Many of the largest rivers flow into the Atlantic Ocean. #3272 It covers around 20 per cent of Earth's surface. #3273 Several spacecraft have landed in Earth's oceans at the end of their space missions. #3274 They include the **Mercury**, **Gemini** and **Apollo** crafts. #3275 The **Indian Ocean** is the warmest ocean in the world. #3276 The surface water can reach temperatures of up to 30°C. #3277 It is the only ocean that shares its name with a country. #3278 The Indian Ocean is home to less marine life than the other oceans. #3279 This is due to the higher water temperature. #3280 Water in the Indian Ocean has one of the lowest oxygen contents in the world. #3281 The Indian Ocean experiences a high number of monsoon storms. #3282 It is land locked to its north by the continent of Asia. #3283 The **Arctic Ocean** is the smallest and shallowest ocean. #3284 The Arctic Ocean and the Southern Ocean are the coldest. #3285 The North Pole is situated in the middle of the Arctic Ocean. There is no land at the North Pole – it is a

# WORLD facts

floating raft of ice. #3286 During the winter the Arctic Ocean is almost completely covered in ice. #3287 The Arctic Ocean gets its name from the Greek word *arctos*, which means bear. #3288 This is because a constellation called the Great Bear can be seen in the sky above it. #3289 The **Dead Sea**, a salt lake, has the saltiest water. #3290 It is so salty that nothing can survive in it. #3291 The Dead Sea is extremely salty because it is surrounded by a hot desert. #3292 The intense heat causes water to evaporate faster, leaving large quantities of salt behind. #3293 Scientists who specialize in the study of oceans are called **oceanographers**. #3294 Scientists who study marine plants and animals are called **marine biologists**. #3295 In the olden days, the only way to observe how fast a ship was sailing was to throw a piece of wood into the water to see how quickly it floated away. #3296 This was called 'heaving the log'. #3297 In modern times, sailing speed is measured in knots. #3298 One knot equals 1.85 km/h. #3299 Many fish living 3,000 m or more below the surface have their own lights. #3300 These lights glow naturally, by bioluminescence. #3301 Fish change colour depending on where they live. #3302 Fish living near the surface are often blue, green or violet. #3303 The twilight zone is 180 m below the water's surface. #3304 It is also known as the disphotic zone. #3305 Fish there are usually silver or light-coloured. #3306 A mangrove is a type of plant that grows on seashores and in estuaries. #3307 80 per cent of all pollution in seas and oceans comes from land-based activities. #3308 40 per cent of the world's population lives within 60 km of a coast. #3309 More than 90 per cent of goods traded between countries are transported by sea. #3310 The busiest port in the world is in **Shanghai** in China. #3311 It handles around 32 million containers a year and is the size of around 470 football pitches. #3312

## 17 FISHY FACTS

The **yeti lobster** is the furriest crustacean in the world. #3313 An **oyster** can change from one gender to another, then back again! #3314 A **catfish** has more than 100,000 taste buds. #3315 **Shrimps** can swim backwards. #3316 A **blue whale's** tongue is so large that 50 people could stand on it. #3317 **Dolphins** jump out of the water to save energy – it's easier to move through the air than through the water. #3318 **Fish** can't close their eyes as they don't have eyelids. #3319 The **stout infant fish** is the smallest freeliving fish in the sea. #3320 It lives in the **Great Barrier Reef in Australia**. #3321 Around 120 million tonnes of fish are caught each year around the world. #3322 **Trouts** can warn us of pollution in rivers. #3323 They need fresh, clean water with lots of oxygen to survive. #3324 If they start disappearing from a river, it means that water has become polluted. #3325 A **salmon** remembers the river it was born in even if that river is 1,000 km away. #3326 They remember where to go using their sense of smell, the Moon and ocean currents. #3327 The heaviest crustacean to live on land is the **robber crab**. #3328 They can weigh up to 4 kg and have a leg span of up to 1 m! #3329

# 10 facts about
# SCHOOLING FISH

Cod can grow to
**1.8 m long – as long
as a tall man**. #3330

The largest cod are
**90 kg** in weight. #3331

The whisker-like barbel on a
cod's chin helps it to find food
on the ocean floor. #3332

A female cod may lay up to
**9 million eggs
in one go**. #3333

Fish that swim together are called a school or a shoal. #3334

Fish of different species often swim together for protection. #3335

Atlantic herring form mega-schools containing **hundreds of millions of individuals.** #3336

Fish shoal with others of a similar size and appearance. #3337

Sardines shoal with mackerel, hake and anchovy. #3338

Each year, sardine schools swim up the coast of East Africa, closely followed by predators such as dolphins, whales and sharks. These hunters travel long distances every year to join in the feast. #3339

The *Apollo* spacecrafts took three days to reach the Moon.

At this speed it would take a rocket

# 96
## YEARS

to reach the planet Neptune, the most distant planet in the solar system.

#3340

# 10 FACTS ABOUT SPACE EXPLORERS

The **first manufactured object to orbit Earth** was a Soviet satellite called *Sputnik* in 1957. #3341

Soviet cosmonaut Valentina Tereshkova became the **first woman in space** in 1963. #3342

In 1961, Soviet cosmonaut Yuri Gagarin became the **first man in space**. #3343

On 20 July 1969, the Americans landed **the first man on the Moon**. #3344

Neil Armstrong was the **first man to walk** on the Moon's surface, but Buzz Aldrin took the first pee on it. #3345

In 1970, the crew of *Apollo 13* **nearly died** when an oxygen tank explosion crippled their craft. #3346

In 1986, space shuttle *Challenger* **exploded** seconds after takeoff. #3347

The American Moon-landing programme cost **£16 billion** – the cost today would be around £93 million. #3348

In 2012, the American probe *Voyager 1* became the **first manufactured object** to leave the solar system. It was launched in 1977. #3349

The rocks collected from the Moon by the *Apollo* astronauts weigh a total of **382 kilograms**. #3350

# 12 **Hummingbird** FACTS

Hummingbirds are the only birds that can fly **backwards**. #3351

Hummingbirds hover in front of flowers to feed on nectar. They have long beaks to reach right inside the flower. #3352

Hummingbirds can even fly **upside down**. #3353

A hummingbird's wings flap between **12 and 100** times a second, producing the

# hum

that gives the bird its name. #3354

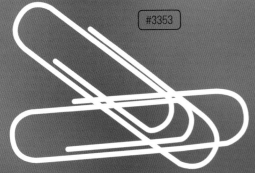

The bee hummingbird is the smallest bird in the world. It weighs **just 2 g** – about the weight of two paperclips. #03355

The vervain hummingbird's egg is **1 cm long** and weighs just 0.3 g. #3356

To save energy, a hummingbird can **slow its heartbeat,** and **reduce its body temperature**. #3357

A resting hummingbird's heart beats **50 times per minute**. #3358

When it flies, its heart rate rises to **1,260 beats per second**. #3359

A hummingbird's feet are **so tiny that it cannot walk**. It uses its feet to hold on to branches when it rests. #3360

A hummingbird **eats half its own weight in nectar and insects** every day. #3361

The female **purple-throated carib** has a long, curved beak. It feeds on different flowers from the male, whose beak is shorter and straighter. #3362

# 50 facts on

According to legend, the city of Rome was founded in **753 BC** by its first king – **Romulus**. #3363 Romans believed in many different gods and goddesses. #3364 **Jupiter**, the god of the sky, was the most important god. #3365 Under Roman law, both the bride and groom had to be Roman citizens in order to marry. #3366 The Romans spoke and wrote in **Latin**. Many words in the English language are based on Latin words. #3367 Roman houses were so well built that the remains of some villas, and even towns, survive today. #3368 The Romans created an early newspaper called *Acta Diurna* ('daily news'). #3369 Guests at Roman dinner parties would eat their food lying down on a sofa.

#3370 Most children in Roman times did not go to school as school fees were expensive. #3371 Roman children played hide and seek, chase and hopscotch. #3372 They also had kites, dolls and building blocks to play with. #3373 Children often wore a special charm, called a **bulla**, around their neck. #3374 It was given to them when they were babies to protect against misfortune. #3375 Roman false teeth were made from the teeth of dead people, or from animals! #3376 Only Roman male citizens were allowed to wear a **toga**. #3377 Certain colours were permitted only for special occasions or to show people's rank. #3378 Only the **emperor** was allowed to wear a completely purple toga. #3379 Rome had four classes (ranks) of people. #3380 The lowest class were the **slaves**. #3381 The next class up were called the **plebeians**. #3382 The second-highest class were the **equestrians**. #3383 The highest class were the noble families. They were called **patricians**. #3384 Amphitheatres were the centre of public entertainment all over the Roman Empire. #3385 People would go to watch men fighting wild beasts – or each other – to the death! #3386 The stadium was also used for chariot

# THE ROMANS

racing, which was a very popular sport. [#3387] The largest amphitheatre in the empire was the **Colosseum** in Rome. [#3388] It could seat up to 50,000 people. [#3389] The Romans loved bathing and built public baths where they could wash and meet their friends. [#3390] The baths also had snack bars, games rooms and libraries. [#3391] There were separate baths for men and women. [#3392] The calendar we use today was started by **Julius Caesar,** a leading Roman general and politician. [#3393] The names of our months are taken from Latin words and the names of Roman gods and people. [#3394] The Romans invaded and ruled other countries all over **Europe**, **Africa** and the **Middle East.** [#3395] The Romans invaded **Britain** twice, in **55** and **54 BC,** before they finally conquered it following an invasion in **AD 43.** [#3396] The **Roman army** could march up to 40 km a day. [#3397] It was made up of groups of soldiers called legions. [#3398] There were about 5,000 soldiers in a legion. [#3399] Each legion had its own number, name, badge and fortress. [#3400] There were about 30 legions based throughout the Roman Empire. [#3401] The Romans stayed in Britain for almost 400 years. [#3402] They called it **Britannia**. [#3403] Before the Romans arrived in Britain, there were no roads as we would recognise them today. [#3404] The Romans built over 9,000 km of roads in Britain. [#3405] They built their roads as straight as possible. [#3406] This was to allow them to travel quickly and avoid bandits hiding around bends. [#3407] Around **AD 50** the Romans founded the city of **Londinium**. [#3408] Londinium became **London**. [#3409] Many roads and the River Thames ran through Londinium. [#3410] These transport links made the city an important trade centre. [#3411] **Hadrian's Wall** marked the northern boundary of the Roman Empire. [#3412]

# 11 LIZARD FACTS

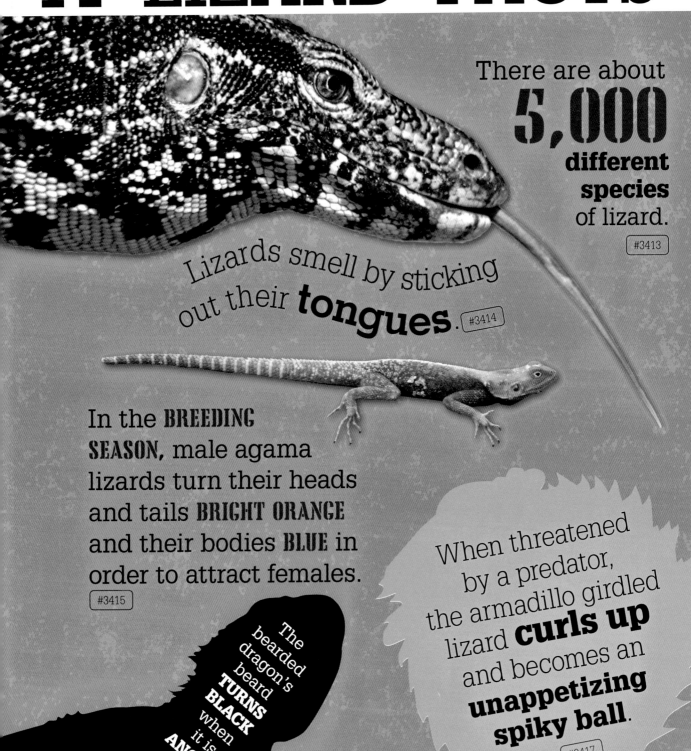

There are about **5,000** **different species** of lizard.
#3413

Lizards smell by sticking out their **tongues**. #3414

In the **BREEDING SEASON**, male agama lizards turn their heads and tails **BRIGHT ORANGE** and their bodies **BLUE** in order to attract females.
#3415

The bearded dragon's beard **TURNS BLACK** when it is **ANGRY.**
#3416

When threatened by a predator, the armadillo girdled lizard **curls up** and becomes an **unappetizing spiky ball**.
#3417

**Skinks** are lizards with **short necks** and **short legs.** Some have no legs at all, and move like snakes. #3418

**Glass lizards** look like snakes, but they have the eyelids and ear openings of a lizard. #3419

Caiman lizards eat almost nothing other than **snails.** #3420

Lizards can give a **painful bite,** but none is as venomous as some snakes. #3421

The **common basilisk** can **run on water,** and is sometimes called the **Jesus Christ lizard**. #3422

Many lizards have a **DEWLAP**, which is a loose flap of skin that grows down under the chin. They use these to **COMMUNICATE WITH EACH OTHER.** #3423

# 100 terrific TRAIN facts

Early trains were powered by horses, ropes and gravity. #3424 Roads or rails called **wagonways** were used around **1550**. #3425 Horse-drawn carts travelled over the wagonways' wooden rails. #3426 In the late **1700s** iron was used, instead of wood, for rails and the wheels on the carts. #3427 Wagonways evolved into **tramways** and spread throughout the world. #3428 In **1803 Samuel Homfray** funded the development of a steam-powered vehicle in Great Britain. #3429 **Richard Trevithick** built him the first steam-engine tramway locomotive. #3430 In **1804** it carried iron and men between **Merthyr Tydfil** and **Abercynnon** in **Wales**. #3431 In **1825** Trevithick went on to build the first passenger steam railway in the world. #3432 It ran between the British towns of **Stockton** and **Darlington**. #3433 In **1828** work began on the **Baltimore and Ohio Railroad**, the first intercity railroad in the **United States**. #3434 More railways swiftly followed but there was some opposition to their development from rival transport companies (such as stagecoach operators). #3435 In **1829 George Stephenson** built the *Rocket* which won the Rainhill Trials, a contest held to find the best designed locomotive to power the new railway system. #3436 Engineers based their train designs on the *Rocket* for the next 150 years. #3437 The first railway to cross a continent was the **Pacific Railroad**. #3438 It ran for 3,069 km and connected Calfornia with the east coast of the United States. #3439 It opened in **1869**. #3440 **New York City** built the first elevated rail system in the United States in the late **1860s**. #3441 It ran using cable cars but constant breakdowns led to the closure of the line. #3442 It was reopened in **1871** with steam engines pulling the cars. #3443 **London**, **England**, built the first underground rail system. #3444 Built in **1890** it now has 270 stations. #3445 The shortest journey between two stations on the **London Underground** is between Leicester Square and Covent Garden. #3446 It takes around 40 seconds to travel between the stations. #3447 The only railway to reach the top of a volcano was built on **Mount Vesuvius** in **Italy** in **1880**. #3448 **Boston** built the United States' first subway in **1897**. #3449 New York City's subway system has the most stations in the world. #3450 There are 468 stations on 10 different lines. #3451 The United States has the most railway tracks in the world. #3452 It has almost 250,000 km of track. #3453 Much of the track is used for freight trains, which are used for transporting goods. #3454 Its passenger network spans around 35,000 km. #3455 **China's** rail network is the second biggest in the world. #3456 It has around 100,000 km of track. #3457 It carries over 2 billion passengers a year. #3458 **Russia** has the third biggest rail network in the world. #3459 It covers almost 85,500 km of track. #3460 The **Indian** rail network is the fourth largest. #3461 It carries the most passengers in the world. #3462 On average it operates around 19,000 trains a day. #3463 They carry about 8 billion passengers a year! #3464 The steepest passenger railtrack in the world is in the **Blue Mountains** in **Australia**. #3465 It has a gradient incline of 52 degrees. #3466 The longest straight stretch of railway is also in Australia. #3467 The part without any curves is 478 km long. #3468 There are 40,000 bridges and tunnels and 9,000 level crossings on **Great Britain's National Rail** network. #3469 The longest station platform in the world is in **Gorakhpur, India**. #3470 It measures around 1,366 m. #3471 The heaviest train in the world was a freight train weighed in **2001**. #3472 Its gross weight was 99,734,000 kg. #3473 It weighed as much as 27,000 elephants! #3474 The longest possible journey on one train is between **Moscow** and **Vladivostok** in **Russia**, on the **Trans-Siberian Express**. #3475 The journey is 9,297 km long. #3476 The highest railway station in the world is at **Condor** in **Bolivia**. #3477 It has an altitude of 4,787 m. #3478 The largest station in the world is **Grand Central** in New York City. #3479 It has 44 platforms. #3480 The longest station seat in the world is at **Scarborough** station in Australia. #3481 It is 139 m long. #3482 The longest railway tunnel in Great Britain is the **Severn Tunnel**. #3483 It is over 7 km long. #3484 In Great Britain around 3.5 million passengers travel by train each day. #3485 **London Waterloo** is the busiest station in Great Britain. #3486 Around 100 million people use it each year. #3487 70 per cent of train journeys taken in Great Britain start or finish in London. #3488 Diesel trains replaced steam trains in the middle of the 20th century. #3489 **France** was one of the first countries to introduce high-speed electric trains. #3490 They introduced the **TGV high-speed train** in

**1981**. #3491 It is the fastest train in the world. #3492 It can reach speeds of 515 km/h. #3493 That's four and a half times faster than a car on the motorway. #3494 **Japan's Shikansen** is also known as 'the bullet train'. #3495 It can reach speeds of 300 km/h. #3496 This train is always on time as it is considered very rude to be late in Japan. #3497 The **Channel Tunnel** between **France** and **England** is the longest undersea tunnel in the world. #3498 Workers in France and England started digging the tunnel from opposite ends and met in the middle. #3499 Construction began in **1988**. #3500 It cost 80 per cent more than originally planned. #3501 The total cost to build it was around £10 billion. #3502 It has three parallel tunnels. #3503 Two running tunnels are for trains and a service tunnel is used by other vehicles. #3504

The running tunnels are 30 m apart. #3505 The lining of the tunnel is designed to last for 120 years. #3506 It was built using chalk marl, a marine deposit made up of small fossils. #3507 The Channel Tunnel was officially opened in **1994**. #3508 In 2013 the Channel Tunnel carried an average of 56,000 passengers per day. #3509 It takes just 2 hours and 15 minutes to travel from **London** to **Paris**. #3510 20 minutes is spent undersea. #3511 The **Seikan** railway tunnel in Japan connects the island of **Honshu** to **Hokkaido**. #3512 It opened in **1988**. #3513 It is the deepest underwater rail tunnel in the world. #3514 Its track level is about 100 m below the seabed and 240 m below the water's surface. #3515 There are two stations located inside the Seikan railway tunnel. #3516 A train created by the **National Belgium Railway Company** holds the record for the longest passenger train. #3517 It measured 1,732 m. #3518 It had 70 coaches in total, including one for dancing! #3519 The train made only one journey, when it travelled 62.5 km to raise money for charity. #3520 The longest **model train** measured 282 m. #3521 It had a total of 1,563 carriages. #3522 People who study trains are sometimes known as **ferroequinologists**. #3523

All snowflakes have **six sides** but no two that have ever been studied are exactly alike. #3524

In 1881, a violent storm rained **crabs and sea snails** on an English town over 60 km from the coast. #3525

In 1934, a **371 km/h** gust of wind was recorded at Mount Washington, USA! #3526

The largest snowball fight in the world was held in Seattle, USA. **5,834 people** participated!. #3527

In 1986, hailstones the size of **grapefruits** fell on a town in Bangladesh, killing 92 people. #3528

If all the moisture in the air fell as rain, it would cover Earth's surface to a depth of **2.5 cm.** #3529

The town of Calama in the Atacama Desert had had no rain for **400 years,** until a shower in 1972. #3530

By the time you've read this sentence, over **900 million tons of rain** will have fallen around Earth! #3531

In 1882, two **frozen frogs** were found inside hailstones in Iowa, USA. #3532

Commonwealth Bay in Antarctica occasionally experiences winds of **320 km/h.** #3533

Earth acts like a **GIANT MAGNET** because of its core of molten metal. That's why compasses point north. #3534

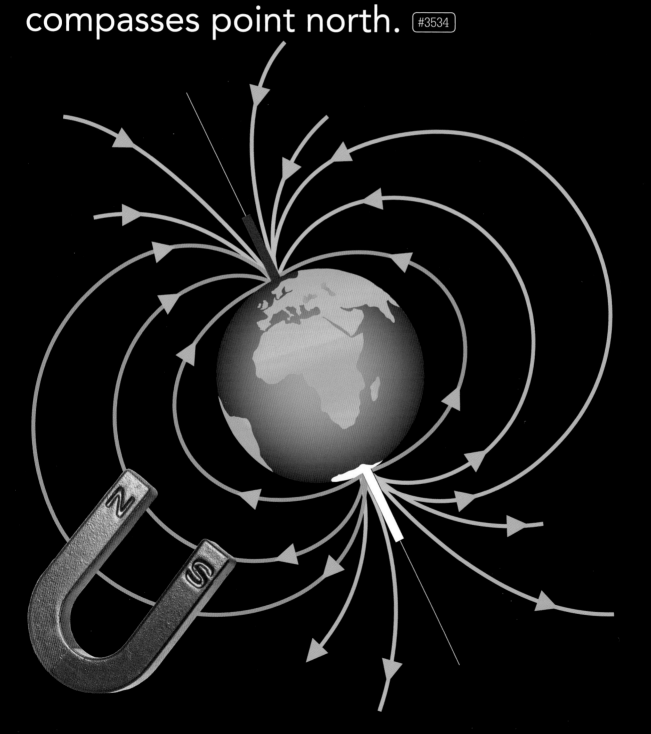

# 5 **CAMEL** FACTS

A camel's hump is **FULL OF FAT.** When there is no food, it can live off its fat reserves for several months without eating. #3535

There are more than **1 million** wild camels in **Australia**. They were introduced to the continent by humans in the **19th century.** #3537

**Camel's milk contains** **10** **times** as much iron as cow's milk. #3536

A camel can drink **135 LITRES** of water in just **15 minutes**. #3538

A **BACTRIAN CAMEL** can carry a load of 250 kg for **four days** without stopping. That's more than the weight of three adult humans. #3539

# 6 GIRAFFE FACTS

The giraffe is the **tallest land animal**, standing as high as **6 m.** #3540

The giraffe has a **blue-black** tongue that is nearly HALF A METRE long. #3541

Giraffes can **run at 56 km/h** in short bursts. #3542

Sometimes a giraffe will rest with its head bending back to its body. #3543

To get enough blood **up its long neck** to the brain, a giraffe has to **pump blood twice as hard as other large mammals**. #3544

**MALE GIRAFFES** fight each other by **smashing their heads** against one another's body. #3545

More copies of the **BIBLE** are **SHOPLIFTED** than of any other book. #3546

# 10 MIND-BENDING FACTS ABOUT GOVERNMENTS

**There are 53 countries in the Commonwealth,** including the UK, Canada, Australia, New Zealand and Jamaica. #3547

The current **longest-serving head of state**, King Rama IX of Thailand, has been in power since 1946. #3548

The five most popular political systems are a democracy, republic, monarchy, communist state and dictatorship. #3549

No king or queen has entered the **UK House of Commons** since 1642... #3550

... when Charles I stormed in with his soldiers and **tried to arrest** five members of Parliament. #3551

The **biggest democracy** in the world is India. #3552

**714 million people** were eligible to vote in the Indian general election of 2009. #3553

A **theocracy** is a system of government based on religion – the head of state is selected by a religious group. #3554

There are two theocracies – the **Vatican City** in Rome, home of the Roman Catholic Church, and **Iran,** an Islamic republic. #3555

In **Australia** it is compulsory for citizens over the age of 18 to vote. #3556

# 9 turtles and tortoises facts

Many turtles live in the oceans. Tortoises are a kind of turtle that live on land.
#3557

The alligator snapping turtle lures fish using its tongue, which **looks like a tasty worm**.
#3559

A turtle's shell has about **60 different bones** in it.
#3558

Turtles have been around on Earth for **at least 220 million years**.
#3560

Turtles do not have teeth. Instead, they have **sharp beaks** to tear their food.
#3562

Green turtles **return to the same beach where they hatched** to lay their own eggs.
#3561

One leatherback turtle was tracked swimming **20,000 km** from Indonesia to the USA.
#3563

Desert tortoises spend **95%** of their time in burrows nearly 2 m underground.
#3564

The hingeback tortoise has a hinge at the back of its shell that allows it to close its shell and protect its legs and tail from predators.
#3565

# 4 CLEVER CAVE FACTS

Krubera Cave in Georgia, western Asia, is the **deepest known cave,** plunging deeper than 2,000 metres. It would take you about 30 seconds to fall that far! #3566

Stalactites are rocky needles hanging from cave ceilings, formed by dripping water. The **WORLD'S LONGEST STALACTITE** is 8.2 metres long in the White Chamber in Lebanon. #3567

Mammoth Cave in Kentucky, USA, is the **WORLD'S LARGEST CAVE SYSTEM,** with over 628 kilometres of linked caves and passages. #3568

The **longest underwater cave** found so far is a **215-kilometre maze** of flooded passages in Mexico. It's not yet been fully explored. #3569

# 5 WINDING FACTS ABOUT RIVERS

The area of land that contributes water to a river is called a basin. The basin of the Amazon River covers **NEARLY HALF OF SOUTH AMERICA!** #3570

The Amazon empties so much water into the Atlantic that freshwater can be found **180 KILOMETRES OUT TO SEA**. #3571

A huge underground river runs under the **NILE**, containing **SIX TIMES MORE WATER** than the Nile itself. #3572

The **WORLD'S SHORTEST RIVER** is the Roe River in Montana, USA, which is only 61 metres long – half the length of a football pitch. #3573

The Yellow River in China is the **WORLD'S MUDDIEST RIVER**, dumping over a billion tons of silt into the sea each year. #3574

# 52 fantastic FOOD facts

In France, children often drink hot chocolate from bowls. #3575 Bagels are the only bread product that is boiled before it is baked. #3576 The **Earl of Sandwich** gave his name to the sandwich. #3577 It was originally always meat between two slices of bread. #3578 Over 10 per cent of an apple is made up of carbohydrates (a main type of nutrient). #3579 More than 80 per cent of an apple is water. #3580 There are more than 7,000 varieties of apples. #3581 Strawberries are the only fruit that have their seeds on the outside. #3582 On average, there are 200 tiny seeds on every strawberry. #3583 Bananas are picked when they are still green. #3584 They are transported at a temperature of 13.3°C in order to increase their shelf life. #3585 The largest hot dog eating contest had 3,189 participants. #3586 The event was organized by **Oscar Mayer** in Valencia, Spain in **2011**. #3587 The record for the most sugared jam doughnuts eaten in three minutes, without licking the lips, is six, and is held by **Lup Fun Yau**. #3588 When cranberries are ripe, they bounce like a ball. #3589 Monkeys peel bananas from the bottom. #3590 Corn dextrin is a common thickener used in junk food. #3591 It is also used in the glue on envelopes and postage stamps! #3592 An average corn on the cob has an even number of kernels. #3593 The tea bag was created by accident as a way to send tea leaves by post. #3594 Fortune cookies are not part of traditional Chinese cuisine; they were invented by Chinese people living in the United States. #3595 The biggest consumers of ketchup are children, aged 6–12 years old. #3596 **Benedikt Weber** holds the world record for the fastest time to drink a bottle of ketchup. #3597 He drank 396 g of ketchup in just 32.37 seconds! #3598 The hottest chilli recorded is the 'Carolina Reaper'. #3599 Generally, the smaller the chilli, the hotter it will be. #3600 The first meals eaten in space were soft, gloopy foods, much like baby food, packed into tubes like toothpaste. #3601

The astronauts squeezed these meals into their mouths. #3602 The process of freeze-drying food is used for space travel, but is now used for everyday foods as well. #3603 Extra large eggs come from more mature hens. The older the hen, the bigger the eggs. #3604 When duck eggs are boiled, the white turns blue-white and the yolk turns a red-orange. #3605 Lachanophobia is the fear of vegetables. #3606 The Japanese sell square watermelons because they stack better. #3607 A hard-boiled egg will spin, while a soft-boiled or uncooked egg won't. #3608 The melting point of chocolate is just below our natural body temperature, which is why it melts in the mouth. #3609 Prior to the turkey tradition, Christmas food included roast swan, pheasants and peacocks. #3610 Every time you lick a stamp, you absorb 5.9 calories. #3611 There are approximately 465 baked beans in a standard 415 g tin. #3612 The British sausage has its own fan club – the British Sausage Appreciation Society – with over 5,000 members in the UK. #3613 Pineapples are international symbols of welcome. #3614 In colonial times, pineapples were so rare and costly that you were able to rent them for the day as a dining table centrepiece while entertaining. #3615 Oranges have been grown since ancient times and originated in South-East Asia. #3616 The carotene in oranges gives them their orange colour. #3617 There are typically ten segments inside an orange. #3618 Orange peel can be used by gardeners to sprinkle over vegetables as a slug repellent. #3619 The mango is the national fruit of India, Pakistan and the Philippines. #3620 Giving someone a basket of mangoes is considered a gesture of friendship. #3621 Cooks of royal families used to add almonds to the food so that the heavy meals of meat were easier to digest. #3622 Crackers have holes in to allow steam to escape during cooking. #3623 Each kernel of popcorn contains a small drop of water stored inside a circle of soft starch. #3624 Popcorn needs between 13–14 per cent moisture to pop – as the kernel heats up, the water begins to expand. #3625 Jelly was first eaten by the Egyptians. #3626

# 50 yucky food facts

The gelling agent used in most jellies is gelatin and is sourced from animals. #3627 You can buy cow tongue ice cream in Tokyo. #3628 Carmine is a red food colouring that comes from boiled cochineal beetle – it is used in sweets. #3629 Honey is made from nectar and bee vomit. #3630 An edible snail is called an escargot. #3631 Snails have been eaten since Roman times. #3632 Haggis is made from the heart, lungs, liver and kidneys of a sheep. #3633 Garum, a fish sauce, was the Ancient Greek and Roman's favourite condiment. #3634 It was made from rotten fish. #3635 More than 1,900 species of insect are eaten around the world. #3636 Fried locusts are a Nigerian delicacy. #3637 They taste a little like prawns. #3638 In Cambodia, large spiders fried with garlic are a popular dish. #3639 American Indians roast beetles and munch on them like popcorn. #3640 People in Bali catch dragonflies with a stick coated in sticky plant juice. #3641

They then fry them and eat them. #3642 Japanese athletes drink giant hornet juice. #3643 Food markets in Beijing in China offer candied scorpions on a stick. #3644 In Laos, people eat red ants tossed with salad. #3645 In **2013** a group of London students opened a restaurant specializing in insects. #3646 Dishes included watermelon with caterpillar risotto and ground-up cricket. #3647 Roman **Emperor Nero** started eating dinner in the afternoon. #3648 He would finish eating around dawn! #3649 Sumo wrestlers eat two giant pots of meat stew every day. #3650 This is to make sure they're heavy enough to fight. #3651 Over 2 billion people around the world are overweight. #3652 About 805 million people around the world are sick from hunger. #3653 A lack of vitamin B can cause hair loss and tiredness. #3654 A type of Sardinian cheese has maggots put in it on purpose. #3655 Cider makers used to add meat to their mixture of apples and water. As the meat rotted, it helped the mixure turn to cider. #3656 The meat was usually livestock, but sometimes it came from the rats that fell into the mixture by accident. #3657 Salami develops a mould around its casing while it's being made. #3658 The mould is left on to give it more flavour. #3659 Some wine makers use mouldy grapes to make sweet wines. #3660 Kopi Luwak is the world's most expensive coffee. #3661 It's made from beans eaten then pooed out by a small animal called a palm civet. #3662 Kiviak is an Inuit meal made by stuffing 500 birds into the body of a seal. #3663 This is then eaten by making a hole in the neck and sucking out the juices. #3664 White truffles are edible fungi that sell for thousands of pounds per kilogram. #3665 Miso is a Japanese paste made from rice, barley and soybeans. #3666 This mixture is then combined with fungus. #3667 In China, it's considered a delicacy to leave eggs to rot for months, turning their yolks green, before they're eaten. #3668 A Limburger sandwich is filled with raw onion, mustard and Limburger cheese, which smells like body odour. #3669 Offal is the internal organs of an animal. #3670 The rubbery lining of a cow's stomach is called tripe. #3671 Black pudding is a blood sausage cooked until it goes solid. #3672 Head cheese is the meat from a pig's head, set in jelly. #3673 Ox brain fritters are popular in Cuba. #3674 Thrips are tiny insects that hide in fruit and vegetables. #3675 Oregano can legally contain up to 1,250 insect fragments per 10g. #3676

# 39 ENERGY facts

Energy can't be created or destroyed; it can only be changed (transformed) from one type of energy to another. #3677 Mechanical energy is the energy connected with the motion and position of an object. #3678 Mechanical energy can either be kinetic energy or potential energy. #3679 Kinetic energy is energy of motion – the energy an object has because of its movement. #3680 Potential energy is stored energy of position – the stored energy an object has because of its position. #3681 In lightning, electrical energy transforms into light, heat and sound energy. #3682 The word 'energy' comes from the Greek word *energeia*. #3683 In **1905 Albert Einstein** discovered that energy is related to mass, which led to the discovery of nuclear energy. #3684 Food contains chemical energy used by humans and animals to grow and reproduce. #3685 Plants use energy from the Sun to grow and create oxygen. #3686 **Fossil fuels** are formed from the remains of plants and animals that lived millions of years ago. #3687 Fossil fuels are coal, oil and natural gas. #3688 Most coal we use today formed before the dinosaurs ruled the planet. #3689 The energy stored in fossil fuels comes from the Sun. #3690 Some pollution is caused by energy generation and use. #3691 The world's biggest source of energy for producing electricity comes from **coal**. #3692 Coal formed around 300 million years ago. #3693 It takes millions of years to form, so is not a renewable energy. #3694 Coal is mined in around 100 countries with China producing the most. #3695 The word 'petroleum' means **rock oil**, or oil from earth. #3696 Russia, Saudi Arabia and the United States produce the most oil in the world. #3697 **Solar energy** is made from sunlight. #3698 The Mojave Desert, in USA, is home to the world's largest solar power plant. #3699 Solar cells convert light energy into electricity. #3700 Solar cells are also called photovoltaic cells. #3701 Spacecraft and space stations, such as the International Space Station (ISS), often use solar cells to generate

power. #3702 **Hydropower** converts the energy of moving water into other types of energy. #3703 The Three Gorges Dam is the world's largest **hydroelectric** power station. #3704 It spans the Yangtze River in China. #3705 Hydroelectric power stations use water held in dams to drive turbines and generators. #3706 These turn mechanical energy into electrical energy. #3707 A small number of countries, including Norway, Canada and Brazil, produce most of their electricity through hydropower. #3708 **Nuclear power** produces around 13 per cent of the world's electricity. #3709 Nuclear power uses energy released when atoms split. #3710 There are over 400 nuclear power reactors in use around the world. #3711 Around 30 different countries have operational nuclear reactors. #3712 The Obninsk Nuclear Power Plant, in Russia, was the first to deliver electricity in **1954**. #3713 The largest producers of nuclear power are the United States, France and Japan. #3714 Nuclear power provides around 20 per cent of the electricity used in the United States. #3715

# 11 WONDERFUL
# WIND ENERGY FACTS

**Wind power** has been used for thousands of years. #3716 Ancient Egyptians used wind energy to sail up and down the river Nile. #3717 Windmills first appeared around the 9th century in Persia. #3718 Around 100 different countries use wind power to generate electricity. #3719 Wind energy is clean and renewable. #3720 China is the world's largest producer of wind power. #3721 The UK has the most offshore wind farms in the world. #3722 The large blades of wind turbines can interfere with some radar systems used by weather stations or air traffic controls. #3723 They can be mistaken for planes or different weather patterns. #3724 Modern wind turbines usually have three blades that can reach speeds of over 320 km/h. #3725 The tips of large wind turbines can reach heights up to 200 m. #3726

# 5 FACTS ABOUT
# BIRDS
## OF PREY

Kestrels hover in the air scanning the ground for prey. When they see movement, they dive. #3727

## The peregrine falcon is the world's fastest animal. It reaches

## 300 km/h

when it dives. That's as fast as a bullet train. #3728

Bald eagles build huge nests up to **4 m tall** – taller than **two people** standing on top of each other. #3729

**The secretary bird catches its prey by chasing it on the ground. It kills the prey by stamping on it.**

#3730

The smallest bird of prey is the Asian black-thighed falconet, which is just 15 cm long. #3731

An owl can turn its head almost all of the way round.

#3732

It needs to turn its head because its eyes cannot move in their sockets. The eyes are very large so that it can see at night. #3733

An owl's wings have special downy feathers that allow it to fly very quietly. This helps them to sneak up on prey at night. #3734

**An owl's neck is very flexible because it has 14 bones in it. The human neck has just 7 bones.** #3735

Owls are long-sighted, and cannot focus on anything closer than a few centimetres away. #3736

# 5 TRULY EXTREME EXPERIMENTS

Sir Isaac Newton poked a **LARGE, BLUNT NEEDLE** into his eye to test his ideas about optics (the properties of light). #3737

Italian priest Lazzaro Spallanzani swallowed **TINY BAGS OF FOOD** attached to threads and pulled them up from his stomach after a few hours to find out how food is digested. #3738

A study in 2009 found that cows that have been given names **PRODUCE MORE MILK** than unnamed cows. #3739

By crushing lumps of amber (made from tree resin) scientists can capture tiny puffs of the atmosphere **THE DINOSAURS BREATHED.** #3740

Stubbins Ffirth, a trainee doctor, tried to show **YELLOW FEVER CANNOT BE PASSED BETWEEN PEOPLE**. He dripped vomit from fever patients into cuts on his arms, into his eyes and even swallowed it. (Although he lived, he was wrong – yellow fever is contagious!) #3741

DAISY

# 3 GOBSMACKING ENVIRONMENTAL FACTS

**Recycling one aluminium can** can save enough electricity to power a TV for three hours, and aluminium cans can be recycled an unlimited number of times. #3742

At least **20 million hectares of rainforest** are lost every year, which is as big as England, Scotland and Wales combined. #3743

The **next ice age** is due to start in about 1,500 years, but might be delayed by climate change. #3744

# 9 Horse FACTS

A horse's height is measured in **hands**.
#3745

One hand
equals 10.16 cm.
#3746

**A PONY is a horse that
is under 14.2 hands tall.**
#3747

The oldest recorded horse
was called **Old Billy**.
He lived to the age of 62.
#3748

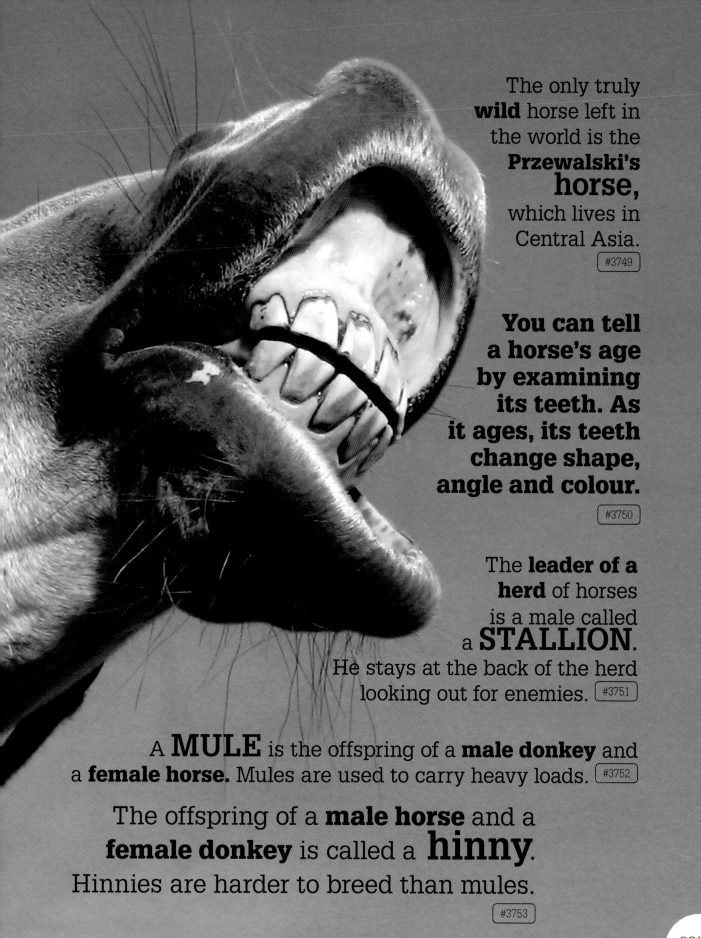

The only truly **wild** horse left in the world is the **Przewalski's horse,** which lives in Central Asia. #3749

**You can tell a horse's age by examining its teeth. As it ages, its teeth change shape, angle and colour.** #3750

The **leader of a herd** of horses is a male called a **STALLION.** He stays at the back of the herd looking out for enemies. #3751

A **MULE** is the offspring of a **male donkey** and a **female horse.** Mules are used to carry heavy loads. #3752

The offspring of a **male horse** and a **female donkey** is called a **hinny.** Hinnies are harder to breed than mules. #3753

# 10 LUDICROUS FACTS ABOUT LAWS

In the UK, it's an **act of treason** to place a postage stamp of the Queen's head upside down. #3754

In France, it is forbidden to call a pig **Napoleon.** #3755

In Singapore, **chewing gum** is banned. #3756

In Florida in the USA, it is illegal to **skateboard** in a police station. #3757

In the UK, the head of any **dead whale** found on the coast is legally the property of the king; the tail belongs to the queen. #3758

In London, it is illegal to **flag down a taxi** if you have the **plague.** #3759

In Alabama in the USA, it's illegal to be **blindfolded** while driving a vehicle. #3760

In Eraclea in Italy, it is forbidden to build **sandcastles.** #3761

In Vermont in the USA, women must obtain written permission from their husbands to wear **false teeth.** #3762

In Switzerland, it's illegal to **flush a toilet** in a flat after 10pm. #3763

# 3 FACTS ABOUT EYE-POPPING PRICES

The world's most expensive camera sold for a record-breaking **£1.74 million**! It was one of only 25 made in 1923. #3764

Napoleon Bonaparte's sword is one of the top-selling antiques on record. It sold for over **£4 million**. #3765

In 1969, the actor Richard Burton paid **£700,000** for a pear-shaped diamond to give to his wife, Elizabeth Taylor. It has since been resold for about **£3.2 million**. #3766

The **skirt** is one of the oldest fashion garments. #3767 It was worn by men and women in Ancient Egyptian times. #3768 The oldest piece of clothing was a loincloth. #3769 This was a piece of material worn like a nappy. #3770 The first lipsticks were made thousands of years ago. #3771 Women used to grind precious gems and decorate their lips with the dust! #3772 In the **1500s** it was very fashionable to pluck your eyebrows. #3773 In **1571 Queen Elizabeth I** declared that everyone over the age of six had to wear hats on a Sunday. #3774 In the 1620s **King Louis XIII** wore a wig to hide his baldness. #3775 Soon, the rest of the court were wearing wigs and the trend spread throughout Europe. #3776 In the 1670s **King Louis XIV** declared that only the aristocracy was allowed to wear red heels. #3777 The first high heels were worn by both men and women. #3778 Men wore them for riding horses, as it kept their feet secure in stirrups. #3779 By around **1740** the trend had died out. #3780 **Napoleon** had brass buttons sewn on the sleeve of his soldiers' uniforms. #3781 This was to discourage them from wiping their noses on their uniforms. #3782 Sandals originated in warm climates where the sole of the foot needed to be protected from the heat, and the top of the foot needed to be cool. #3783 In **1896** the first right-footed and left-footed shoes for children were created by a shoemaker. #3784 He was called **Gustav Hoffmann.** #3785 Before **1822**, all shoes had been identical. #3786 Wearing the wrong shoes can damage your spine. #3787 Before the 19th century, designers used dolls rather than models to showcase their designs. #3788 Up until the 19th century, children were dressed like adults. #3789 The first modern lady's boot was designed for **Queen Victoria** in **1840.** #3790 Victorian widows were expected to wear black for two years after their husbands' deaths. #3791 During the **1860s** dresses were so wide, those wearing them often got stuck in doorways. #3792 The invention of cars in the **1900s** led the way for shorter skirts, so women could get into cars more easily.

#3793 The first *Vogue* magazine was published in the USA in **1892.** #3794 During World War I, the magazine couldn't be delivered in Europe so in **1916** the first UK edition was printed. #3795 The first French issue followed in **1920.** #3796 The first commercial mascara was created by a French chemist called **Eugène Rimmel.** #3797 It became so popular that 'rimmel' is the word for mascara in several languages. #3798 **Perfume** can make you feel better. #3799 Experts have linked scent to emotion – a lavender scent helps you to relax and a lively citrus one will give you an energy boost. #3800 The two most commonly used flower essences in perfume are rose and jasmine. #3801 One of the most expensive **beauty treatments** in the world is a gold-leaf facial. #3802 Pieces of gold are rubbed into the skin to improve the complexion. #3803 It costs around £200 for an hour-long session. #3804 Both the pencil skirt and the A-line **skirt** were created by French designer **Christian Dior.** #3805 Christian Dior was born in **1905.** #3806 His parents wanted him to become a diplomat, but he liked art and wanted to do something more creative. #3807 When he was young, he sold sketches on the street for pocket money. #3808 During World War II, his sister **Catherine Dior** joined the French Resistance, but was captured and put into a concentration camp. #3809 She survived, and in **1947** Dior named his first perfume Miss Dior as a tribute to her. #3810 One of the richest designers in the world is Italian designer **Giorgio Armani.** #3811 Giorgio Armani was born in **1934.** #3812 He originally studied to be a doctor, but after three years, he left university to join the army. #3813 His first job in fashion was as a window dresser in Milan. #3814 In 1916, the US Rubber Company created the first **trainers** – rubber soles with canvas tops. #3815 Soon after, in 1917, the Converse Rubber Shoe Company produced trainers especially for basketball. #3816 The shoes got the nickname 'sneakers' because a person wearing them could sneak up on someone. #3817 The discovery of **Tutankhamun**'s tomb in Egypt in the

# 80 fabulous

**1920s** led to Egyptian-style art on handbags and purses. #3818 **Vintage** clothing dates from the **1920s**. #3819 Anything made in the current time that includes styles or ideas of the past is considered **retro**. #3820 **Lacoste**'s little crocodile was the first designer logo. #3821 It was created in **1933**. #3822 The first fashion week was held in New York in **1943**. #3823 There are about 40 'Fashion Week' events in different cities throughout the world. #3824 The biggest are held in New York, Milan, Paris and London. #3825 The average fashion show is just over ten minutes long. #3826 The **bikini** dates back to ancient times. #3827 Ancient Roman artwork shows women wearing them. #3828 In the **1890s** women would enter the sea through a changing room on wheels. #3829 They would also sew weights into the hems of their swimming garments to prevent them from rising up and revealing their legs. #3830 In **1907** Australian swimmer **Annette Kellerman** was arrested in USA for wearing a revealing bathing suit on the beach. #3831 In **1946** a French engineer called **Louis Réard** created the modern bikini. #3832 He named it after a nuclear testing plant, Bikini Atoll, hoping it would be an explosive item in the history of fashion. #3833 Bikinis were banned from Miss World in **1952** and also in several countries. #3834 In Majorca, holidaymakers can be fined if they refuse to cover up when not on the beach. #3835 Anyone wearing their bikini or swimsuit in a bar, restaurant or shop can be fined £500. #3836 Men's **shirts** are buttoned up on the right and women's on the left. #3837 Around 2 billion t-shirts are sold in a year. #3838 Astronaut **Chris Hadfield** claims astronauts don't wash their clothes in space. #3839 They throw them out into the Earth's atmosphere, where they burn up. #3840 The low-hanging, baggy-pants style originated in prisons, where inmates are not allowed to wear belts. #3841 A person who collects ties is known as a grabatologist. #3842 The largest fashion franchise is **Benetton**. #3843 It has more than 6,000 stores around the world #3844 They sell around 150 million garments a year. #3845 The highest-paid model in the world is **Gisele Bündchen**. #3846

## 10 FACTS ABOUT COCO CHANEL

French designer **Coco Chanel** changed the way women dressed in the early 20th century. #3847 She created loose and comfy clothing that freed them from tight and fussy styles. #3848 She was born in **1883**. #3849 She spent some of her childhood in an orphanage. #3850 Her first perfume Chanel No. 5 was introduced in **1922**. #3851 It was the first perfume to mix natural and artificial ingredients. #3852 She popularised the Little Black Dress in **1926**. #3853 She also made costume jewellery popular, mixing real and fake jewels. #3854 She died in **1971** at the Ritz Hotel in Paris. #3855 She was 87 years old. #3856

## 12 JEAN GEMS

The first **denim** fabric was made in Nimes, France. #3857 Denim got its name from the french for 'fabric of Nimes'. #3858 In **1872 Jacob Davis** created the first jeans. #3859 He couldn't afford the patent so asked his fabric supplier **Levi Strauss** for help. #3860 They first called their invention waist overalls. #3861 They were created for mine workers. #3862 Rivets were sewn onto jeans to make them stronger, especially on the pockets. #3863 In **1934** the first pair of women's jeans were called Lady Levis. #3864 They were designed for women who worked on ranches. #3865 Jeans were banned in schools, restaurants and theatres in the **1950s** because they were seen as a sign of rebellion. #3866 The average American owns seven pairs of jeans. #3867 You can buy jeans for your pets! #3868

# FASHION facts

# 4 ROCKING FACTS ABOUT ROCKS

The **oldest known rock** is in Canada and is 4 billion years old. #3869

There are **bacteria** that live in the spaces between crystals inside rocks. #3870

Sound travels **TEN TIMES FASTER** through rock than through air. #3871

Although rubies are red and sapphires are blue, they are the **SAME ROCK** – impurities make them different colours. #3872

# 5 FACTS ABOUT EARTH SCIENCE

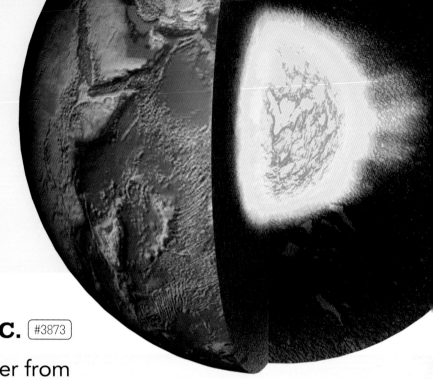

The temperature at the Earth's core is over **5,500°C.** #3873

Much of this is heat left over from when the Earth first formed. #3874

The last magnetic pole reversal (the North and South Poles swapping over) happened around 780,000 years ago and experts believe the next flip could happen soon. #3875

Scientists can sample the ancient atmosphere – from around **800,000 YEARS AGO** – from the bubbles in ice they collect in Antarctica. #3876

**FOSSILS** of **MARINE ANIMALS** are found on Mount Everest and throughout the Himalayas, as the land that forms them was once under the sea. #3877

# 7 BLUE WHALE FACTS

The blue whale is the **BIGGEST ANIMAL** that has ever lived, at up to

## 30 M long. #3878

It weighs **150 tonnes**

as much as **24 elephants.** #3879

Its heart weighs **600 kg,** and is the size of a small car. #3880

It can eat **up to 4 tonnes of krill** in one day. #3881

A baby blue whale puts on about **90 KG** in weight per day for the first year of its life. #3882

Its **TONGUE** can weigh **as much as a whole elephant**. #3883

Its **tail** is **8m wide** – almost as long as the world long jump record. #3884

# 50 SUPER SPY facts

**John Dee** was an astrologer and one of the best-known secret agents for **Queen Elizabeth I**.
#3885

He signed any letters he sent to her as 007.
#3886

**Daniel Defoe**, author of *Robinson Crusoe,* was also a spy.
#3887

One of America's first spies was soldier **Nathan Hale**.
#3888

At the age of 21, he spied on British troop movements in the American Revolutionary War.
#3889

He was arrested and executed, but became a hero following his bravery.
#3890

**Abraham Lincoln** created the United States Secret Service in **1865**.
#3891

Its main function was to stop people making fake money.
#3892

Abraham Lincoln was shot on the day he created the service and died the following day.
#3893

It was the first time a US president had been assassinated.
#3894

After two more presidents were shot, the Secret Service was assigned to protect the president.
#3895

Until **2003**, it was under the charge of the Department of the Treasury.
#3896

The British Secret Intelligence Service was formed in **1909**.
#3897

Royal Navy Commander **Mansfield Smith-Cumming** and British Army Captain **Vernon Kell** were its leaders.
#3898

Their objective during World War I was to find German spies.
#3899

During the war, around 120 spies were sent to Britain.
#3900

Around 65 of them were caught.
#3901

The service is commonly known as MI6 (Military Intelligence, Section 6).
#3902

Before he became a famous writer **Roald Dahl** was a fighter pilot, then worked at the British Embassy in Washington.
#3903

The MI6 operates alongside the Security Service (MI5).
#3904

MI5 deals with threats to national security within the UK.
#3905

MI6 deals with threats abroad.
#3906

MI6's headquarters are at Vauxhall Cross, in London, England.
#3907

MI5 estimates there are as many Russian agents in London today as there were during the Cold War.
#3908

The real name of the spy **Mata Hari** was **Margaretha Geertruida Zelle**.
#3909

While working as a dancer in France she was arrested for spying for Germany.
#3910

At her execution in **1917** she wore a stylish new outfit.
#3911

The escape artist **Harry Houdini** may have been a spy for Britain and the USA. #3912

It's believed he passed on information he found out while performing for important kings and rulers around the world. #3913

During World War II, some German leaders were suspicious of the UK Scouts – they thought it was a spy movement. #3914

The Americans recruited the Mafia to help in the invasion of Italy in World War II. #3915

The help that Mafia boss **Lucky Luciano** gave led to his release from prison. #3916

The Cambridge Five were British double agents who passed information to Russia during World War II and into the **1950s**. #3917

Only four were ever caught, nobody knows who the fifth agent was. #3918

Married couple **Julius** and **Ethel Rosenberg** were American Communists executed in **1953** for passing nuclear secrets to the Soviet Union. #3919

**George Koval** was another Soviet spy who stole America's nuclear secrets. #3920

It was only discovered he was a spy in **2002**. #3921

The Russians once made a lipstick for their agents that was also a gun. #3922

A place where secret messages are left is known as a 'drop'. #3923

**Ian Fleming**, author of the James Bond books, was a real-life spy. #3924 He served in the British Naval Intelligence during World War II. #3925

During World War II, the explorer **Jacques Cousteau** posed as a diver in France so he could spy on German naval movements. #3926

He received France's Legion of Honour for his efforts. #3927

In the **1960s**, the US Central Intelligence Agency (CIA) spent millions of dollars on a spy kit for a cat. #3928

The cat would then be able to follow Russian spies without suspicion. #3929

Sadly the cat was run over on its first mission. #3930

The CIA headquarters is in Virginia, USA. #3931

Located there is a museum that only spies can visit. #3932

All kinds of amazing gadgets are on display, including a dollar coin that holds microfilm and an underwater spy drone that looks like a catfish, codename Charlie. #3933

All new CIA agents are given a tour on their first day. #3934

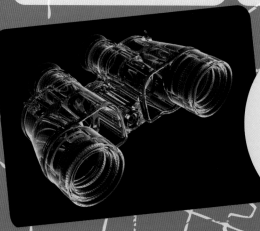

# 5 SECRETS OF THE UNIVERSE

In 2012, a British space scientist used a special maths equation called the **DRAKE EQUATION** to predict that we have four intelligent alien civilizations in our galaxy. #3935

Instead of 'little green men', the scientist also predicts that they may look like **FOOTBALL-PITCH SIZED JELLYFISH,** with onion-shaped limbs and an orange underbelly! #3936

In 2011, astronomers discovered a star that they believe is composed **ENTIRELY OF DIAMOND.** It measures 60,000 kilometres across – five times the size of Earth. #3937

Earth may have **FOUR MORE MOONS.** In 1986, a scientist discovered an asteroid in orbit around the Sun that appeared to be following Earth. Since then, at least three similar asteroids have been discovered. #3938

Earth is **NOT FLAT** – but **THE UNIVERSE MIGHT BE**! Using Einstein's Theory of General Relativity and scientific measurements, scientists believe it is. #3939

The things we know – planets, stars, galaxies, black holes – make up just **4%** of the Universe.

The rest is unknown stuff – **23% DARK MATTER** and **73% DARK ENERGY** that scientists still can't really explain. #3940

# 13 FACTS ABOUT

## STRANGE
### SEA
### CREATURES

The blobfish's body is mostly made of light jelly-like tissue. This helps it to float using very little energy. #3941

The mantis shrimp's eyes are mounted on long stalks. #3942

**Young boxfish** have bodies shaped like cubes. #3943

The gurnard takes its name from the 'gurr' sound it makes when it is caught. #3944

The male anglerfish is just a couple of centimetres long. He is dwarfed by the female, which is 20 cm long. #3945

The male anglerfish fuses his head to the side of a female, and taps into her bloodstream for food. #3946

**The body of the leafy sea dragon is covered in stalks, which make it look like seaweed.** #3947

The female jawfish lays eggs, but the male carries them around in his mouth. #3948

# GIANTS OF THE SEA

The giant spider crab can grow to 3 m wide. #3950

**The sunflower starfish has up to 40 arms.** #3951

Manta rays have wingspans of up to 3.5 m. #3952

The lion's mane jellyfish has a bell-shaped body that is up to 2 m wide. #0349

The lion's mane jellyfish's tentacles can reach up to 37 m – the height of a ten-storey building. #3953

While dinosaurs roamed on land during the Mesozoic era, amazing flying creatures soared overhead. #3954 Pterosaurs were flying reptiles that evolved in the Triassic period. #3955 They were the first vertebrates (animals with backbones) to evolve powered flight. #3956 They were the largest creatures ever to fly. #3957 They had short bodies and long legs and tails. #3958 Each wing was made from a flap of skin, which stretched from the hind leg to the forearm. #3959 Pterosaurs would flap their wings to fly and tuck their wings away when walking on land. #3960 150 different species of pterosaur have been discovered. #3961 Experts believe there are probably thousands more. #3962 Recent research has revealed that pterosaurs might have been a little bit fluffy. #3963 Their eggs were soft-shelled and only a few have been found so far. #3964 Dinosaur eggs, by comparison, were hard shelled. #3965 By the time a pterosaur hatched, its wings were fully formed. #3966 Fish was their favourite food, so they mostly lived by water. #3967 Some scientists believe they lived in large groups, like birds today. #3968 Many pterosaurs had head crests, possibly to counterbalance their long beaks. #3969 **Eudimorphodon** was one of the first pterosaurs, evolving in the late Triassic period, around 210 million years ago. #3970 It gobbled fish out of the sea with its 110 teeth!

#3971 Its wingspan was around 1 m. #3972 At the end of its tail was a diamond-shaped flap, which may have helped it steer through the sky. #3973 **Nemicolopterus** is the smallest pterosaur known and was about the size of a sparrow. #3974 Its curved claws led experts to believe it perched high up in the trees to feed on foliage and probably to avoid huge meat-eaters like **Tyrannosaurus rex** below. #3975 **Pteranodon** lived during the Cretaceous period, around 85–75 million years ago. #3976 It was named by Othniel C Marsh. #3977 Its name means 'winged' and 'toothless'. #3978 Pteranodon was a carnivore – it ate fish and small marine animals. #3979 Its wingspan was around 6 m. #3980

# 42 fantastic facts on PREHISTORIC FLIERS

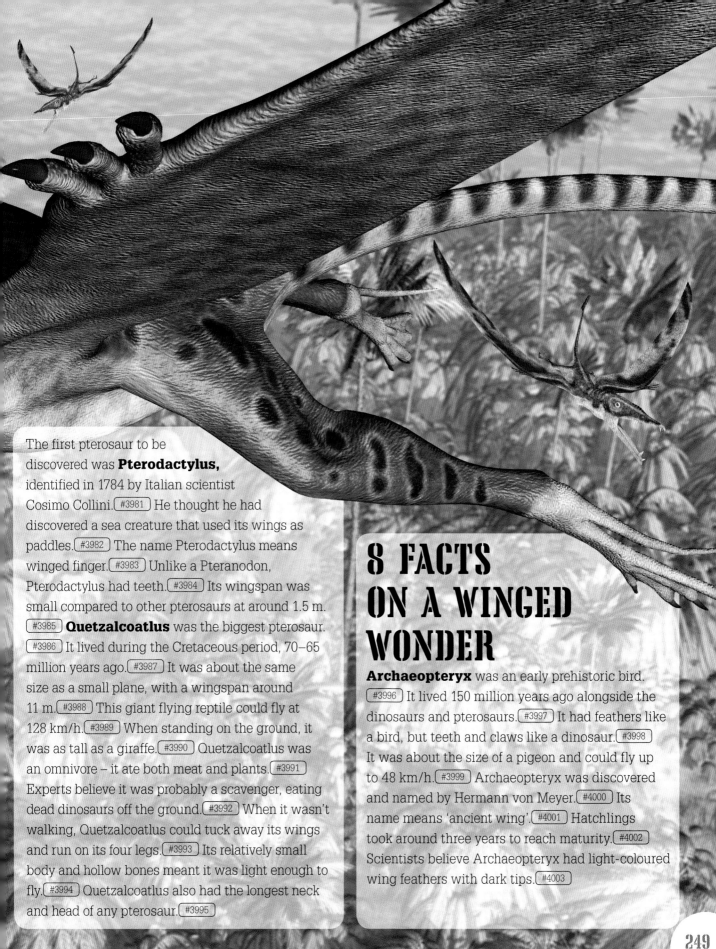

The first pterosaur to be discovered was **Pterodactylus,** identified in 1784 by Italian scientist Cosimo Collini. #3981 He thought he had discovered a sea creature that used its wings as paddles. #3982 The name Pterodactylus means winged finger. #3983 Unlike a Pteranodon, Pterodactylus had teeth. #3984 Its wingspan was small compared to other pterosaurs at around 1.5 m. #3985 **Quetzalcoatlus** was the biggest pterosaur. #3986 It lived during the Cretaceous period, 70–65 million years ago. #3987 It was about the same size as a small plane, with a wingspan around 11 m. #3988 This giant flying reptile could fly at 128 km/h. #3989 When standing on the ground, it was as tall as a giraffe. #3990 Quetzalcoatlus was an omnivore – it ate both meat and plants. #3991 Experts believe it was probably a scavenger, eating dead dinosaurs off the ground. #3992 When it wasn't walking, Quetzalcoatlus could tuck away its wings and run on its four legs. #3993 Its relatively small body and hollow bones meant it was light enough to fly. #3994 Quetzalcoatlus also had the longest neck and head of any pterosaur. #3995

# 8 FACTS ON A WINGED WONDER

**Archaeopteryx** was an early prehistoric bird. #3996 It lived 150 million years ago alongside the dinosaurs and pterosaurs. #3997 It had feathers like a bird, but teeth and claws like a dinosaur. #3998 It was about the size of a pigeon and could fly up to 48 km/h. #3999 Archaeopteryx was discovered and named by Hermann von Meyer. #4000 Its name means 'ancient wing'. #4001 Hatchlings took around three years to reach maturity. #4002 Scientists believe Archaeopteryx had light-coloured wing feathers with dark tips. #4003

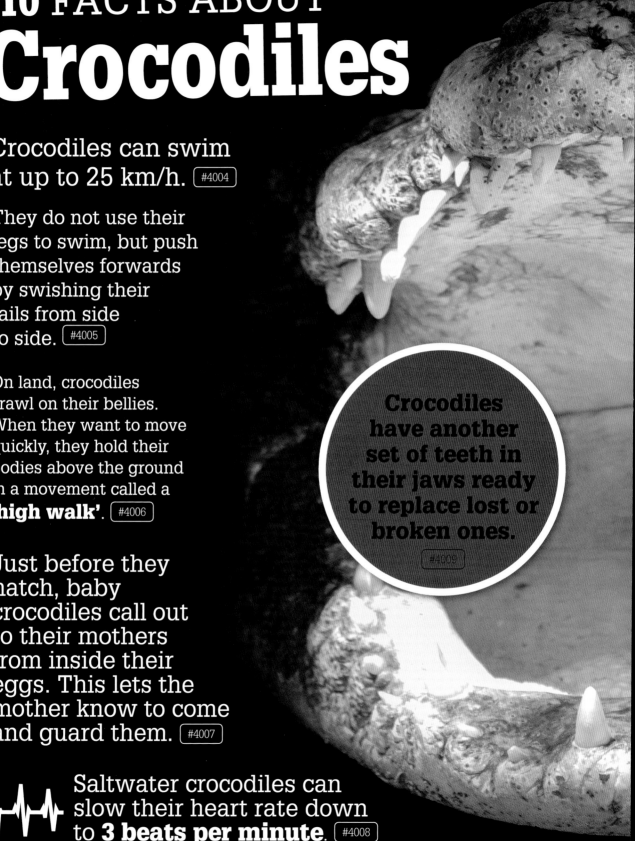

# 10 FACTS ABOUT
# Crocodiles

Crocodiles can swim at up to 25 km/h. #4004

They do not use their legs to swim, but push themselves forwards by swishing their tails from side to side. #4005

On land, crocodiles crawl on their bellies. When they want to move quickly, they hold their bodies above the ground in a movement called a **'high walk'**. #4006

Just before they hatch, baby crocodiles call out to their mothers from inside their eggs. This lets the mother know to come and guard them. #4007

**Crocodiles have another set of teeth in their jaws ready to replace lost or broken ones.** #4009

Saltwater crocodiles can slow their heart rate down to **3 beats per minute**. #4008

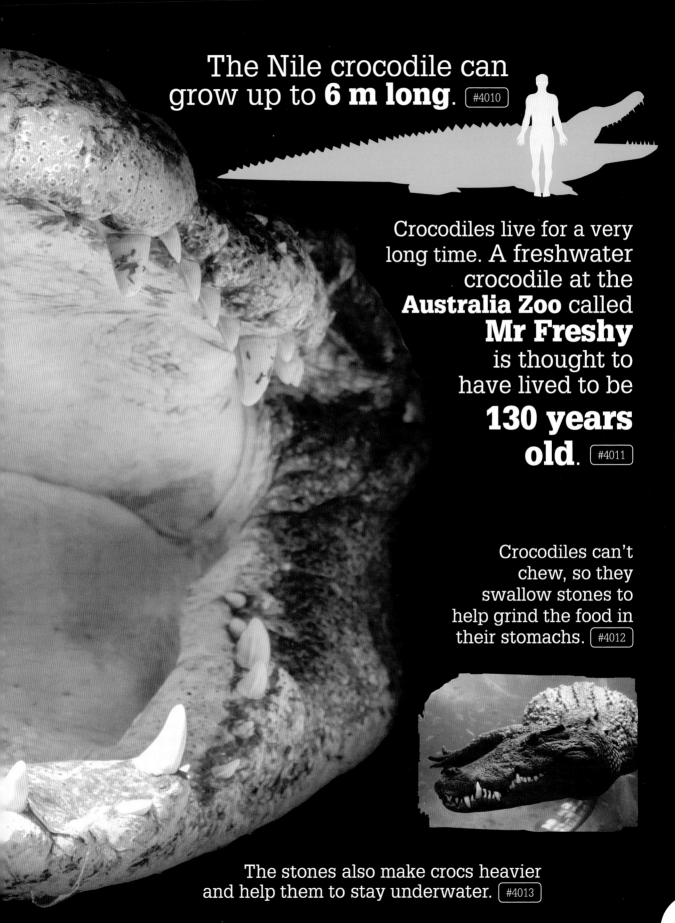

# The Nile crocodile can grow up to **6 m long**. #4010

Crocodiles live for a very long time. A freshwater crocodile at the **Australia Zoo** called **Mr Freshy** is thought to have lived to be **130 years old**. #4011

Crocodiles can't chew, so they swallow stones to help grind the food in their stomachs. #4012

The stones also make crocs heavier and help them to stay underwater. #4013

The **world's largest swamp,** the Pantanal in Brazil, covers an area larger than England. #4014

The vast **Ganges Delta** in Asia, a swampy area where two mighty rivers meet, covers an area the size of Scotland and Wales. #4015

The **Great Rift Valley** is a **6,000 kilometre trench** that has been created where two of the giant plates that make up Earth's crust are pulling apart. #4016

Earth's deepest mine is TauTona Goldmine in South Africa, 3,900 metres deep. #4017

The deepest hole ever bored, Kola Borehole in Russia, descends 12,200 metres! #4018

All the gold mined in a year would fit inside the average living room. #4019

The largest gold nugget ever found is the 'Welcome Stranger', found in 1869 in Australia. #4020

The first diamond found in South Africa was picked up by children on a beach. #4021

The world's largest diamond, the Cullinan Diamond, was the size of a large egg. #4022

The world's most valuable gem is painite, a small crystal found only in Myanmar. #4023

Earth's oldest fossils are 3.4 billion years old. #4024

The world's largest pearl, the Pearl of Lao Tzu, is about the same size as a football. #4025

Only one in a thousand oysters contains a pearl. #4026

# 5 FACTS ABOUT FISHING BIRDS

A wood stork can snap its beak shut around a fish in

## 25 milliseconds.

#4027

The American white pelican can hold 11.5 lt of water in its bill. #4028

As well as doing their own fishing, **pelicans poach food from other birds**, chasing them until they drop their prey.

#4029

When it lands, a **CORMORANT** will **STRETCH ITS WINGS OUT** to dry them after diving in water.

#4030

## Gannets dive
into the sea at speeds of up to 100 km/h from heights of up to 30 m.

#4031

# 5 FACTS ABOUT
# GULLS

Gulls drop molluscs onto rocks to break them open to eat. #4032

Seagulls are **CARING PARENTS**. Males and females pair for life, and take turns incubating their eggs. #4033

A herring gull chick taps on a red spot on its parents' beaks to get them to **regurgitate their food** for the chick to eat. #4034

Gulls are omnivores, and will **scavenge human bins** for anything remotely edible. #4035

Gulls **STAMP ON THE GROUND** to imitate rainfall. This **TRICKS WORMS** into coming to the surface. #4036

# 10 WATERY OCEAN WONDERS

The Atlantic Ocean is getting **2.5 centimetres wider each year**! #4037

The **Mariana Trench** in the Pacific is so deep, it could submerge Mount Everest. #4038

The Pacific Ocean has an average depth of **4,200 metres**. #4039

The Pacific Ocean has more than **25,000 islands**. #4040

Sea water freezes at a **lower temperature** than fresh water, at -1.9°C. #4041

In 1933, a US Navy ship caught in a Pacific storm survived a **34-metre high wave** – the biggest wave at sea ever recorded. #4042

The world's **longest mountain range** is called the mid-ocean ridge – it spans 65,000 kilometres around the globe. #4043

The water in a wave doesn't travel forwards like you might think, it goes **round in a circle**. #4044

If you could remove all the **salt** from the oceans, it would cover Earth's dry land to a depth of **1.5 metres**. #4045

In 1900, 6,000 people died when the town of **Galveston, USA**, was swamped by waves. #4046

The **Amazon River** carries more water than the next eight biggest rivers combined. #4047

Lake Nyos in West Africa, which lies in the crater of an inactive volcano, once released a cloud of **poisonous volcanic gas** that killed 1,700 people. #4048

The Iguazu Falls in South America consists of **275 waterfalls** along 2 km of the Iguazu River. #4049

# 61 incredible INVENTIONS

The **abacus** was invented in **2400 BC** in Babylonia. #4050 **Boomerangs** were first used by Indigenous Australians thousands of years ago as a hunting weapon. #4051 **Paper** was invented in China in the 2nd century. #4052 **Johann Gutenberg** created the first **printing press** with movable type in about **1440**. #4053 The first **pocket watch** was invented by **Peter Henlein** around **1510**. #4054 During his lifetime, **Galileo Galilei** came up with ideas for a compass, telescope and thermometer. #4055 **Leonardo da Vinci** drew designs for a tank, a helicopter, a submarine and a parachute. #4056 **Sir Francis Bacon** invented frozen chicken in **1626**. He died from a chill caught while experimenting with his freezing method. #4057 In **1656 Christiaan Huygens** invented the pendulum clock. #4058 The first piano, exhibited in **1709**, was invented by an Italian called **Bartolomeo di Francesco Cristofori**. #4059 It was originally called a *gravicembalo col piano e forte*, which means soft and loud keyboard instrument. This was shortened to pianoforte and finally piano. #4060 16th-century author **Sir John Hartington** came up with the idea of the toilet. #4061 He installed a working prototype in the bathroom of his godmother – **Queen Elizabeth I**. #4062 The first patent for a flushing water closet was issued to **Alexander Cumming** in **1775**. #4063 **Thomas Crapper** later came up with three patented inventions to improve the workings of the flushing water closet. #4064

In **1822 Charles Babbage** designed the first mechanical computer. #4065 He called it his 'difference engine'. #4066 The rubber band was invented by **Stephen Perry** around **1845**. #4067 **Alfred Nobel** created dynamite in **1867**. #4068 In **1898 Nikola Tesla** created the first remote control using radio waves. #4069 **John Hetrick** invented the airbag in **1952**. #4070 Airbags were first introduced to cars by General Motors in **1973**. #4071 In **1770 William Addis** was in jail for rioting when he came up with a good idea for cleaning teeth by threading some bristles through holes drilled in an animal bone. #4072 In **1795** the French military offered a cash prize to anyone who could come up with a way to keep food fresh. #4073 **Nicolas Appert** took 15 years, but won the prize in **1810** with his idea for canned food. #4074 The first can opener didn't appear for another 48 years, until **Ezra Warner** patented one in **1858**. #4075 The can opener most people use today, with a wheel that rolls around the edge of the can, was invented in **1870** by **William Lyman**. #4076 **Alessandro Volta** made the first electrical battery in around **1800**. #4077 In **1826 John Walker** created the first matches. He called them 'Friction Lights'. #4078 Morse code was invented by **Samuel Morse** in **1832**. #4079 In **1838** Morse demonstrated the first telegraph machine. #4080 **Thomas Edison** has over 1,000 patents in his name. #4081 He invented the phonograph, which could record and play back sound. In **1877** he made the world's first recording, using the song 'Mary Had A Little Lamb'. #4082 The safety pin was invented in three hours in **1849** by **Walter Hunt**. #4083 **Joseph Glidden** came up with the idea for barbed wire in **1876**. #4084 **Alexander Graham Bell** patented the first telephone in **1876**. #4085 The Yale lock was invented by **Linus Yale** in **1865**. #4086 Around **1880 William Upjohn** created a pill that could dissolve in the stomach. #4087 **Charles Cretors** operated the first popcorn-making machine and sold his popcorn on the streets of Chicago in **1885**. #4088

Around **1888 John Dunlop** came up with the idea for the world's first pneumatic (operated by gas or air) tyre. #4089 Inventor **Whitcomb Judson** has around 30 patents to his name. #4090 His most famous patent is for the zipper, which he patented in **1892**. #4091 An air-conditioning machine was invented in **1902** by **Willis Carrier.** #4092 **Albert J. Parkhouse** came up with the idea for a wire coathanger in **1903.** #4093 The crossword puzzle was invented in **1913.** #4094 Its creator was a journalist called **Arthur Wynne.** #4095 In **1928 Alexander Fleming** accidentally discovered penicillin, an antibiotic. #4096 In **1927 Otto Frederick Rohwedder** invented a machine to slice bread. #4097 In **1938 Chester Carlson** invented a new process of printing images and the first photocopy was made. #4098 **Laszlo Biro** invented the first ballpoint pen in **1938.** #4099 The ejection seat was invented by **James Martin**. The first human used one in **1946.** #4100 The idea for double yellow lines on roads came from a man called **George Musgrave** in **1947.** #4101 Velcro was invented in **1948** after a scientist found sticky seeds stuck to his dog's fur. Under a microscope, he saw that the seeds had tiny hooks which latched on to the hairs. #4102 Barcodes were designed in **1949** by **Norman Woodland**. #4103 He extended the dots and dashes of Morse code into bands. #4104 **Martin Cooper**, and his Motorola team, created the world's first mobile phone. #4105 The first mobile handset was created in **1973** and weighed around 2 kg. #4106 The first phone cost around £3,000. #4107 The battery only lasted 20 minutes. #4108 In **2007** a woman invented a bra that converts into two emergency gas masks. #4109 The Wasabi fire alarm, invented in **2009**, releases the smell of wasabi (a strong horseradish) to warn deaf people there is a fire. #4110

# 39 facts about ANCIENT EGYPT

## 11 FACTS ABOUT THE BOY PHARAOH

The most famous Egyptian pharaoh (ruler) is **Tutankhamun**. #4111 He was born about **1336 BC** and became pharaoh when he was nine years old. #4112 His tomb was discovered by a team of archaeologists in **1922**, nearly 3,000 years after his death. #4113 Over 3,000 treasures had been placed in his tomb to help him in the afterlife. #4114 These included oars, toys and a trumpet. #4115 X-rays of his mummy show that he was about 18 years old when he died. #4116 The cause of his death is still a mystery. #4117 Tutankhamun's mummy was inside the smallest of three coffins, stacked one inside the other. It was made of solid gold. #4118 The coffins were inside a sarcophagus – a box and lid carved from stone. #4119 Rubble from the hillside above later fell and buried the entrance of the tomb. #4120 Tutankhamun's tomb is the only intact pharaoh's tomb ever found. #4121

**Ancient Egyptians** believed that the world was flat and the River **Nile** flowed through the centre of it. #4122 The Ancient Egyptians lived along the banks of the River Nile. #4123 Farmers first settled in Egypt around **5000 BC**. #4124 About 95 per cent of Egypt's population still live in the Nile Valley (the area next to the river). #4125 All of Ancient Egypt depended on the Nile for water, food and transportation. #4126 Before modern dams were built the River Nile would flood the surrounding area each year. #4127 The flood would coat the land on either side of the river with thick black mud. #4128 This mud was ideal for growing crops. #4129 Egyptians **mummified** (preserved) a dead person's body so the person would live on forever in the afterlife. #4130 During mummification, most of the major organs were removed and placed in jars. #4131 The brain was removed through the nostrils

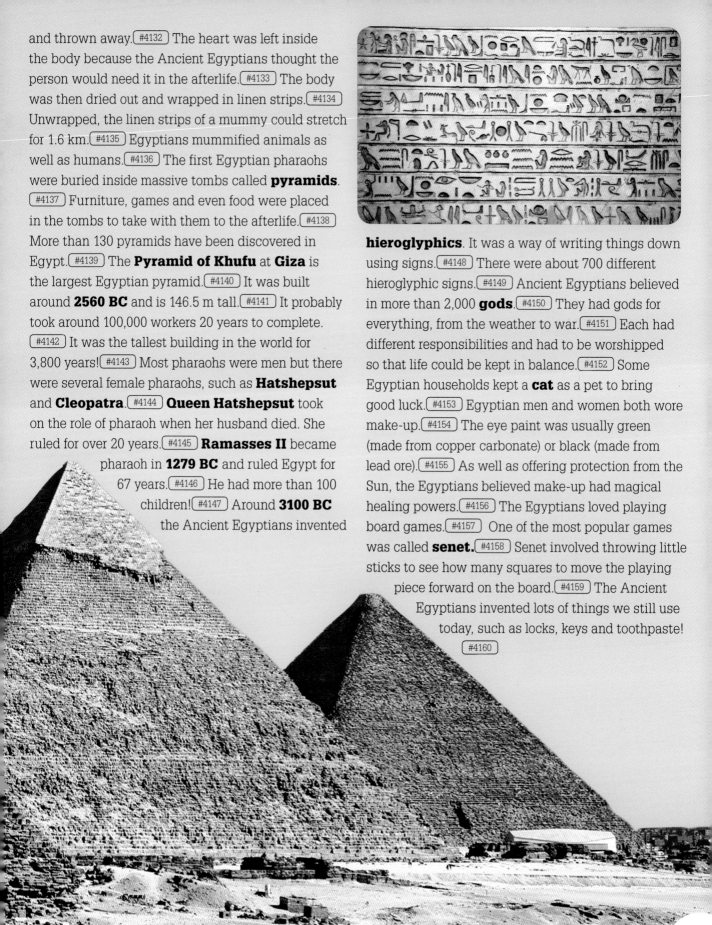

and thrown away. #4132 The heart was left inside the body because the Ancient Egyptians thought the person would need it in the afterlife. #4133 The body was then dried out and wrapped in linen strips. #4134 Unwrapped, the linen strips of a mummy could stretch for 1.6 km. #4135 Egyptians mummified animals as well as humans. #4136 The first Egyptian pharaohs were buried inside massive tombs called **pyramids**. #4137 Furniture, games and even food were placed in the tombs to take with them to the afterlife. #4138 More than 130 pyramids have been discovered in Egypt. #4139 The **Pyramid of Khufu** at **Giza** is the largest Egyptian pyramid. #4140 It was built around **2560 BC** and is 146.5 m tall. #4141 It probably took around 100,000 workers 20 years to complete. #4142 It was the tallest building in the world for 3,800 years! #4143 Most pharaohs were men but there were several female pharaohs, such as **Hatshepsut** and **Cleopatra**. #4144 **Queen Hatshepsut** took on the role of pharaoh when her husband died. She ruled for over 20 years. #4145 **Ramasses II** became pharaoh in **1279 BC** and ruled Egypt for 67 years. #4146 He had more than 100 children! #4147 Around **3100 BC** the Ancient Egyptians invented **hieroglyphics**. It was a way of writing things down using signs. #4148 There were about 700 different hieroglyphic signs. #4149 Ancient Egyptians believed in more than 2,000 **gods**. #4150 They had gods for everything, from the weather to war. #4151 Each had different responsibilities and had to be worshipped so that life could be kept in balance. #4152 Some Egyptian households kept a **cat** as a pet to bring good luck. #4153 Egyptian men and women both wore make-up. #4154 The eye paint was usually green (made from copper carbonate) or black (made from lead ore). #4155 As well as offering protection from the Sun, the Egyptians believed make-up had magical healing powers. #4156 The Egyptians loved playing board games. #4157 One of the most popular games was called **senet.** #4158 Senet involved throwing little sticks to see how many squares to move the playing piece forward on the board. #4159 The Ancient Egyptians invented lots of things we still use today, such as locks, keys and toothpaste! #4160

# 6 FACTS ABOUT WEASELS, STOATS AND MINKS

The weasel can take down prey **ten times its own weight.** #4162

Weasels need to eat **a quarter of their own body weight** of food every day. #4163

The fur of a weasel **turns white in the winter** to hide it against the snow. #4161

Stoats are **strong swimmers,** and have been known to swim for more than a kilometre. #4164

The American mink **hisses** when it is threatened, and **purrs** when it is feeling contented. #4165

*Mink are fast swimmers, and will hunt fish that are bigger than themselves.* #4166

# 3 SHOCKING SPACE FACTS

Your skin would **inflate like a balloon** if you went to space without a spacesuit. #4167

The Sun is about **halfway** through its 10 billion-year lifetime. #4168

Saturn's famous rings are made of **millions of chunks of rock and ice**. #4169

# 10 WOW FACTS ABOUT OUTER PLANETS

Jupiter spins **faster than any other planet.** A day there only lasts about 10 hours. #4170

The giant Red Spot on Jupiter is a **whirling storm** that has been raging for at least 300 years. #4171

Jupiter is **so huge** that all the other planets in the solar system would **fit inside it.** #4172

Jupiter has the **most moons** of any planet – at least 63. #4173

There are a total of **seven rings** orbiting Saturn. #4174

Saturn is the **lightest planet** in the solar system – it is mostly made up of hydrogen and helium. #4175

Seasons last over **20 years** on the planet Uranus. #4176

Uranus is **tilted on its side** so one of its poles always faces the Sun. #4177

Neptune has howling winds **10 times stronger** than those on Earth. #4178

Neptune's moon, Triton, is one of the **coldest places in the solar system**, with a temperature of -235°C. #4179

# 79 fantastic FILM facts

The first machine patented in the United States that showed animated pictures was called zoopraxiscope. Most people called it the wheel of life. `#4180` Patented in **1867** by **William Lincoln**, moving drawings or photographs were watched through a slot in the zoopraxiscope. `#4181` Brothers **Louis** and **Auguste Lumière** were the first to present projected, moving, photographic pictures to a paying audience. `#4182` Louis is commonly credited as inventing the first motion picture camera in **1895**. `#4183` Silent films were often accompanied by a pianist or a narrator. `#4184` The oldest continuously working film studio in the world is Ealing Studios (previously known as Will Barker Studios). `#4185` It has created movies since **1902**. `#4186` Universal Studios was named by its founder **Carl Laemmle** after he saw a van with the words Universal Pipe Fittings on. `#4187` The first stuntman was ex-cavalryman **Frank Hanaway**. `#4188` He starred in *The Great Train Robbery* in **1903** and could fall off a horse without hurting himself. `#4189` The author with the most films is **William Shakespeare**. `#4190` **Count Dracula** is the most played horror movie character. `#4191` The Hollywood star who has played the most leading roles in feature films was **John Wayne**. `#4192` He appeared in 153 movies. `#4193` The first film ever made in Hollywood was **D. W. Griffith's** *In Old California* in **1910**. `#4194` The first custard pie thrown in a film was in *A Noise from the Deep* in **1913**. `#4195` It was thrown by **Mabel Normand** at **Fatty Arbuckle**. `#4196` The world's oldest open-air cinema is in Broome, Australia. `#4197` It has been showing films since **1916**. `#4198` *The Jazz Singer* made in **1927** was the first 'talkie' picture (a film with a soundtrack, rather than a silent film). `#4199` *To Have and Have Not* made in **1945** is the only instance when a Nobel prize-winning author's work was adapted by another Nobel prize-winning author. `#4200` **Ernest Hemingway**'s novel of the same name was adapted for the screen by **William Faulkner**. `#4201` The first patent for a drive-in cinema was issued in **1933** to **Richard Hollingshead**. `#4202` He opened the first one in New Jersey, USA, on a site for 400 cars. `#4203` The first movie to gross over £65 million was *Jaws* in **1975**. `#4204` *Star Wars* was originally prefixed by the word 'the'. `#4205` During filming of *Wallace & Gromit: The Curse of the Were-Rabbit*, animators used 2,844 kg of plasticine. `#4206` The previous record was held by *Chicken Run* which used 2,380 kg. `#4207` The ruby slippers worn by **Judy Garland** in *The Wizard of Oz* sold in auction in **2000** for nearly £451,000. `#4208` No one is sure how many pairs were made for the film, or where they all are. `#4209` The most films seen in one year is 1,132 by **Maggie Correa-Avilés** in Puerto Rico. `#4210` The first film to have a budget of £65 million was *True Lies*. `#4211` It starred **Arnold Schwarzenegger** and **Jamie Lee Curtis**. `#4212` *Toy Story*, made in **1995**, was the first feature film created entirely with computer-generated imagery (CGI). `#4213` Over 800,000 hours of mathematical equations went into the film, which works out to more than a week of computer time for every second on the screen. `#4214` The largest permanent IMAX theatre is in Sydney, Australia. `#4215` It measures around 35 m by 29 m. `#4216` It opened in **1996** and can seat 540 people. `#4217` With an alleged budget of £184 million, *Avatar* is one of the most expensive movies of all time. `#4218` **Marlon Brando**'s personal script from *The Godfather* sold for around £175,000 in an auction in **2005**. `#4219` **Audrey Hepburn**'s little black dress from *Breakfast at Tiffany's* sold for almost £660,000 in **2006**. `#4220` *Avatar* was the first movie to gross over £1.2 billion. `#4221` This made it the most successful movie in history. `#4222` **Johnny Depp** earned a huge £47 million in just one year, making him the actor with the highest annual earnings ever. `#4223` The longest red carpet at a world premiere was for *Harry Potter and the Deathly Hallows Part 2* in **2011**. `#4224` The red carpet stretched from Trafalgar Square to Leicester Square in London, England. `#4225` Stars had to walk a total of 455 m. `#4226` The multi-language independent feature film *The Owner* was directed by 25 directors from 13 countries. `#4227` The fastest film ever produced was called *Shotgun Garfunkel*. #4228 Shot in South Africa in **2013**, it took just 10 days, 10 hours and 30 minutes to make. #4229 In *Despicable Me*, the movie's directors provide the voices of the minions. #4230 The Hollywood Walk of Fame had just eight stars on when it was unveiled in **1958**. #4231 On average, two stars are added every month. #4232 The stars are made of thin marble. #4233 The walk features seven types of stars – each recognizing a different area in the entertainment business. #4234 Stars have also been awarded to events – like the *Apollo 11* moon landing. #4235 **Charlie Chaplin** was initially refused a star. #4236 His son later sued and in **1972** Charlie finally got his star. #4237 The Indian movie industry, Bollywood, makes the most films in the world. #4238 It produces around 800 movies a year. #4239 This is more than double the number produced by Hollywood. #4240 The first Bollywood film was made in **1913** when India was still part of the British Empire. #4241 It was called *Raja Harishchandra*. #4242 Bollywood refers to the origins of cinema in Bombay and Hollywood. #4243 The formal name for Indian cinema is Hindi cinema. #4244 The largest film studio in the world is Ramoji Film City in India. #4245 It opened in **1996**. #4246 It has 47 sound stages and permanent sets, including a railway station and temple. #4247 The most successful films in Oscar history are *Titanic*, *Ben Hur* and *Lord of the Rings: Return of the King*. #4248 They all won 11 Oscars each. #4249 *Lord of the Rings: Return of the King* won all 11 Oscars it was nominated for. #4250 **Meryl Streep** is the actress with the most nominations. #4251 She has been nominated 14 times. #4252 **Katherine Hepburn** holds the record for most wins, with four. #4253 **Laurence Olivier** and **Spencer Tracy** hold the record for most Best Actor nominations. #4254 **Daniel Day-Lewis** has had the most wins with three. #4255 An Oscar weighs just over 3 kg and is 34 cm tall. #4256 The first British film to win a Best Film Oscar was *Hamlet* in **1948.** #4257 Laurence Olivier directed and starred in it and won a Best Actor award for his role. #4258

Hollywood is a district in Los Angeles, California. #4259 In the late **1800s**, a man called **Harvey Wilcox** bought some of the land where Hollywood now is. He planned to form a religious community there. #4260 As he sold off bits of his land for people to build homes on, his wife raised money to build churches and schools. #4261 By **1900** there were about 500 people living there and the area had been formally registered as Hollywood. #4262 Hollywood's first street was called Prospect Avenue, which later changed to Hollywood Boulevard. #4263 In **1910** the population voted to become a part of Los Angeles. #4264 Many film companies moved from the east coast to the west coast, USA, to avoid being fined by **Thomas Edison's** Motion Pictures Patents Company, which was based in New Jersey and owned all the patents for film-making equipment. #4265 The Nestor Motion Picture Company opened the first Hollywood studio in **1911**. #4266 **Adolph Zukor**, from Hungary, founded Paramount Pictures in **1912**. #4267 Its original name was Famous Players Film Company. #4268 In **1918** four brothers from Poland set up another new film studio and called it Warner Brothers. #4269 One of the greatest Hollywood film studios was never actually in Hollywood. #4270 Metro-Goldwyn-Mayer (MGM) was located in Culver City, around 11 km away from Hollywood. #4271 **Marcus Loew** organized the merger of Metro Pictures Corporation, with Louis B. Mayer Productions and Goldwyn Productions, to form MGM in **1924**. #4272 During its peak, MGM produced around one film a week. #4273 From around **1928** to **1948** the major Hollywood studios owned all the film theatres across USA and would only show films they had produced. #4274 Film stars had to sign up with a specific studio and could only act in films produced by that studio. #4275 In **1948** the US Supreme Court ruled it was illegal for the studios to own theatres that only showed their films. #4276 The only US film studio located in Hollywood in **2014** was Paramount. #4277 The Hollywood sign was built in **1923** to help promote and sell houses in the area. 4278 Originally the large letters spelled out the word 'Hollywoodland'. #4279 The sign was lit up by 4,000 light bulbs, was about six stories tall and around the length of a football pitch. #4280 In **1978** a trust was put in place to take care of the sign and protect it from vandals. #4281

# 3 MAD FACTS ABOUT MEASUREMENTS

The largest unit of measurement for distance is a **gigaparsec**. It's about 3.26 billion light years or 31,000 trillion kilometres. #4282

The Scoville heat unit (SHU) is used to measure the **heat of chillies**. The Trinidad Moruga Scorpion pepper has a rating of up to 2,000,000 SHU. #4283

**Horsepower** is used to measure the power of engines – it began when people running steam-powered vehicles paid a fee based on the number of horses they had been saved from using. #4284

# 4 TEENY-TINY ATOM FACTS

The number of atoms in the **WHOLE UNIVERSE** is thought to be around $10^{80}$ – which is 1 followed by 80 zeroes. #4285

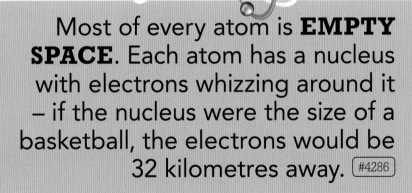

Most of every atom is **EMPTY SPACE**. Each atom has a nucleus with electrons whizzing around it – if the nucleus were the size of a basketball, the electrons would be 32 kilometres away. #4286

If you took all the space out of atoms, the whole human race would be the size of a **sugar cube.** #4287

Atoms are very tiny – about **25,000,000,000,000,000,000,000 carbon atoms make up the lead of a pencil.** #4288

# ZOOPLANKTON

Most zooplankton are **small marine animals** that cannot swim. They drift in the ocean currents, **feeding on tiny plants**. #4289

There are more than

# 14,000

species of **copepod**, tiny crustaceans about **1 mm** wide.

#4292

**Copepods** are found wherever there is water, including ditches and damp soil. #4290

The smallest zooplankton are just **2 millionths of a metre** wide. #4291

Zooplankton can drift **thousands of kilometres** ….

Krill start life as drifting zooplankton, before they develop the ability to swim.
#4293

**Adult krill often eat their own young.**
#4294

The total weight of the

KRILL

in the Antarctic Ocean is greater than the weight of all human beings – it may be more than

# Without krill, most life in the Antarctic would DIE!
#4295

# 500 MILLION TONNES.
#4296

Whales travel **thousands of kilometres** to the polar regions in summer to feed on krill.
#4297

**Krill eggs sink** to depths of more than 200 m **before hatching**, to keep them safe from predators.
#4298

Although they are only tiny, **krill can live for up to** 10 years.
#4299

across the ocean in their lifetimes.
#4300

# 10 TERRIFIC TRANSPORT FACTS

A **Boeing 747** travels **800 metres** on each litre of fuel. As it can carry 550 passengers, it's more fuel efficient than most cars. #4301

**Early airships** were filled with hydrogen, a highly flammable gas. #4302

After some deadly explosions, helium was used instead. #4303

The **earliest known successful flight** was by hot air balloon in Paris in 1783. #4304

The word **'juggernaut',** a huge lorry, is Indian – it's the name of a Hindu temple cart said to be used to crush people. #4305

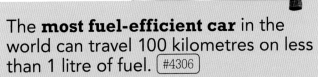

The **most fuel-efficient car** in the world can travel 100 kilometres on less than 1 litre of fuel. #4306

**Maglev** trains have **no wheels** – they are suspended above a rail by magnetic force. #4307

In 1972, Jean Boulet landed a helicopter safely after the **engine failed** at a height of 12,440 metres. #4308

The South American Aztecs didn't make use of the **wheel,** so didn't have carts or carriages. Instead they travelled and transported things via canoe. #4309

There will be around **200,000** aeroplane flights in the world today. #4310

The **GREAT PACIFIC GARBAGE PATCH** is a floating mass of around 100 million tons of plastic waste and chemical sludge that has collected in the Pacific Ocean. #4311

# 63 facts about TECHNOLOGY

## 17 FACTS ABOUT HOW IT ALL BEGAN...

**James Watt** was a Scottish inventor who improved the steam engine during the late **1700s**. #4312 Factories and mining companies began to use Watt's steam engine for their machinery. #4313 This helped kickstart the Industrial Revolution in the **1800s**. #4314 After his death, Watt's name was used to describe the electrical unit of measurement. #4315 Italian professor **Alessandro Volta** was born in **1745**. #4316 He used zinc, copper and cardboard to invent the first battery. #4317 The unit of voltage is now named after Volta. #4318 **André-Marie Ampère**, a French physicist and science teacher, played an important part in discovering electromagnetism. #4319 He also came up with a way to measure the flow of electricity. #4320 The ampere, which is the unit for measuring electric current, was named in his honour. #4321 German physicist and teacher **Georg Ohm** studied the relationship between voltage, current and resistance. #4322 In **1827** he proved that the amount of electrical current that can flow through a substance depends on its resistance to electrical flow. #4323 This is known as Ohm's Law. #4324 English scientist **Michael Faraday** was born in **1791**. #4325 He discovered that moving a magnet near a coil of copper wire creates an electric current in the wire. #4326 **Nikola Tesla** was a Serbian scientist who invented the first electric motor by reversing the flow of electricity on **Thomas Edison**'s generator. #4327 In **1893** Westinghouse Electric Company used Tesla's ideas to light the Chicago World's Fair with around 250,000 lights. #4328

The earliest known surviving photograph was taken by **Joseph Nicéphore Niépce** in **1827**. #4329 He took it with a camera obscura, a pinhole camera that dates back to Ancient China. #4330 The photo showed the view from his home. #4331 Today it is in the Gernsheim Collection, in the University of Texas, USA. #4332 **George Eastman** created the Kodak **camera**. #4333

It went on sale in **1888** and was a simple box camera with a fixed focus lens. #4334 His company then produced the first daylight-loading camera. #4335 This meant the photographer could reload the camera without using a darkroom. #4336 In **1914 Oskar Barnack** created the Leica camera. #4337 Polaroid cameras hit the market in **1948**, producing photos in under a minute. #4338 In 1969 **Willard S. Boyle** and **George E. Smith** made the first successful imaging technology, using a digital sensor. #4339 They were awarded a Nobel Prize for Physics in **2009** for paving the way for digital photography. #4340 Around the **1860s Dr Mahlon Loomis** claimed to have been the first person to communicate using **wireless** technology. #4341 The dentist, from Virginia, USA, transmitted telegraphic messages between mountain tops. #4342 He developed a method of transmitting and receiving messages by using the Earth's atmosphere as a conductor and launching kites with copper screens that were linked to the ground with copper wires. #4343 The US Congress awarded Loomis with a £33,000 research grant. #4344 **Claude Elwood Shannon** is considered the founding father of **electronic communications**. #4345 Shannon noticed the similarity between Boolean algebra and telephone switching circuits. #4346 He applied Boolean algebra to electrical systems while at the Massachusetts Institute of Technology (MIT) in **1940**. #4347 While working at Bell Laboratories, he formulated a theory explaining the communication of information – now called the Information Theory, which helped bring about the digital age. #4348 In **1973 Dr Martin Cooper** invented the first portable **handset** for Motorola. #4349 People in Chicago were the first to try out the new mobile phones, in **1977**. #4350 Other cities and countries soon followed. #4351 The industry is now worth billions of dollars a year. #4352 In **2002** Sanyo created a phone that could take pictures. #4353 The Apple iPhone, released in **2007**, was the first phone without a keyboard that was operated by touch. #4354 It also integrated a video with a phone and web browser. #4355 More 5-year-olds can use an iPhone than can tie their shoelaces. #4356 After **Charles Babbage** came up with his Difference Engine, he designed an Analytical Engine. #4357 This included a central processing unit and memory, which are both inside computers today. #4358 Babbage's ideas were only on paper though, as at the time the technology to build them didn't exist. #4359 In **1991** the Science Museum in London finally built his Difference Engine. #4360 It is more than 3 m long and 2 m tall and contains 8,000 moving parts. #4361 In **1953** International Business Machines (IBM) came out with their first **computer**. #4362 In **1958** the first bank computers were used. #4363 **Jack Kilby** and **Robert Noyce** invented the integrated circuit, also known as the **microchip**, in 1958. #4364 Jack Kilby won a Nobel Prize for Physics for his work in **2000**. #4365 According to Moore's Law, microchips double in power every 18 to 24 months. #4366 By the mid-**1960s** there were around 20,000 computers in the world. #4367 Over the years computers got smaller and cheaper. #4368 **Doug Engelbart** invented the computer mouse in the early **1960s**. #4369 He invented it in his research lab at Stanford Research Institute. #4370 The first prototype was built in **1964**. #4371 Over the years, the mouse has been developed to include more buttons and wireless connection – but its functionality remains much the same. #4372 In **1975 Bill Gates** and **Paul Allen** formed Microsoft. #4373 They dreamed of every home having a computer. #4374 In **1983** they announced their Windows program, but it took a while to develop and didn't go on sale until **1985**. #4375 By **1988** Microsoft was the largest software company based on sales. #4376 Apple Computers was formed by **Steve Wozniak**, **Steve Jobs** and **Ronald Wayne** in **1976**. #4377 Ronald Wayne sold his share in the business for a small amount, just after they started out. #4378 The first Apple computer was built by Steve Jobs in **1975**. #4379 He introduced the first Macintosh in **1984**. #4380 The videocassette recorder **(VCR)** was introduced around **1976**. #4381 Originally the film industry was opposed to the new technology, thinking it would affect box office takings. #4382 Instead a whole new industry of home entertainment was created. #4383 #4384 In **1977** Atari launched the first **game system** with plug-in cartridges. #4385 Over 40 manufacturers created 200 games for the system. #4386 The first video games copyrighted in the US were *Asteroids* and *Lunar Lander* in

186 million **Walkmans** between **1979** and **1999**. #4388 By **1983** cassette tapes outsold vinyl records. #4389 Early MP3 players stored around 8 songs, then along came the Apple iPod in **2001** – which could store around 1,000. #4390 By **2005,** 8 out of 10 digital music players sold were iPods. #4391

# 20 RANDOM FACTS ABOUT THE INTERNET

The Internet and World Wide Web are two different things. #4392 The Internet is a huge network that links computers together all over the world using a range of wires and wireless technologies. #4393 The web is a collection of linked pages accessed using the Internet. #4394 The Internet is also used for emails, file sharing and video calls. #4395 The Internet is the fastest-growing communications tool ever. #4396 It took radio broadcasters 38 years to reach an audience of 50 million, TV 13 years, and the Internet just 4 years. #4397 The world's first website was created by **Tim Berners-Lee** at CERN (the European Organization for Nuclear Research). #4398 The website was about the World Wide Web project itself. #4399 It described the basic features of the web, how to access other websites and build your own. #4400 In **1993** CERN shared the World Wide Web software with the general public. #4401 This enabled others to create websites and for the World Wide Web to grow. #4402 US President **Bill Clinton**'s inauguration in **1997** was the first to be webcast. #4403 On average a web-surfing session lasts about an hour. #4404 China is the country with the most Internet users in the world. #4405 But only around 45 per cent of people living there use it. #4406 The first Google doodle was a Burning Man symbol. #4407 Google founders **Larry Page** and **Sergey Brin** went to the Burning Man festival in **1998** and added the doodle to let users know they were away from the office that weekend. #4408 The US hosts 43 per cent of the world's top 1 million websites. #4409 Google, Facebook and YouTube are the three most visited websites in the world. #4410 Americans spend most time on Facebook – on average 40 minutes a day. #4411

# 19 awesome ART facts

The world's most famous painting, the *Mona Lisa*, was painted by **Leonardo da Vinci** around 1503.
#4412

The *Mona Lisa* is displayed in the Louvre museum in Paris, France, and seen by about 9 million vistors a year.
#4413

Some of the world's oldest art can be found in the Lascaux caves in France.
#4414

Cave paintings of large animals were discovered in the Lascaux caves in **1940** by a group of teenage boys.
#4415

In **1911** the *Mona Lisa* was stolen by **Vincent Peruggia**, a worker at the Louvre. It was found two years later in Italy.
#4416

**Pablo Picasso** completed his first work of art, *Le Picador*, at just nine years of age.
#4417

Before becoming a museum, the Louvre was a medieval fortress and then a palace for the kings of France.
#4418

Experts believe the Lascaux paintings are almost 20,000 years old.
#4419

Picasso was a suspect in the theft of the *Mona Lisa* and was questioned by the police over its disappearance.
#4420

Around 1,000 of Picasso's paintings are missing or stolen.
#4421

The *Ghent Altarpiece* is the most stolen artwork of all time.
#4422

In 1961 **Henri Mattisse's** painting *Le Bateau* was hung upside down in a museum in New York, USA, for 47 days before anyone noticed it was the wrong way up.
#4424

Despite being one of the world's best artists, Dutch painter **Rembrandt Harmenszoon van Rijn** was declared bankrupt in 1656.
#4425

The Winter Palace (within the State Hermitage Museum) has 322 galleries, housing nearly 3 million works of art.
#4426

Today Rembrandt's paintings sell for millions.
#4429

**Vincent van Gogh** produced more than 2,000 paintings during his lifetime but only sold one while he was alive.
#4427

**Paul Cezanne's** most famous painting, *The Card Players*, was of local farm workers painted in around 1890.
#4428

Before becoming a painter, Cezanne was studying to be a lawyer.
#4430

## 6 WACKY ARTIST FACTS

➜ Surrealist artist **Salvador Dali** hid a silhouette of himself in all of his paintings. #4431

➜ English artist **Andy Brown** created a portrait of the **Queen** by stitching 1,000 used teabags together. #4432

➜ In **2004** the Chilean artist **Marco Evaristti** used 3 fire hoses and 3,000 litres of paint to paint the tip of an iceberg in Greenland red. #4433

➜ UK artist **Millie Brown** swallows dyed milk, which she then vomits onto canvas to create her paintings. #4434

➜ There is a group of painters in the Ukraine who like to create their masterpieces underwater. #4435

➜ **Hong Yi** from Malaysia painted a portrait of a basketball player... using a basketball. #4436

# 25 MONEY facts

Ancient Egyptians used ring money – actual rings made of bronze, copper or gold.
#4437

Ancient Chinese coins had holes in the centre.
#4438

Thousands of years ago, the Aztecs used small doll figures made of solid gold as currency.
#4439

The first metal coins appeared in Ancient Greece around **700 BC**.
#4440

In Ancient Greece, coins were believed to have magical powers.
#4441

To pay their bills, the Egyptians pulled off a ring or two to use as payment.
#4442

Chinese coins were strung together on a string or rope, called a 'string of cash'.
#4443

In other places around the world, people used rice, bread or chocolate as money.
#4444

Paper money originated in China around **1024**.
#4445

The Ancient Greeks introduced the idea of engraving pictures of people and gods on coins around 400 BC.
#4446

Each year the **International Bank Note Society** (IBNS) names a 'banknote of the year' based on its beauty.
#4447

Founded in Italy in **1472**, and originally a pawn shop, **Banca Monte dei Paschi di Siena** is the world's oldest surviving bank.
#4448

Food was not very good currency, because it went bad or was eaten.
#4449

The pound sterling, used in the UK, is the world's oldest currency still in use.
#4450

Qatar has the richest population in the world.
#4451

The first ATM machine was built in **1967** by Scottish inventor, **John Shepherd-Barron**.
#4452

In **1950**, **Frank X. McNamara** created the first credit card, the Diners Club Card.
#4454

More Monopoly money is printed in USA every year than real money.
#4455

The first sterling coin was a silver penny introduced around 1,300 years ago.
#4456

Rare and old coins can sell for millions of pounds at auction.
#4457

The ATM machine was based on a chocolate-bar dispenser.
#4453

In the UK and US more than 50 per cent of all purchases are now made on plastic card.
#4458

A 'pound' was made up of 240 silver pennies, equal to a pound in weight.
#4459

The Flowing Hair Dollar is believed to be one of the first coins minted in the US in **1794**.
#4461

In 1940, a tornado disturbed a hoard of buried treasure, raining gold coins down on a Russian town.
#4460

# **7** FACTS ABOUT Cats

Cats have much better **night vision** than humans. We need **six times** more light to see as clearly as a cat.

#4462

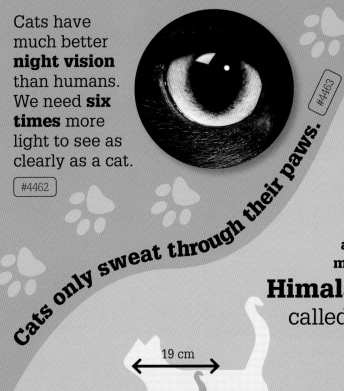

#4463

Cats only sweat through their paws.

Cats purr when they are ill. The vibrations may help their bones and muscles to heal.

#4464

The **smallest adult cat ever measured** was a

**Himalayan-Persian** called **Tinker Toy**.

#4465

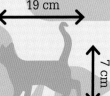

19 cm

7 cm

**Tinker Toy**, was only **7 cm** tall and **19 cm** long – about the size of a rat.

#4466

There are currently

# 55

recognized **breeds** of house cat.

#4467

Cats sometimes **chew grass** to make themselves **throw up fur balls**.

#4468

# 6 BIG CAT FACTS

The **cheetah** is the **fastest land mammal,** and can accelerate from **0 to 95 km/h** in just 3 seconds. That's the same as an F1 racing car. #4469

Most **jaguars** are orange with black spots, but about **6 per cent** are black all over. #4470

A lion's ROAR can be heard from **8 km** away. #4471

Tigers are known to imitate the sounds of other animals to lure in prey. #4472

Tigers now inhabit only 7 per cent of the areas that they lived in **100 years ago**, because humans are taking over their land. #4473

LIONS do most of their HUNTING at night. #4474

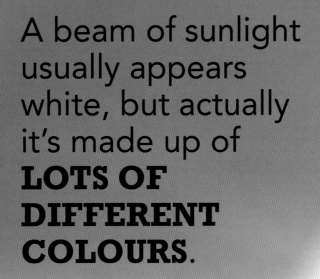

A beam of sunlight usually appears white, but actually it's made up of **LOTS OF DIFFERENT COLOURS**.

If the beam happens to hit raindrops on the way down at the right angle, the colours separate so that we can see them – creating a rainbow. #4475

# 4 FACTS TO SEND YOU HOT AND COLD

The iceberg that sank the *Titanic* was made from the snow that fell over Greenland **3,000 years ago**.

#4476

Scientist believe that the atmosphere around the sun is heated by **nanoflares** – tiny bursts of hot energy. #4477

A **microbe** known just as 'strain 121' lives in holes under the sea that pour out water at temperatures of **121°C** – much hotter than boiling water.

#4478

Nothing can be colder than **ZERO KELVIN (-273°C)**. #4479

# 49 facts on EARLY WORLD HISTORY

Around **3.8 billion** years ago, the first signs of life appeared on our planet. [#4480] Around **1.8 million** years ago the species **Homo erectus** (meaning 'upright man') was the first to look and act like modern humans. [#4481] One of the first specimens identified as Homo erectus was the **Java Man fossil**. [#4482] It was discovered in **1891** on **Java**, an island in **Indonesia**. [#4483] Some scientists believe it is the missing link between apes and humans. [#4484] **Neanderthals** first appeared about 200,000 years ago. [#4485] They looked much like modern humans only shorter and more heavily built. [#4486] They were also much stronger; their arms and hands were especially powerful. [#4487] Their chins and foreheads sloped backwards. [#4488] They had a slightly larger brain than that of modern humans. [#4489] Neanderthals hunted animals with long wooden spears. [#4490] They also used fire and other tools. [#4491] Our own species, **Homo sapiens**, evolved in **Africa** about 200,000 years ago. [#4492] Homo sapiens have small faces, tucked under a high, domed braincase. [#4493] On average, Homo sapien bodies are less muscular than earlier hominins such as Neanderthals. [#4494] Homo sapiens began to develop highly crafted tools, food-gathering strategies and social organization. [#4495] Changes from **10,000 BC to 4,000 BC** saw the development of settlements into towns and cities. [#4496] **Ancient Mesopotamia** is known as the cradle of civilization. [#4497] **Sumerian, Akkadian, Babylonian** and **Assyrian** people all formed empires in this territory (today known as **Iraq**). [#4498] Writing was invented by the Sumerians, about **3,100 BC**. [#4499] The Sumerians also introduced a number system based on counting in units of 60, which we still use today.

[#4500] They wrote on small pieces of soft clay, which were left in the sun to dry until hard. [#4501] By **3,200 BC** they had begun to use wheels. [#4502] From **539 BC** to around **331 BC** the **Persian Empire** was the most powerful state in the world. [#4503] It stretched from **Egypt** to **India**. [#4504] Its long-lasting war with **Greece** eventually led to its downfall. [#4505] The Greeks, led by **Alexander the Great**, conquered much of the civilized world. [#4506] He established **Alexandria** as the capital of Egypt. [#4507] A great library was built there. It housed many of the books of the ancient world. [#4508] During the following years the **Roman Empire** grew in strength. [#4509] By **146 BC** Greece had become a province of the Roman Empire. [#4510] The **Justinian Plague** broke out in the 6th century. It killed It killed thousands of people in the lands around the eastern Mediterranean. [#4511] The **Middle Ages** is the name given to the period from the 5th to the 15th centuries. [#4512] The majority of people in the Middle Ages worked as farmers. [#4513] People at this time thought the world was flat! [#4514] In **1484 Pope Innocent VIII** published the *Summis desiderantes* in which he states that witchcraft exists and must be stopped. [#4515] This officially began a witch hunt throughout Europe, which lasted for the next 200 years. [#4516] Women suspected of being witches were burned or drowned. [#4517] **The Renaissance** was a period of enlightenment from the early 14th century to the late 16th century. [#4518] The invention of the printing press in **1440** allowed ideas to spread more easily. [#4519] The word 'renaissance' is a **French** word and means 'rebirth'. [#4520] The Renaissance was a time of great beauty and art. [#4521] Many masterpieces by great artists such as **da Vinci** and **Michelangelo** were created at this time. [#4522] It was also the age of exploration, sometimes known as the **Age of Discovery**. [#4523] **Europeans** discovered new routes to **India** and the **Americas**. [#4524] Much of the previously unknown world was mapped during this time. [#4525] **Venice** in **Italy** was the world's busiest port at the time. [#4526] New scientific, mathematical and political thought challenged the teachings of the Catholic Church (the main religious power in Europe at the time). [#4527] **Martin Luther** broke away from the Catholic Church and began to spread the Protestant religion throughout northern Europe. [#4528]

# 52 FACTS ON AMERICAN HISTORY

**Native Americans** are the indigenous people of **North America**. [#4529] They lived throughout what is now the USA, including Alaska and the mainland. [#4530] From the 16th to 19th century, following the arrival of European settlers, Native American population numbers decreased. [#4531] One of the major causes of this was the arrival of new diseases such as smallpox. [#4532] There was also conflict with the new settlers over land and customs. [#4533] The British were the first outsiders to attempt to colonize North America, but initially failed to do so. [#4534] **Roanoke Colony** was established in **1587**. [#4535] 17 women, 11 children and 90 men set up home there, but they mysteriously disappeared just three years later. [#4536] The British established a second colony in **Jamestown**, **Virginia**, in **1607**. [#4537] **The Pilgrim Fathers** were a group of settlers who left Britain in search of religious freedom. [#4538] Around 102 passengers and 30 crew sailed to North America on the *Mayflower* in **1620**. [#4539] Just two people died on the voyage. [#4540] These Pilgrims eventually developed 13 colonies along the east coast. [#4541] They became increasingly independent and resentful of the taxes they had to pay to the British government. [#4542] In **1775** the **Revolutionary War** broke out. [#4543] The first shot fired was on 19 April **1775**. [#4544] It is known as 'the shot heard around the world'. [#4545] The French helped the North American colonies to victory, and independence from the British, in **1783**. [#4546] Less than 100 years later, in **1861**, another war began. [#4547] Over 600,000 soldiers died in the **American Civil War**. [#4548] 11 southern states wanted to become independent and make their own laws. [#4549] They were concerned that President **Abraham Lincoln** would outlaw slavery. [#4550] The states wanted to form their own

country called the Confederacy. [#4551] They had their own president – **Jefferson Davis.** [#4552] The 25 northern states fighting against the Confederacy were known as the Union – they wanted to remain unified as a single country. [#4553] The north was bigger, richer and more industrial than the south. [#4554] One-third of all soldiers who fought for the Union were immigrants. [#4555] 1 in 10 were African American. [#4556] African American soldiers were paid lower wages than white soldiers doing the same jobs. [#4557] In **1864** African American soldiers finally received equal pay. [#4558] **General Robert Lee** led the Confederate army. [#4559] In **1863** his family home, Arlington Estate in Virginia, was confiscated by the Union. [#4560] President Lincoln gave permission for a cemetery to be built on the land. [#4561] After the war, Lee's son successfully sued the government for taking the land illegally. [#4562] He sold the land back to the government. It is now **Arlington National Cemetery**. [#4563] General Lee surrendered to **General Ulysses Grant**, leader of the Union army, in **1865**. [#4564] 10 days later President Lincoln was assassinated by **John Wilkes Booth**. [#4565] Booth was an actor and a Confederate sympathizer who supported slavery. [#4566] He was shot dead trying to escape capture. [#4567] Eight other conspirators in the assassination plot were tried and convicted. [#4568] The **Civil Rights Movement** was a fight for racial equality that began after the end of the Civil War. [#4569] In **1865** slavery was abolished (made illegal) by the 13th Amendment to the US Constitution. [#4570] Many southern states then introduced laws to ensure former slaves would not become part of their society. [#4571] These laws were known as Jim Crow laws. [#4572] They enforced segregation (the separation of people) in public places such as restaurants, schools, toilets and on public transport. [#4573] In the **1950s** the Supreme Court ruled that segregation in schools was illegal. [#4574] Federal troops had to be sent to **Little Rock High School**, **Arkansas**, to ensure everyone was able to attend the desegregated school. [#4575] In **1955** **Rosa Parks** was arrested for not giving her seat on a bus to a white passenger. [#4576] This sparked the Montgomery Bus Boycott, which lasted a year. [#4577] **Martin Luther King** took part in the boycott. Eventually the Supreme Court ruled that segregation on buses was illegal. [#4578] In **1964** the **Civil Rights Act** was signed by President **Lyndon Johnson**. [#4579] It outlawed discrimination based on gender or race. [#4580]

The **Victoria Cross** is the highest British military decoration, awarded for bravery. #4581

First given by Queen Victoria in 1857, the Victoria Cross has been awarded **1,357 times**. #4582

The **Purple Heart** is awarded to US servicemen or women wounded or killed in service. #4583

US presidents have awarded almost **2 million** Purple Hearts. #4584

The **Freedom Award** from the International Rescue Committee is for extraordinary contributions to the cause of refugees and human freedom. #4585

The **Turner Prize** is an annual visual arts prize in the UK. In 1999, Tracey Emin's controversial shortlisted piece featured an unmade, messy bed! #4586

The highest award in Denmark is called the **Order of the Elephant**, usually given to heads of state and members of the royal family. #4587

The **British Order of the Bath** gets its name from the old ceremony of ritually bathing a new knight to purify him. #4588

Swedish inventor **Alfred Nobel** left money in his will for international prizes for peace, chemistry, physics, medicine, economics and literature. #4589

Nobel Prizes bring prestige for winners – and a small fortune! In 2012, each prize was worth around **£700,000**! #4590

# **3** FASCINATING FACTS ABOUT WORLD RELIGIONS

There are around **2.5 billion Christians** in the world today, around one third of the world's population, making Christianity the most popular religion in the world. #4591

One of the world's oldest and smallest religions is Samaritanism, practised by around 700 people. #4592

The **Zoroastrian** religion began around 1200 BC and was the main religion of the Persian Empire – and the world – during the 500s BC. Now it has fewer than 200,000 followers worldwide. #4593

# 10 FACTS ABOUT
# GECKOS

The eyes of a gecko are

## 350

times more **SENSITIVE TO LIGHT** than human eyes.

#4594

Most geckos **HUNT AT NIGHT**.

#4595

A gecko can hold its **whole body weight** on one toe. #4596

Geckos shed their skin every two to four weeks, then eat it. #4597

Most geckos **CLING** to smooth vertical surfaces **USING MILLIONS OF TINY HAIRS** on their feet.

#4598

Leopard geckos have claws instead of **sticky pads**. #4599

The flying gecko cannot actually fly but **glides** to escape from predators. #4600

If attacked, a gecko can **BREAK OFF ITS TAIL**, escape and then grow another. #4601

Most geckos have fixed eyelids and

# CANNOT BLINK.
#4602

Like all lizards, geckos are

# COLD-BLOODED.
They must lie in the Sun all day to make them warm enough to hunt through the night.
#4603

287

# 3 MOVEMENT FACTS

When you're **sitting still,** you're actually **moving!** #4604

That's because Earth rotates at **1,670 kilometres per hour** and moves around the Sun at **107,280 kilometres per hour.** #4605

Then the solar system moves at **70,000 kilometres per hour** through the galaxy, and the galaxy spins at **792,000 kilometres per hour.** #4606

# 10 FANTASTIC FACTS ABOUT FORCES

When you jump, you exert a **tiny force on Earth,** shifting it very slightly in space. #4607

**Light** doesn't always travel in straight lines – it can be bent by gravity, so it curves around planets and stars. #4608

**Pigeons** navigate using special brain cells that detect the strength and direction of magnetic fields. #4609

A full bottle **breaks more easily** than an empty bottle. #4610

A **feather** and a **bowling ball** dropped at the same time on the **Moon** would reach the ground together. #4611

Every object has **its own gravity**. #4612

A ship trapped in a **freezing sea** would be crushed by the force of ice forming around it. #4613

Sledges move over **water**, not snow. Heat from **friction** melts a layer of snow and the sledge glides over. #4614

If you break a **magnet** in half, each half will instantly get its own north and south poles. #4615

Earth is protected from the Sun by a magnetic field which stretches out into space. #4616

# 76 cool **CASTLE** facts

Castles were built as both homes and fortresses all over the world. #4617 They were often built to provide safety or to show how rich the owners were. #4618 **The Normans** introduced the British to castles when they invaded in **1066**. #4619 Originally castles were made of wood. #4620 **Motte-and-bailey castles** were built on raised ground, so enemies had to attack from below. #4621 Later wood was replaced with stone to make castles stronger. #4622 A **donjon** is the main tower within the walls of a medieval castle. #4623 It is also known as a 'keep' and was the last place of defence if the castle was attacked. #4624 The number of floors and height of its walls depended on how rich the castle's owner was. #4625 The **bailey** was the enclosed area between the outer walls and the donjon. #4626 The strong wall built around the outside of the donjon and bailey is called the **curtain wall**. #4627 They are very thick walls which act like a strong shield. #4628 To limit access to the castle, there were few doors in the curtain wall. #4629 Originally towers were built with square tops, but these were later replaced by round towers offering better defence. #4630 Round towers were also harder for attackers to knock down. #4631 Unlike square towers, they had no weak corners which collapsed if holes were dug under their foundations. #4632 At the top of the castle walls were the **battlements**. #4633 Castle defenders could fire arrows through square gaps called **crenels** along the top

of the wall. #4634 The raised sections between crenels were called **merlons**. #4635 They helped to shelter the defenders during an attack. #4636 The word **'portcullis'** (a heavy grate used to block an entrance) comes from the French word *porte coleice*, meaning 'sliding door'. #4637 **Murder holes** were openings in a ceiling, usually near a gate or doorway. #4638 They were used by defenders to drop harmful items, such as hot liquids, onto attackers. #4639 A **moats** is a deep, wide ditch surrounding the whole castle complex. #4640 Moats were used to defend the castle, but also for punishment. #4641 If you broke the laws of the castle you could be strapped into a **ducking stool** and dropped into the moat. #4642 Other punishments included being put in an **oubliette**, a small space, and left to die in the castle's **dungeons**. #4643 *Oubliette* means 'to forget' in French. #4644 **Medieval** castles did not have flushing toilets. #4645 Instead they had small rooms called **garderobes**. #4646 These were built over a hole or chute which would send waste into the moat. #4647 *Garderobe* means 'wardrobe' in French and these rooms were also used to store clothes. #4648 Sometimes attackers cut off supplies to people living inside a castle until they surrendered. This was called a **siege**. #4649 Devices called siege engines were used to attack castles. Examples include **battering rams** and **catapults**. #4650 Almost all castles had a water source, usually a well, within their walls. #4651 This was essential if someone laid siege to the castle. #4652 Cats and dogs were kept in castles to kill rats, which would have eaten important grain stores. #4653 While hunting would contribute meat to the table of any medieval castle, the most common food was bread. #4654 Castles stopped being built around the **1500s**. #4655 By this time gunpowder was widely used so the castle was no longer the invincible fortress it had been. #4656 **Prague Castle** is one of the biggest castle complexes in the world. #4657 It dates back to the 9th century. #4658 It's around 570 m long and 130 m wide. #4659 There has been a castle on the site of **Alnwick Castle** in **England** for over 1,000 years. #4660 For the past 700 years it has been the home of the **Percy** family. #4661 The 12th Duke of Northumberland, **Ralph Percy**, and his wife still live there today. `#4662` During the Middle Ages the castle was used to defend England against Scottish attacks. `#4663` Today it is a home and a tourist attraction. `#4664` More than three million people visit the monastery **Mont Saint Michel** every year. `#4665` Its location on an island about 1 km off the coast of France made it an important strategic stronghold in the 8th century. `#4666` Strong tides connect and disconnect the island from the mainland every day. `#4667` **Warwick Castle** in England was begun in **1068** by the Normans. `#4668` It was home to the Earls of Warwick for hundreds of years. `#4669` One owner, **Sir Fulke Greville**, was killed by a servant in **1628** and is said to haunt the castle. `#4670` In **1978** it was opened up as a tourist attraction. `#4671` One of the world's largest working **trebuchets** (huge catapults used in sieges) has been built at Warwick Castle. `#4672` It can hurl a 150 kg boulder over 300 m at 250 km/h. `#4673` **Edinburgh Castle** in **Scotland** is built on an extinct volcano called **Castle Rock**. `#4674` People have lived on Castle Rock since the **Bronze Age**, around **850 BC**. `#4675` Over the years ownership of the castle has switched back and forth between the English and the Scots. `#4676` The castle was used as a prison during the 18th and 19th centuries. `#4677` Prisoners from the **Seven Years' War**, the **American War of Independence** and **Napoleonic Wars** were locked in its dungeons. `#4678` The castle is home to the **Mons Meg cannon**, made around **1449**. `#4679` The cannon could fire huge cannonballs – each one was around three times the size of your head! `#4680` **Hohensalzburg Castle** in **Austria** was built in the 11th century and is one of the largest castles in Europe. `#4681` It is around 250 m long and 150 m wide. `#4682` **Malbork Castle** in **Poland** is the largest castle in the world. `#4683` Malbork Castle was founded in **1274** by the Teutonic Knights from **Germany**. `#4684` They used it as their headquarters to help defeat Polish enemies. `#4685` **Himeji Castle** in **Japan** has a maze of paths leading up to it. They are used to confuse attackers and prevent them finding a way inside. `#4686` It has never come under attack, which is unusual for a castle that has been around since **1331**. `#4687` **Neuschwanstein Castle** in Germany was built by **King Ludwig II** of Bavaria. `#4688` He built the fairytale castle as a place of retreat from his public life. `#4689` After his death in **1868** his castle was opened to the public. `#4690` **Balmoral Castle** in Scotland was originally a smaller medieval building. `#4691` **Prince Albert** bought the castle for **Queen Victoria** in **1852**. `#4692`

# 25 FACTS ABOUT WINDSOR CASTLE

Windsor Castle is the oldest and largest occupied castle in the world. `#4693` The castle covers around 52,000 m² of land. `#4694` That's the size of around 11 football pitches! `#4695` Today around 150 people live there, including the **Queen**. `#4696` Built by **William I** 900 years ago, it was originally made from wood. `#4697` The location was chosen as it was within a day's march of the Tower of London. `#4698` **Henry I** was the first monarch to use the castle as a home, in **1110**. `#4699` 40 monarchs have called the castle their home since then. `#4700` St George's Chapel was built within the castle's walls in **1348** by **King Edward III**. `#4701` He built it as a headquarters for the Order of the Garter, a fellowship of knights. `#4702` The Order is made up of members of the Royal Family plus 24 Knight Companions. `#4703` Companions are chosen by the Royal Family as a reward for their loyalty or military service. `#4704` The Order attends a special service once a year in the chapel. `#4705` For the rest of the time the chapel is used for royal weddings or funerals and also holds a daily service for the general public. `#4706` **Henry VIII** is buried in the chapel. `#4707` The Great Kitchen is the oldest working kitchen in the UK. `#4708` The Queen has 33 kitchen staff, including 20 chefs. `#4709` Windsor Castle is home to many treasures including works of art by **da Vinci**, **Rembrandt** and **Rubens**. `#4710` It also has the world's largest doll's house. `#4711` This was built in the early **1920s** and includes a real miniature library, running water and working lifts. `#4712` When the Queen is at home, the Royal Standard flag is flown at Windsor Castle. `#4713` When she's away, the Union Jack flag is flown in its place. `#4714` A huge fire in **1992** destroyed one fifth of the castle. `#4715` It took around 15 hours and 225 firefighters to put it out. `#4716` It cost around £35 million to repair the damage. `#4717`

# 25 BRAIN-busting facts

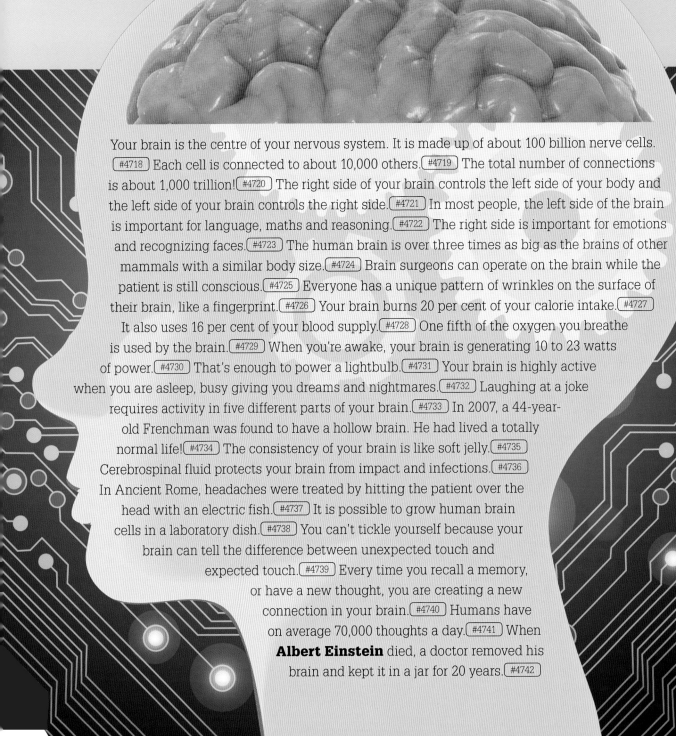

Your brain is the centre of your nervous system. It is made up of about 100 billion nerve cells. `#4718` Each cell is connected to about 10,000 others. `#4719` The total number of connections is about 1,000 trillion! `#4720` The right side of your brain controls the left side of your body and the left side of your brain controls the right side. `#4721` In most people, the left side of the brain is important for language, maths and reasoning. `#4722` The right side is important for emotions and recognizing faces. `#4723` The human brain is over three times as big as the brains of other mammals with a similar body size. `#4724` Brain surgeons can operate on the brain while the patient is still conscious. `#4725` Everyone has a unique pattern of wrinkles on the surface of their brain, like a fingerprint. `#4726` Your brain burns 20 per cent of your calorie intake. `#4727` It also uses 16 per cent of your blood supply. `#4728` One fifth of the oxygen you breathe is used by the brain. `#4729` When you're awake, your brain is generating 10 to 23 watts of power. `#4730` That's enough to power a lightbulb. `#4731` Your brain is highly active when you are asleep, busy giving you dreams and nightmares. `#4732` Laughing at a joke requires activity in five different parts of your brain. `#4733` In 2007, a 44-year-old Frenchman was found to have a hollow brain. He had lived a totally normal life! `#4734` The consistency of your brain is like soft jelly. `#4735` Cerebrospinal fluid protects your brain from impact and infections. `#4736` In Ancient Rome, headaches were treated by hitting the patient over the head with an electric fish. `#4737` It is possible to grow human brain cells in a laboratory dish. `#4738` You can't tickle yourself because your brain can tell the difference between unexpected touch and expected touch. `#4739` Every time you recall a memory, or have a new thought, you are creating a new connection in your brain. `#4740` Humans have on average 70,000 thoughts a day. `#4741` When **Albert Einstein** died, a doctor removed his brain and kept it in a jar for 20 years. `#4742`

# 25 facts on BATTLES that changed history

A legendary and heroic group of 300 **Spartans** sacrificed themselves to enable the rest of the Greek army to escape during the **Battle of Thermopylae** in **480 BC**. [#4743] The **Battle of Pharsalus** in **48 BC** saw **Julius Caesar** defeat **Pompey Magnus**. [#4744] Pompey was fighting for the Roman senators and people of Rome against Caesar's tyrant rule. [#4745] Caesar's victory paved the way for the Roman republic to become an empire. [#4746] The **Battle of Hastings** in **AD 1066** saw England's **King Harold II** defeated by the Frenchman **Duke William** of Normandy. [#4747] Duke William then became king. [#4748] In **1415 King Henry V** led an army of just 8,000 knights, archers and soldiers in the **Battle of Agincourt**. [#4749] They defeated a French army of around 36,000 men. [#4750] A young peasant girl called **Joan of Arc** led the French to victory against the English in the **Siege of Orleans** in **1429**. [#4751] The **Battle of Naseby** in **1645** saw England's **King Charles I** lose to **Oliver Cromwell** and his parliamentarian troops, allowing Cromwell to win the English Civil War. [#4752] The **Battle of Yorktown** in **1781** was a victory for American and French forces over the British. It marked the end of the American Revolutionary War. [#4753] This resulted in the creation of the United States of America as a separate country. [#4754] After Yorktown, British troops began to leave America. The last of them left in November **1783**. [#4755] The **Battle of Trafalgar** in **1805** was Britain's greatest victory during the Napoleonic Wars. [#4756] The British Royal Navy defeated the French and Spanish navies off the coast of Spain which gave Britain control of the sea. [#4757] The **Battle of the Nations** saw Prussia, Russia, Austria and Sweden join forces in **1813** to fight Napoleon's French army. [#4758] The battle took place in **Leipzig**, **Saxony** (now part of Germany). [#4759] It involved 600,000 soldiers and was the largest land battle of the Napoleonic Wars. [#4760] Napoleon was defeated and returned to France. [#4761] Napoleon's final battle, which ended his rule as Emperor of France, took place in **1815** at **Waterloo**, in Belgium. [#4762] The allied armies were led by the British and Prussian generals **Wellington** and **Blücher**. [#4763] Around 1,000 RAF planes were shot down in the **Battle of Britain** in **1940**, during WWII. [#4764] The RAF fought back to defend Britain. [#4765] With the help of radar the RAF shot down around 1,600 German planes. [#4766] This action by the RAF prevented **Hitler** from invading Britain. [#4767]

# 3 MOMENTOUS MILITARY FACTS

**Nine countries** in the world have **nuclear weapons**. #4768

15 countries, including Costa Rica, have **no military forces at all**. #4769

There are about **1.4 million** men and women on active duty in the **US military** and roughly the same in the Reserve. #4770

# 5 COUNTRY NUMBER-CRUNCHERS

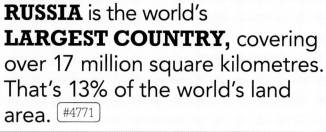

**RUSSIA** is the world's **LARGEST COUNTRY,** covering over 17 million square kilometres. That's 13% of the world's land area. #4771

The world's **SMALLEST COUNTRY** is the **VATICAN CITY** in Rome. It covers just 0.44 square kilometres or around 62 football pitches. #4772

At their tallest point, the coral islands of the Maldives in the Indian Ocean peek out of the sea at a maximum height of **JUST 2.4 METRES**. #4773

Tibet is the highest region in the world, towering above sea level at a height of **4,900 METRES**. #4774

The border between Canada and the United States is the **LONGEST INTERNATIONAL BORDER IN THE WORLD** between two countries at **8,891 KILOMETRES**. #4775

# 8 FACTS ABOUT HOW
# FISH BREATHE

Fish breathe by absorbing oxygen in the water through their gills. #4776

Very active fish have larger gills to take in more oxygen. #4777

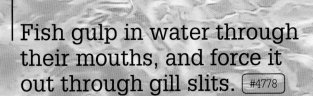

Fish gulp in water through their mouths, and force it out through gill slits. #4778

**The gills of a 1-kg mackerel have a surface area of 1 square metre – that's the same size as a beach towel.** #4779

# Sharks have between five and seven gill slits on either side of their heads. #4780

Lungfish have both gills and lungs to breathe. During a dry season when the water dries up, the lungfish survive by burrowing into the mud, and breathing with their lungs. #4781

**Mudskippers can breathe through their skin.** #4782

They must keep their skin wet at all times in order to breathe. #4783

# 4 SNOOZY SLEEP FACTS

Some **SNORES** are as loud as a road drill. #4784

You spend around a **third** of your life fast **asleep.** #4785

You can have up to 12 **dreams** a night - but you don't always remember them when you wake. #4786

The record for a human lasting without sleep is **18 DAYS, 21 HOURS AND 40 MINUTES.** #4787

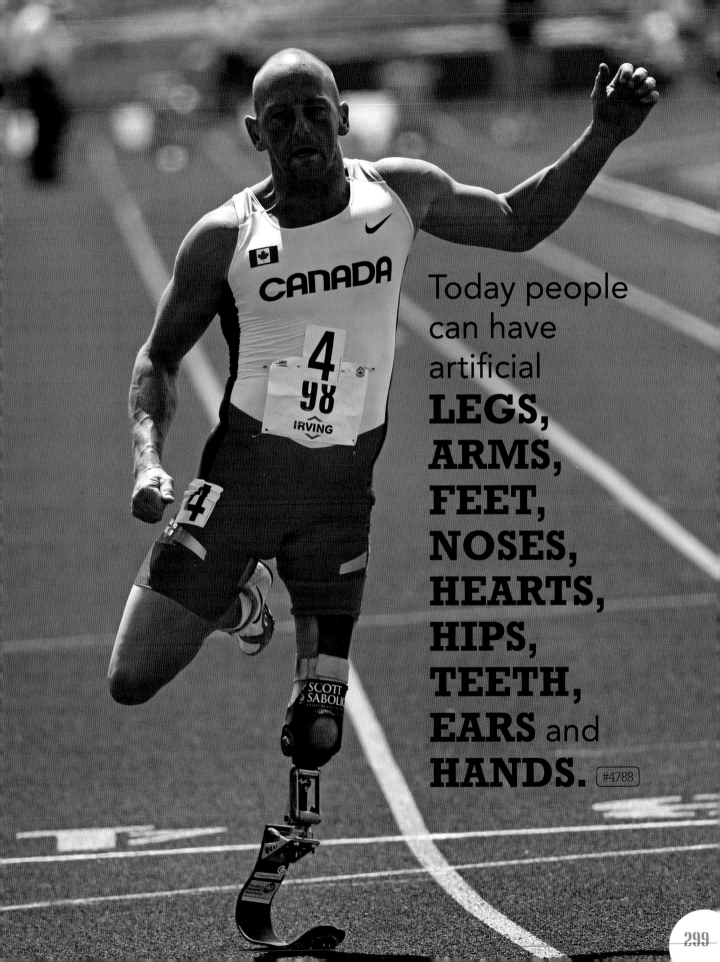

Today people can have artificial **LEGS, ARMS, FEET, NOSES, HEARTS, HIPS, TEETH, EARS** and **HANDS.** #4788

299

# 26 CHOCOLATE FACTS
## AND SWEET TREAT

Chocolate grows on trees. #4789 It is made using the beans from the cacao tree. #4790 Between **AD 250** and **900** cacao beans were used as money by people in **Mexico**. #4791 Around the year **1502 Hernando Cortes**, the Spanish Conquistador exploring Mexico, discovered chocolate and sent it home to **Spain**. #4792 At first, chocolate was only made into drinks. #4793 The first chocolate house (a shop selling drinking chocolate) opened in **London**, **England** in **1657.** #4794 In **1847 Joseph Fry** introduced the first solid chocolate bar to England. #4795 It was made from a mixture of cacao powder, cacao butter and sugar. #4796 It takes a year's crop from one cacao tree to make 450 g of chocolate. #4797 White chocolate isn't really chocolate as it contains no cacao. #4798 Chocolate has been to space on every **Russian** and **American** space voyage! #4799 Mondelez International is the biggest chocolate company in the world. #4800 It employs people in 33 countries around the world. #4801 The largest chocolate bar ever made weighed 5,792.5 kg – about the same as an African elephant! #4802 It was made in **2011** by Thorntons PLC. #4803 The **United States** produces the most chocolate in the world. #4804 The **Swiss** eat the most chocolate in the world, per person! #4805

Candy floss used to be called fairy floss. #4806

5,000-year-old chewing gum, made from birch bark tar, has been found in Finland – with teeth imprints still in it! #4807

The first sweets created in factories were boiled sweets and marshmallows. #4808

In **1848** an American called **John B. Curtis** developed and sold the first commercial chewing gum. #4809

It was called **The State of Maine Pure Spruce Gum**. #4810

**William James Morrison** invented candy floss in **1897**. #4811

Before he made candy floss, he was a dentist. #4812

The **Ancient Egyptians** made the first sweets around 4,000 years ago by combining fruit and nuts with honey. #4813

In **1908** American **George Smith** invented the lollipop, named after his favourite racehorse – Lolly Pop. #4814

# 21 SLEEP facts

that causes you to fall asleep suddenly at any time. #4832 Humans usually **dream** for about two hours a night. #4833 Sleep helps you remember important information.. #4834 During sleep your brain works out what's important and stores it for future use. #4835

The largest sleepover, or pyjama party, was held by 1,626 Girl Guides in 2008. #4815 **Sleep** is just as important to your health as diet and exercise. #4816 Humans can survive longer without food than we can without sleep. #4817 When you sleep, you grow about 8 mm. #4818 You shrink back to normal height during the day. #4819 Most healthy adults need between seven and nine hours of sleep a night. #4820 Newborn babies can sleep up to 18 hours a day. #4821 We naturally feel tired at two different times of the day – around 2am and 2pm. #4822 Humans are the only mammals that willingly delay sleep. #4823 **Exercising** regularly makes it easier to fall asleep and helps

you to sleep better. #4824 But exercising right before going to bed will make sleeping more difficult. #4825 **Snoring** is caused by vibrations of the soft palate and tissue in the mouth, nose and throat. #4826 The loudest snorer in the UK is a granny. Her snores have been recorded at 111.6 decibels. #4827 That's around eight times louder than a jet engine! #4828 **Sleepwalking**, also known as somnambulism, can start at any age but is more common in children. #4829 You're more likely to sleepwalk if one or both of your parents have done so. #4830 **Dysania** is the state of finding it hard to get out of bed in the morning. #4831 **Narcolepsy** is a sleep disorder

# 13 ANIMAL sleep facts

**Giraffes** sleep for up to four hours a day at the most. #4836 They sleep in short 10-minute bursts. #4837 This is to ensure they're alert if a predator attacks. #4838 **Brown bats** sleep for up to 20 hours a day. #4839 **Sloths** sleep for around 10 hours a day. #4840 A **desert snail** can snooze for three years! #4841 **Horses** and **cows** can nap standing up. #4842 They only go into a deep sleep when they lie down. #4843 **Sea otters** will often sleep in groups called rafts. #4844 Big **cats** are cathemeral, which means they only take short naps. #4845 This is so they can easily hunt at any time of day. #4846 **Platypuses** sleep in burrows in the ground. #4847 Platypuses make the same movements when they sleep as they do when they kill their prey! #4848

# 10 FACTS ABOUT BEARS

During late summer and early autumn, GRIZZLY BEARS EAT CONTINUOUSLY **without getting full**. They eat as much as they can to get fat for the winter. #4849

All bears share the same ancestor – the dawn bear. #4850 They lived more than 20 million years ago. #4851

The **spectacled** bear gets its name from the **circular marks** around its eyes, which make it look like it is **wearing spectacles**. #4853

The brown bear is the **largest and heaviest** of all bears, weighing as much as **1 tonne** – the weight of a small car. #4852

Female grizzly bears can lose **40 per cent** of their body weight over the winter. #4854

Over a short distance, a grizzly bear can **outrun a horse**.

#4855

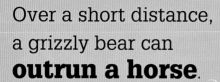

Sun bears **love honey...**

...they will rip open tree trunks...

...in search of **beehives**.

#4856

Polar bears are very strong swimmers, and have been seen more than **100 km** from land. #4857

Grizzly bears usually give birth to

# TWINS.

#4858 The cubs will stay with their mother for **two years** before going off on their own. #4859

# 10 STAR-SPANGLED FACTS ABOUT THE USA

The USA was **declared independent from Britain** on 4 July 1776. #4860

The American national anthem is called **'The Star Spangled Banner'.** #4862

Four presidents have died **natural deaths** while in office. #4861

Due to unusual circumstances, two **unelected men** were running the USA between 1974 and 1976. #4863

The term **'First Lady'** for a president's wife comes from President Zachary Taylor in 1849, when he used it for his late wife at her funeral. #4864

Four USA presidents – Lincoln, Garfield, McKinley and Kennedy – were **assassinated**. #4865

Eight of the first nine **presidents** were British, because they were born before the country became independent! #4866

The government met in eight different cities before settling on **Washington DC** as the US capital in 1790. #4867

Before joining the USA, the states of **Vermont, Texas and Hawaii** were all independent republics with their own governments. #4868

Grover Cleveland is the only president to serve **two non-consecutive terms,** so he was both the 22nd and the 24th president. #4869

The **NAZCA** people of South America cut **HUNDREDS OF SHAPES** of animals, birds, trees and flowers into the desert between AD 400 and 650. #4870 Some were as big as 270 metres across. #4871

As they didn't have aeroplanes, they would **NEVER HAVE KNOWN** what they really looked like. #4872

# 11 DEADLY CREATURES

The
## STARGAZER FISH
protects itself by giving a sharp **electric shock** to attackers.
#4873

## DISGUISED
as a chunk of coral, the reef stonefish kills passing fish with a touch from its venomous spines. #4874

The spines on a **lionfish's** needle-like dorsal fins give a painful sting to predators. #4875

A single **puffer fish** contains enough **poison** to kill **30** people. #4876

The toxic saliva of the blue-ringed octopus can kill a human being in minutes.
#4877

The **banded sea krait**

is a sea snake that has venom

**ten times** more toxic

than a **rattlesnake's**. #4878

**Nudibranches,** or sea slugs, are brightly coloured. #4879 This is a warning that they are **poisonous** to eat. #4880

The **STINGRAY** uses its venomous tail spines to protect it from sharks and killer whales. #4881

The **Caribbean fire coral** gets its name from the burning sensation its stinging polyps produce when you touch them.

#4882

**THE ELECTRIC EEL** can produce an electric shock of up to 500 volts – the equivalent of 40 car batteries.

#4883

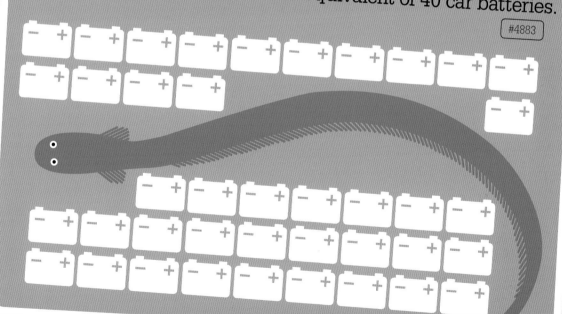

# 52 MASSIVE mountain facts

Mountains exist on every continent and even under the sea.
#4884

...or peak is the highest point on a mountain.
#4885

Around 20% of the Earth's surface is covered in mountains.
#4886

Fold mountains are formed when the Earth's plates run into each other, forcing the Earth's crust to crumple and fold.
#4887

The **Mid-Atlantic Ridge** is a mountain range under the Atlantic Ocean.
#4888

The biggest mountain ranges in the world, such as the **Himalayas** and the **Andes**, are fold mountains.
#4889

Great mountain ranges, like the **Andes** in South America, lie along the edges of continents.
#4890

The scientific study of mountains is called orology.
#4891

Mountains which are formed when volcanoes erupt are known as **volcanic mountains**.
#4892

Fault-block mountains form where cracks in Earth's crust force some rocks up and others down.
#4893

The air is thinner on mountains and the air pressure is lower, so climbers often need oxygen masks to breathe.
#4894

The **Andes** is the longest mountain range on land. They stretch for 7,000 km.
#4895

The **Rockies** in North America stretch for around 4,830 km.
#4896

Most of the world's rivers start in the mountains.
#4897

The **Andes** mountain range passes through seven countries.
#4898

Rock nearly 2 billion years old tops the **Rockies'** summits.
#4899

Mountains are home to about 10 per cent of Earth's population.
#4900

**Table Mountain** is a flat-topped mountain overlooking Cape Town in South Africa.
#4901

**Mount Everest** is the world's highest mountain, but **Mauna Kee** in Hawaii, rises further from the ocean floor.
#4903

**Table Mountain** is often covered in cloud, which is known as the 'table cloth'.
#4902

# EVEREST

→ **Mount Everest** is the world's highest mountain at 8,444 m. #4919

→ It is part of the Himalayas, which cover around 2,410 km in Asia. #4920

→ In **1856** the mountain was named after **George Everest**. #4921

→ George was the General Surveyor of India but was born in Wales. #4922

→ The mountain was first conquered by **Sir Edmund Hillary** and sherpa **Tenzing Norgay** in **1953**. #4923

→ Over 200 people have died trying to climb Everest. #4924

→ Winds on the mountain have been recorded at more than 280 km/h. #4925

→ **Jordan Romero** is the youngest person to climb Everest. #4926

→ He was just 13 at the time. #4927

→ A Nepalese government permit to climb Everest can cost up to £17,000. #4928

→ Everest grows about 4 mm higher every year. #4929

→ In **2000**, a Slovenian called Davorin Karničar skied down Everest. #4930

→ In Nepal, Everest is known as Sargamatha, meaning 'forehead of the sky'. #4931

→ Everest is also called Chomolangma or 'mother of the universe'. #4932

→ The first tweet from the summit was sent in **2011** by Kenton Cool. #4933

→ The summit of Everest is only slightly lower than the height a jet airliner flies at. #4934

→ A couple from Nepal got married on top of the mountain in **2004**. #4935

---

After **Everest,** the world's second highest mountain is **K2**, on the border of Pakistan and China. #4904

The **Great Dividing Range** is the world's third longest mountain chain, stretching around 3,500 km in Eastern Australia. #4905

International Mountain Day is on 11 December and celebrates the importance of mountains. #4906

**K2** is considered the world's most dangerous mountain to climb and is nicknamed 'the savage mountain'. #4907

At 3,776m tall **Mount Fuji** is the most climbed mountain in the world. Around 200,000 people trek up it every year. #4908

**Mount Fuji** is a volcano and last erupted in 1707. #4909

On a clear day **Mount Fuji** can be seen from Tokyo, nearly 100 km away. #4910

The **Alps** is a range of mountains that covers a distance of 1,200 km in Europe. #4911

**Ben Nevis** is the highest mountain on the British Isles, at 1,344 m tall. #4912

In the **Alps** there are 82 official summits, but **Mont Blanc** is the highest, at 4,810 m. #4913

Around 1,500 people climb **Ben Nevis** each year. #4914

**Kilimanjaro** in Africa is, at 5,895 m, the highest mountain in the world that is not part of a mountain range. #4915

The highest mountain on the Moon is **Mons Huygens**. #4916

Most scientists agree that the **Barberton Greenstone Belt** in eastern Africa is the world's oldest mountain range, formed around 3.5 billion years ago. #4917

The **Barberton Greenstone Belt** is made up of three volcanic cones; the highest one, **Kibo,** is dormant but could erupt again. #4918

# 3 SUPER SPACE FACTS

Venus is surrounded by clouds of poisonous **sulphuric acid**. #4936

There may be up to **100,000 million comets** orbiting the Sun. #4937

Neptune is the **stormiest planet** in the solar system. #4938

# 4 SPACE-TASTIC INVENTIONS

**Smoke detectors** were used on a space station in the 1970s. #4939

Silvery **SPACE BLANKETS** used by marathon runners were invented when 1960s' scientists discovered that metal film used in satellites kept people warm. #4940

The **CORDLESS DRILL** was first invented to gather rock samples on the Moon. #4941

The world's **largest telescopes** are on high mountains in Hawaii, where the thin air allows for a great view of the stars. #4942

# 30 BUTTERFLY and MOTH facts

There are around 17,500 species of **butterfly**. #4943 Butterflies prefer to feed in the day. #4944 A butterfly's life cycle is made up of four parts. #4945 They are the egg, larva (caterpillar), pupa (chrysalis) and adult. #4946 When a butterfly emerges from its chrysalis, it will wait a few hours before it flies for the first time. #4947 Butterflies have two large eyes that are made up of many parts and called compound eyes. #4948 Most butterflies live for just two to four weeks. #4949 The largest butterfly in the world is the **Queen Alexandra's Birdwing** butterfly. #4950 Its wingspan is around 30 cm. #4951 The **painted lady** butterfly is found in more places around the world than any other butterfly. #4952 Butterflies cannot fly if they are cold. #4953 Female butterflies can taste through their feet. #4954 They drum leaves with their feet to see if they are a good place to lay eggs. #4955

Butterflies attach their eggs to leaves with a special glue. #4956 Many butterflies and moths have eye spots on their wings to confuse predators. #4957 Butterflies can fly at up to 10 km/h. #4958 Every autumn, **monarch** butterflies migrate 3,000 km from Canada to Mexico. #4959 The **brimstone** butterfly has the longest lifespan of an adult butterfly. #4960 It lives for around 10 months. #4961 **Moths** and butterflies suck up liquid nectar using their proboscis (long flexible snout). #4962 There are 160,000 species of moth. #4963 Moths are mostly nocturnal. #4964 The proboscis of the **Morgan's sphinx** moth can be over 30 cm long. #4965 **Hawkmoths** are the world's fastest moth. #4966 They can reach speeds of up to 50 km. #4967 **Cloth** moths eat natural fibres in cloth. #4968 The largest moth in the world is the **atlas moth**, with a wingspan of 25 cm. #4969 Moths can produce as many as 10 broods per year. #4970 The adult **luna moth** has no mouth. #4971 It lives for just one week, in which time it does not eat. #4972

# 28 ROLLER COASTER facts

The idea for roller coasters developed from the ice-covered wooden slides constructed in **Russia** in the **1400s**. #4973 One of the first roller coasters, **The Russian Mountains of Belleville,** opened in **1817** in **France**. #4974 By the **1930s** there were more than 1,500 roller coasters in the world. #4975 The **United States** has the most roller coasters in the world. #4976 Most roller coasters do not have an engine. #4977 They run by turning potential energy into kinetic energy. #4978 The fastest roller coaster in the world is the **Formula Rossa** ride, at **Abu Dhabi's** Ferrari World theme park. #4979 The ride's top speed is almost 240 km/h. #4980 The **Kingda Ka** roller coaster at Six Flags Adventure Park in **New Jersey** in the United States is the tallest roller coaster in the world. #4981 Its highest point is around 140 m. #4982 Kingda Ka has the largest drop of any roller coaster. #4983 It drops 127 m from the top of the drop to the bottom. #4984 **The Steel Dragon 2000** in **Japan's** Nagashima Spa Land is the longest roller coaster. #4985 Its track covers 2,478 m. #4986 **The Smiler** roller coaster at Alton Towers in **England** has 14 loops – the most in the world. #4987 The world's oldest working roller coaster stands in Lakemont Park in the United States. #4988 It was built in **1902**. #4989 Six Flags Magic Mountain amusement park in **California** in the United States has the most roller coasters to choose from. #4990 It has a total of 18 different rides. #4991 In **2001** four American men broke the record for the most roller coasters ridden in 24 hours. #4992 They managed to ride 74 roller coasters, in 10 different parks, using helicopters to travel between them. #4993 On a roller coaster you experience the thrill of **cognitive dissonance**. One part of you understands you are in no real danger but another part of you experiences genuine fear. #4994 Wooden roller coasters rarely go upside down but almost every steel roller coaster does. #4995 The longest wooden roller coaster in the world is in the United States and is called the **Beast**. #4996 Its track runs for 2,243 m. #4997 Sitting at the back of a roller coaster will make you feel more weightless. #4998 In **2012** an American called Richard Rodriguez broke the record for the most consecutive days spent on a roller coaster. #4999 He rode the UK's tallest roller coaster, the **Big One**, for eight hours a day for 112 days in a row. #5000

# INDEX

# ACKNOWLEDGEMENTS

**The publisher would like to thank the following sources for the photographs used in this book:**

Shutterstock.com PP4-5: tristan tan/Shutterstock.com, Nacho Such/Shutterstock.com, Anton_Ivanov/Shutterstock.com PP10-11: tratong/Shutterstock, Jan Martin Will/Shutterstock, Armin/Dreamstime.com PP14: Featureflash/Shutterstock.com PP24-25: Joseph Scott Photography/Shutterstock, Sokolov Alexey/Shutterstock PP31: FilmMagic/Getty Images PP34-35: Robert Taylor/Shutterstock.com, Pixies/Dreamstime.com PP42-43: mark higgins/Shutterstock.com, Patsy A. Jacks/Shutterstock.com PP45: Phil64/Shutterstock.com PP46-47: Popartic/Shutterstock.com, Julie Clopper/Shutterstock.com, Levent Konuk /Shutterstock.com PP50-51: George Dolgikh/Shutterstock.com PP54: Getty Images PP56-57: Stu Porter/Shutterstock.com, Villers Steyn/Shutterstock.com, Johann Swanepoel/Shutterstock.com PP60-61: Eric Isselee/Shutterstock.com, Steffen Foerster/Shutterstock.com, Roman Klementschitz/Creative Commons Attribution-Share Alike, Stephen Dalton/Nature PL PP68-69: lightpoet/Shutterstock.com, Steve Bower/Shutterstock.com, Cusson/Shutterstock.com PP71: Featurefl ash/Shutterstock.com PP73: Scubaluna/Shutterstock.com PP80-81: Peter Wollinga/Shutterstock.com, Hill2k/Shutterstock.com PP88-89: Mashe/Shutterstock.com PP90: St. Nick/Shutterstock.com PP97: Fred Goldstein/Shutterstock.com PP102-103: Aleksey Stemmer/Shutterstock.com, Dreamstime.com, DiscoDad/Shutterstock.com PP104: Carrie Vonderhaar/Ocean Futures Society/Getty Images PP106-107: dtpearson/istockphoto.com, Aleynikov Pavel/Shutterstock.com PP110-111: Eduard Kyslynskyy/Shutterstock.com, Steffen Foerster/Shutterstock.com PP116-117: AnetaPics/Shutterstock.com PP18-19: tomashko/Shutterstock.com PP121: Kiev.Victor/Shutterstock.com PP128: Undy/Dreamstime.com PP132-133: Tom_robbrecht/Dreamstime.com PP133: Kanuman/Shutterstock.com, Dubai - Ilona Ignatova/Shutterstock.com, littlewormy/Shutterstock.com PP134: Nguyen Anh An/Shutterstock.com, Anthony Ricci/Shutterstock.com PP136: m.bonotto/Shutterstock.com PP140-141: SantiPhotoSS/Shutterstock, Peter Massas/CC Attribution, Daniel Alvarez/Shutterstock, Anthony Hathaway/Dreamstime.com PP142-143: Snowshill/Shutterstock.com PP148-149: 184347200 Elzbieta Sekowska/Shutterstock.com PP152-153: Ian Scott/Shutterstock.com, Photomyeye/Dreamstime.com PP160-161: rook76/Shutterstock.com PP162-163: Chris Howey/Shutterstock.com PP172: DJmattaar/Dreamstime.com, Cbpix/Dreamstime.com, istockphoto.com PP174-175: Nicku/Shutterstock.com, Olga Popova/Shutterstock.com, catwalker/Shutterstock.com, Neftali/Shutterstock.com, Peter Scholz/Shutterstock.com, drserg/Shutterstock.com, Andy Lidstone /Shutterstock.com PP176-177: Stanislav Fosenbauer/Shutterstock.com PP180 SSPL/Getty Images PP182-183: Tooykrub/Shutterstock.com PP184: SSPL/Getty Images PP188-189: Rich Carey/Shutterstock.com PP190-191: Rodrigo Garrido/Shutterstock.com PP194-195: Emi/Shutterstock.com, Ahturner/Shutterstock.com, Daniel Rose/Shutterstock.com PP197: Nicku/Shutterstock.com PP199: Pr2is/Dreamstime.com PP202-203: alterfalter/Shutterstock.com PP205: Getty Images, Michael Dunning/Getty Images PP206-207: Kiyoshi Takahase Segundo/Dreamstime.com, Charlesjsharp/CC Attribution PP208-209: Georgy Kuryatov/Shutterstock.com PP216-217: David Steele/ Shutterstock.com, Colin Edwards Wildside/Shutterstock.com, davidstockphoto/Shutterstock.com PP220-221; abcphotosystem/Shutterstock.com, Ryan M. Bolton/Shutterstock.com, reptiles4all/Shutterstock.com PP228-229: Gerrit_de_Vries/Shutterstock, Chris Zwaenepoel/Dreamstime.com PP232-233: tomashko/Shutterstock.com PP234: Eldad Yitzhak/Shutterstock.com, JeremyRichards/Shutterstock.com, urosr/Shutterstock.com PP236-237: Gertan/Shutterstock.com PP241: idreamphto/Shutterstock.com PP246-247: Jenny/Creative Commons Attribution, Dzain/Dreamstime.com, Kletr/Shutterstock.com PP250-251: Yentafern/Shutterstock.com, Netfalis - Ryan Musser/Shutterstock.com PP253: TsuneoYamashita/Getty Images PP254-255: Fotograf77/Dreamstime.com, Luckynick/Dreamstime.com PP262-263: Ronnie Howard/Shutterstock.com PP267: Featureflash/Shutterstock.com PP270: LebendKulturen.de/Shutterstock.com PP273: AFP/Getty Images PP278-279: Maksim Shmeljov/Shutterstock.com, Maros Bauer/Shutterstock.com PP283: Anthony Correia / Shutterstock.com PP285: Kobby Dagan/Shutterstock.com PP286-287: Ecophoto/Dreamstime.com, Lodimup/Shutterstock.com PP292: jorisvo/Shutterstock.com PP297: Cbpix/Dreamstime.com, izarizhar/Shutterstock.com, Khoroshunova Olga/Shutterstock.com PP299: Jamie Roach/Shutterstock.com PP302-303: lighttraveler/Shutterstock.com PP306-307: Paul Cowell/Shutterstock.com, Alexander R. Jenner/Creative Commons Attribution-Share Alike